D0033914

VETERANS' BENEFITS
HANDBOOK

Lee E. Sharff • Eugene Borden
Fred Stein

PRENTICE HALL
New York • London • Toronto
Sydney • Tokyo • Singapore

Prentice Hall General Reference
15 Columbus Circle
New York, NY 10023

An Arco Book

Arco, Prentice Hall, and colophons are
registered trademarks of Simon & Schuster, Inc.

Manufactured in the United States of America

1 2 3 4 5 6 7 8 9 10

Library of Congress Cataloging-in-Publication Data

Sharff, Lee E.
    Veterans' benefits handbook / Lee E. Sharff, Eugene P. Borden,
Fred Stein.
    p. cm.
    At head of title: Arco.
    ISBN 0-13-952896-2
    1. Veterans—Services for—United States—Handbooks, manuals, etc.
I. Borden, Eugene P. II. Stein, Fred. III. Title. IV. Title: Arco veterans'
benefits handbook.
UB357.S49   1992   92-2536
362.86'0973—dc20   CIP

PLEDGE OF ALLEGIANCE TO THE FLAG

"I PLEDGE ALLEGIANCE TO THE FLAG OF THE UNITED STATES OF AMERICA AND TO THE REPUBLIC FOR WHICH IT STANDS, ONE NATION UNDER GOD, INDIVISIBLE, WITH LIBERTY AND JUSTICE FOR ALL."

The Pledge of Allegiance received official recognition by Congress in an Act approved on June 22, 1942. However, the pledge was first published in 1892 in the Youth's Companion magazine in Boston, Massachusetts to celebrate the 400th anniversary of the discovery of America, and was first used in public schools to celebrate Columbus Day on October 12, 1892.

In its original version, the pledge read "my flag" instead of "the flag of the United States." The change in the wording was adopted by the National Flag Conference in 1923. The rationale for the change was that it prevented ambiguity among foreign-born children and adults who might have the flag of their native land in mind when reciting the pledge.

The phrase "under God" was added to the pledge by a Congressional act approved on June 14, 1954. At that time, President Eisenhower said:

"in this way we are reaffirming the transcendence of religious faith in America's heritage and future; in this way we shall constantly strengthen those spiritual weapons which forever will be our country's most powerful resource in peace and war."

FOREWORD

This first edition of the *Veterans Benefits Handbook* is a compilation of the benefits available to veterans from many sources. Its intention is to describe these well-earned benefits in simple, direct terms to make them as explicit and useful as possible to every veteran. I hope we have succeeded in accomplishing this goal.

For some 30 years I was publisher/executive editor of an annual production of four almanacs for the military — the *Uniformed Services Almanac,* the *Reserve Forces Almanac*, the *National Guard Almanac*, and the *Retired Military Almanac*. Undoubtedly, many of the readers of this Handbook will be familiar with these almanacs. And now, it's extremely satisfying for me to be a part of a team meeting the challenge of producing another publication of service to our veterans.

This Handbook has been prepared by veterans for veterans. My associates, Eugene Borden and Fred Stein, have contributed unstintingly in preparing this Handbook. We have endeavored to include every bit of important and timely information available at the time the book went to press.

We have relied heavily on information provided by a number of federal agencies and wish to express our sincere appreciation to those in these agencies who gave us excellent assistance and cooperation. We acknowledge in particular the assistance of Donald R. Smith and Christopher J. Scheer of the Public Affairs Office, Department of Veterans Affairs (VA), and William Layer and others in the VA's News Service Office. Other contributing federal agencies include the Public Affairs Offices of the Social Security Administration, the Department of Labor, the Small Business Administration, and the Office of Personnel Management.

We also appreciate the valuable assistance of Diana Stein, as well as that of Richard A. Lohr of Lohr Typesetting and Graphics, Falls Church, Virginia, in the production of the Handbook.

Although information on State benefit programs was obtained, time and space constraints prohibited the inclusion of this data.

Lee E. Sharff

TABLE OF CONTENTS

Department of Veterans Affairs

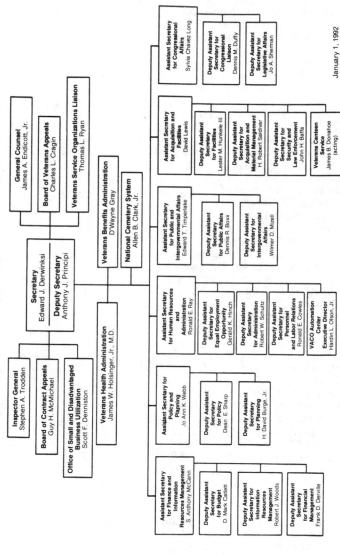

Secretary
Edward J. Derwinksi

Deputy Secretary
Anthony J. Principi

Inspector General
Stephen A. Trodden

General Counsel
James A. Endicott, Jr.

Board of Contract Appeals
Guy H. McMichael

Board of Veterans Appeals
Charles L. Cragin

Office of Small and Disadvantaged Business Utilization
Scott F. Denniston

Veterans Service Organizations Liaison
Thomas L. Ryan

Veterans Health Administration
James W. Holsinger, Jr., M.D.

Veterans Benefits Administration
D'Wayne Gray

National Cemetery System
Allen B. Clark, Jr.

Assistant Secretary for Finance and Information Resources Management
S. Anthony McCann

Deputy Assistant Secretary for Budget
D. Mark Catlett

Deputy Assistant Secretary for Information Resources Management
Robert J. Woods

Deputy Assistant Secretary for Financial Management
Frank D. Derville

Assistant Secretary for Policy and Planning
Jo Ann K. Webb

Deputy Assistant Secretary for Policy
Dean E. Sharp

Deputy Assistant Secretary for Planning
H. David Burge, Jr.

Assistant Secretary for Human Resources and Administration
Ronald E. Ray

Deputy Assistant Secretary for Equal Employment Opportunity
Gerald K. Hinch

Deputy Assistant Secretary for Administration
Robert W. Schultz

Deputy Assistant Secretary for Personnel and Labor Relations
Ronald E. Cowles

VACO Automation Center Executive Director
Hardin L. Olson, Jr.

Assistant Secretary for Public and Intergovernmental Affairs
Edward T. Timperlake

Deputy Assistant Secretary for Public Affairs
Dennis R. Boxx

Deputy Assistant Secretary for Intergovernmental Affairs
Wilmer D. Mizell

Assistant Secretary for Acquisition and Facilities
David Lewis

Deputy Assistant Secretary for Facilities
Lester M. Hunkele III

Deputy Assistant Secretary for Acquisition and Material Management
H. Robert Saldivar

Deputy Assistant Secretary for Security and Law Enforcement
John H. Baffa

Veterans Canteen Service
James B. Donahoe (acting)

Assistant Secretary for Congressional Affairs
Sylvia Chavez Long

Deputy Assistant Secretary for Congressional Liaison
Dennis M. Duffy

Deputy Assistant Secretary for Legislative Affairs
Jo A. Sherman

January 1, 1992

810 Vermont Avenue N.W. Washington, D.C. 20420

viii

OVERVIEW OF
THE DEPARTMENT OF VETERANS AFFAIRS

The United States traditionally has maintained the most comprehensive program of any nation for providing assistance to veterans. These programs had their start with the Pilgrims of Plymouth Colony in 1636 and continued through the nineteenth century when the earlier programs for direct medical and hospital care were expanded. Such expansions included monetary benefits including pensions, not only for veterans but also for their widows and other dependents. Many veterans' homes were established after the Civil War and the U.S. Congress established a new system of veterans benefits when the U.S. entered World War I in 1917.

The Veterans Administration (VA) was established in 1930. At that time the VA operated 54 hospitals, and had 31,600 employees to serve the needs of 4.7 million veterans. The responsibilities of the VA and the benefit programs it administers have grown enormously over the last 60 years. World War II resulted not only in a dramatic increase in the veteran population but also in a large number of new veterans' benefits. Most significant was the GI Bill, signed into law in 1944. With the exception of the social security program, the GI Bill has had a greater impact on Americans than any law since the Homestead Act more than a century ago.

In the decades since World War II, additional assistance laws were passed benefiting veterans of the Korean conflict and the Vietnam involvement. The Department of Medicine and Surgery was established in 1946. The Department of Veterans Benefits was established in 1953. In 1973, the VA assumed another major responsibility when the National Cemetery System was transferred to the VA from the Department of the Army.

On March 15, 1989, the Veterans Administration was renamed the Department of Veterans Affairs, and elevated to Cabinet status. Former Congressman Edward J. Derwinski was appointed as its first Secretary.

VA MISSION, GOALS, AND STRUCTURE

The VA mission is to serve America's veterans and their families as their principal advocate in ensuring that they receive the care, support, and recognition they have earned in service to their country. Thus, a number of broad goals guide the VA in fulfilling its mission and responsibilities, including the following:

• Providing quality medical care on a timely basis to all eligible veterans;
• Providing an appropriate level of benefits to eligible veterans and beneficiaries;
• Ensuring that memorial affairs are handled with honor and dignity;
• Exercising leadership within the Federal government to represent concerns and needs of veterans and their families;
• Ensuring that employees receive high quality leadership in an adequate work environment; and
• Integrating up-to-date technology and innovative management techniques to provide high quality care and appropriate benefits.

In addition to elevating the VA to Cabinet status, the Department of Veterans Affairs Act of October 25, 1988 mandated a reorganization of the VA. It resulted in the creation of six Assistant Secretary positions responsible for the following areas: Finance and Planning, Information Resources Management, Human Resources and Administration, Veterans Liaison and Program Coordination, Acquisitions and Facilities, and Congressional and Public Affairs. Major components of the VA were renamed the Veterans Health Services and Research Administration, the Veterans Benefits Administration, and the National Cemetery System.

MAGNITUDE OF VA PROGRAMS

Care for veterans and their dependents includes a vast universe of recipients and potential recipients. The last dependent of a Revolutionary War veteran died as recently as 1911; the War of 1812's last dependent died in 1946; the Mexican War's in 1962. Widows and children of Civil War and Indian War veterans still receive VA benefits. As late as June 1991, a veteran of the Spanish-American War remained alive and more than 4,300 widows and dependents were receiving compensation or pension benefits.

The present veteran population of 27.2 million represents about 56% of all American veterans who ever served. Nearly 80% of living veterans served during periods when the U.S. was in a declared war. Almost one-third of the Nation's population — approximately 80 million people who are veterans, dependents of veterans, or survivors of deceased veterans — are potentially eligible to receive VA services and benefits.

Through September 1990, the VA and its predecessor agencies spent a total exceeding $551 billion for benefits and services to veterans, their dependents, and survivors. Expenditures for the year which ended in September 1990 amounted to $28 billion. About **57%** of that year's outlays were for direct benefits such as compensation, pension, and education checks. Approximately 38% were for hospital and medical care, and about 2% for national cemeteries, VA hospitals, and other construction programs. The remaining 3% covered general operating expenses. At present there are about 2.7 million veterans who receive disability compensation or pension payments from the VA. In addition, 819,000 widows, children, and parents of deceased veterans are being paid survivors compensation or death pension benefits. This number includes about 90,585 survivors of Vietnam veterans.

A grand total of $551 billion was spent through the year ending in September 1990, with $32 billion budgeted for 1991, and $32.5 billion for FY 1992.

INFORMATION AND CLAIMS

Many state governments and some municipalities operate agencies or offices devoted to administering state and local veterans programs and assisting veterans in filing claims for VA and other federal benefits. Many veterans service organizations also provide information and assistance.

VA regional offices process claims for VA benefits and administer those benefits which include: disability compensation, pension, home loan guaranty, life insurance, education, vocational training for disabled veterans, burial allowance, and survivor's compensation, pension and education.

VA medical center admissions offices are the immediate source for information regarding medical care eligibility, admissions procedure and scheduling. They can provide information on all types of medical care, including nursing home, dental, drug and alcohol dependency, prosthetics, readjustment counseling, and Agent Orange or radiation exposure examinations.

VA national cemeteries or regional offices can answer questions about eligibility of veterans and dependents for burial. Documentation of service must be shown to the director of the cemetery when burial is requested. The cemetery will schedule an interment service, and provide burial and perpetual care of a gravesite as well as an inscribed government marker.

EDUCATION AND TRAINING

Since the first GI Bill went into effect in 1944, more than 20 million beneficiaries have received education and training under the Bill. This includes 7.8 million World War II veterans, 2.4 million Korean conflict veterans, and 8.2 million veterans and active duty service personnel from subsequent military actions. Some 8.4 million veterans attended college under the GI Bill and 9.9 million received technical, farm, and other training under the Bill.

The VA also has assisted in the education of almost 630,000 children, wives, and widows of veterans whose deaths or permanent and total disabilities were service-connected.

Through 1989, the cost of educational benefits totaled more than $70 billion, or about $34 billion more than the U.S. spent in conducting World War I.

HOME LOAN ASSISTANCE

The VA's 47-year-old loan guaranty program has benefited more than 13 million veterans and their dependents. From 1944, when this program was established as part of the original GI Bill, through September 1990, VA home loan guarantees totaled more than $353.8 billion. In addition, the VA has made 333,000 direct loans valued at $3.5 billion. In 1990, the VA guaranteed 196,600 loans valued at $15.8 billion.

LIFE INSURANCE

Five life insurance programs are operated by the VA. In 1990, these programs involved $203 billion in life insurance policies for 6.8 million veterans and military personnel. The 1991 GI life insurance dividends returned more than $1 billion to 2.7 million policyholders.

MEDICAL CARE AND RESEARCH

From the 54 hospitals operated in 1930, the VA hospital system has grown to include 172 medical centers, 350 outpatient and community outreach clinics, 126 nursing home care units, and 35 domiciliaries. These health care facilities provide a wide spectrum of medical, surgical, and rehabilitative care.

The VA operates at least one medical center in each of the 48 contiguous states, Puerto Rico, and the District of Columbia. With 90,000 beds, the medical centers treat 1.1 million patients in VA hospitals, 73,000 in nursing home care units and 25,000 in domiciliaries. More than 21 million outpatient visits are registered in an average year.

VA researchers have played important roles in eradicating tuberculosis, developing the pacemaker and CT scan, and improving artificial limbs. Current high priority VA research projects involve AIDS, drug addiction, Agent Orange exposure, etc.

The VA medical care system employs more than 13,000 physicians, some 60,000 registered nurses, and approximately 120,000 other health care specialists.

NATIONAL CEMETERIES

Since 1973, when the VA took over the National Cemetery System, 10 new national cemeteries have been established and another has been approved for northern California. Environmental and other planning studies have been undertaken preparatory to establishing other national cemeteries.

At present, the National Cemetery System includes 114 operating cemeteries in 38 states and Puerto Rico. Of these cemeteries, 64 are open to new interments. Total acreage in the system has increased from 4,000 acres in 1973 to the present 10,000 acres. Annual interments are expected to increase from 63,000 conducted in 1991 to 94,900 in the year 2000.

The VA also provides approximately 300,000 headstones or markers each year to mark veterans' graves in private and national cemeteries.

VA PERSONNEL

As of July 31, 1991, the VA had 258,116 employees. Among all departments and agencies of the federal government, only the Department of Defense had a larger work force. One of every 8 federal government full-time employees works for the VA. Of the total VA work force, 234,177 were in the Veterans Health Services and Research Administration, 13,793 were employed by the Veterans Benefits Administration, and 1,400 in the National Cemetery System. The remaining VA personnel were in the various staff offices.

VA is a leader in hiring veterans. Some 54 percent of all male employees are veterans. As of June 30, 1991, VA employed 6,465 women veterans or women with veterans' preference. Sixty-nine percent of male and female veteran employees served during the Vietnam Era. Five percent of all VA employees were disabled veterans.

BENEFITS FOR VETERANS AND DEPENDENTS

WHO'S ELIGIBLE

Eligibility for most VA benefits is based on discharge from active military service under "other than dishonorable" conditions for a minimum period specified by law. Men and women veterans with similar service are entitled to the same VA benefits.

The Department of Defense issues each veteran a military discharge form, DD 214, identifying the veteran's condition of discharge — honorable, general, other than honorable, dishonorable or bad conduct.

Honorable and general discharges qualify a veteran for most VA benefits. Educational benefits under the Montgomery GI Bill, however, require an honorable discharge.

Dishonorable and some bad-conduct discharges issued by general courts martial bar VA benefits. Benefits eligibility of veterans with other "bad conduct" discharges and discharges described by military branches as "other than honorable" must be determined by VA. VA decides, after reviewing the facts of each specific case, whether separation from service was under "dishonorable" or "other than dishonorable" conditions.

Those who enlisted in the military after Sept. 7, 1980, and officers commissioned or who entered active military service after Oct. 16, 1981, must have completed two years of active duty or the full period of their initial service obligation to be eligible for most VA benefits. Veterans with service-connected disabilities or those discharged for disability or hardship near the end of their service obligation are not held to this provision. Also, the provision does not apply to participation in veterans insurance programs.

Veterans in prison and parolees may still be eligible for certain VA benefits. VA regional offices can clarify their eligibility.

Service in 21 groups during periods that include World Wars I and II has been certified as active military service by the Department of Defense (DoD) for purposes of laws governing VA. Depending on their periods of service, members of these groups are eligible for certain VA benefits. Individuals must have their service documented with DoD to obtain a discharge from DoD under honorable conditions.

WARTIME SERVICE

Certain VA benefits and medical care require wartime service. As specified in law, VA recognizes these war periods:

Mexican Border Period — May 9, 1916, through April 5, 1917, for veterans who served in Mexico, on its borders or in adjacent waters.
World War I — April 6, 1917, through Nov. 11, 1918; for veterans who served in Russia, April 6, 1917, through April 1, 1920; extended through July 1, 1921, for veterans who had one day of service between April 6, 1917, and Nov. 11, 1918.
World War II — Dec. 7, 1941, through Dec. 31, 1946.
Korean Conflict — June 27, 1950, through Jan. 31, 1955.
Vietnam Era — Aug. 5, 1964, through May 7, 1975.
Persian Gulf War — Aug. 2, 1990, through a date to be set by law or Presidential Proclamation.

While most veterans served in the regular armed forces, there are thousands of individuals whose military service was not recognized as "active" because it was not certified by the Secretary of Defense at the time. However, many of these groups are now recognized and certified as active. They include:

Women's Airforces Services Pilots (WASPs)
Female telephone operators serving with the Army Signal Corps in WWI
Army Corps of Engineers field clerks
Women's Army Auxiliary Corps
Civilian employees, Pacific Naval Air Bases who acted in defense of Wake Island
Female civilian clerks with Army Quartermaster Corps serving with the AEF in WWI
Reconstruction aides and dietitians in WWI
Male civilian ferry pilots
Wake Island defenders from Guam
OSS Secret Intel. Element
Guam Combat Patrol
Quartermaster Corps *Keswick* crew on Corregidor
US civilian volunteers in defense of Bataan
US merchant seamen serving in blockships in Operation Mulberry
Merchant seamen
Flying Tigers
US Coast & Geodetic Survey sailors (selected)

FILING A CLAIM

Those filing a claim with VA for the first time must submit a copy of their service discharge form (DD 214, which documents service dates and type of discharge) or give their full name, military service number, branch of service and dates of service. Once a claim is filed, the veteran's VA file number ("C" number) or Social Security number serves as the veteran's identifier.

Most veterans are aware that the DD Form 214 "REPORT OF SEPARATION FROM ACTIVE DUTY" is one of the most important documents in their possession. Each person separated from the military service is given the *original copy*. Those who have lost or misplaced their original copy also know how difficult it is to get a copy from the National Personnel Records Center, even when the request is submitted under urgent conditions.

The veteran's family should be aware of the location of his/her separation papers. Retirees who have not already done so should take their original DD-214 and other service documents to their local County Clerk/Recorder's office to have them recorded. It is recommended that each DD-214 issued to a person be recorded, not just the last one.

The state veterans affairs offices are chartered by Congress to assist in obtaining copies of military service record documents. Their representative is listed in the local telephone book under County Government.

KEEP IMPORTANT DOCUMENTS

The veteran's DD 214 form and other information mentioned above should be kept in a safe, convenient location accessible to the veteran and next of kin or designated representative. The veteran's preference regarding burial in a national cemetery and use of a headstone provided by the VA should be doumented and kept with this information.

The following documents, if not included in VA files, will be needed for claims processing related to a veteran's death:

— marriage certificate if the claim is for a surviving spouse or children.
— death certificate if the veteran did not die in a VA medical facility.
— children's birth certificates.
— veteran's birth certificate, if parents want to establish benefits eligibility.

If the deceased veteran carried government life insurance at the time of death, the policy's designated beneficiary is entitled to the proceeds. Those managing the veteran's affairs must send the veteran's complete name and insurance policy number to one of two VA insurance centers. Assistance is available at VA regional offices or at 1-800-669-8477. If the policy number is unknown, send the veteran's VA file number, Social Security number, military serial number or military service branch and dates of service with date of birth.

For states east of the Mississippi River, send to:

— Department of Veterans Affairs
  Regional Office and Insurance Center
  P.O. Box 8079
  Philadelphia, PA 19101

  For states west of the Mississippi River, and the states of Minnesota, Wisconsin, Illinois, Indiana and Mississippi, send to:

— Department of Veterans Affairs
  Regional Office and Insurance Center
  Bishop Henry Whipple Bldg.
  Fort Snelling
  St. Paul, MN 55111

Veterans Benefits Timetable

Time	Benefits	Where to apply
90 days	DENTAL TREATMENT: VA provides necessary dental care for veterans who were not provided dental examination and treatment within 90 days of discharge or separation from service. The time limit does not apply to veterans with dental disabilities resulting from combat wounds or service injuries.	Any VA office or medical center
90 days	REEMPLOYMENT	Former employer
Limited time	UNEMPLOYMENT COMPENSATION: The amount of benefit and payment period varies among states. Apply soon after separation.	State employment service
120 days or up to one year it totally disabled	SGLI: Servicemen's Group Life Insurance may be converted to VGLI (Veterans Group Life Insurance), a five-year nonrenewable term policy. At the end of the five-year term, VGLI may be converted to an individual policy with any participating insurance company.	Office of Servicemen's Group Life Insurance, 213 Washington St., Newark, NJ 07102-9990
Two years (from date of notice of VA disability rating)	GI INSURANCE: Life insurance (up to $10,000) is available for veterans with service-connected disabilities. Veterans who are totally disabled may apply for a waiver of premiums on these policies.	Any VA office
10 years from release from active duty or required Selected Reserve	EDUCATION: You may be eligible for educational assistance while you pursue approved training if you participated in either the Post-Vietnam Era Veterans' Educational Assistance Program (VEAP) (Chapter 32) or the Montgomery GI Bill (Chapter 30) while on active duty; or, if you had entitlement under the Vietnam Era GI Bill (Chapter 34) remaining on Dec. 31, 1989, and were on active duty	Any VA Office

from Oct. 19, 1984, through June 30, 1988, without a break; or were on active duty from Oct. 19, 1984, through June 30, 1987, and subsequently entered into the Selected Reserve under a four-year enlistment.

10 years	For members of the Montgomery GI Bill — Selected Reserve (Chapter 106), benefits will end on the date of separation from the Selected Reserve or 10 years from the date eligibility began, whichever happens first.	
12 years (generally from date of notice of VA disability rating)	VOCATIONAL REHABILITATION: For disabled vets, VA will pay tuition and fees, and the cost of books, tools and other program expenses as well as provide a monthly living allowance. Upon completion of the vocational rehabilitation program, VA will assist in finding employment.	Any VA office
No time limit	DISABILITY COMPENSATION: VA pays compensation for disabilities incurred in or aggravated by military service.	Any VA office
No time limit	MEDICAL CARE: VA provides a wide range of care benefits, including help for alcoholism and other drug dependency, to veterans with a service-connected disability and to nonservice-connected veterans who qualify. Readjustment counseling benefits is available at VA vet centers for veterans with readjustment problems.	Any VA office or Medical center
No time limit	GI HOME LOANS: VA will guarantee a loan for the purchase of a home, farm with a residence, manufactured home, or condominium.	Any VA office
No time limit	EMPLOYMENT ASSISTANCE: Assistance is available in finding employment in private industry, in federal and local government.	Local Offices of State Employment Service, U.S. Office of Personnel Management

Benefit Programs for Veterans
Disability Compensation

ELIGIBILITY

Monetary benefits are paid to veterans who are disabled by injury or disease incurred or aggravated during active military service in the line of duty. The disability cannot be a secondary effect of willful misconduct or abuse of alcohol or drugs. The service of the veterans must have been terminated through separation or discharge under conditions that were other than dishonorable. Monetary benefits are related to the residual effects of the injury or disease. The amounts of the benefits, which are not subject to federal or state income tax, are changed periodically by Congress.

BENEFIT

Disability compensation is paid in monthly payments. Currently these range from $83 for a 10 percent degree of disability to $1,680 for a 100-percent disability rating.

Compensation for
Service-Connected Disability   **Rate**

10 percent	$83
20 percent	157
30 percent	240
40 percent	342
50 percent	487
60 percent	614
70 percent	776
80 percent	897
90 percent	1,010
Total disability	1,680

In addition, specific rates, up to $4,799 per month, are paid when the eligible veteran is adjudged to have suffered certain specific, severe disabilities. These are all decided on an individual basis. The law prohibits the award of VA disability compensation concurrently with military retirement pay, except to the extent the retirement pay is waived.

Additional monthly payments to veterans with service-connected disabilities vary widely, depending upon the severity and type of disability. Local VA offices should be contacted to determine additional payments in specific cases.

Veterans whose service-connected disabilities are rated at 30 percent or more are entitled to additional compensation for dependents. The current payments, which are based upon 100 percent disability, are listed below. The payments for 30 percent or more are payable at the same ratio that the degree of disability bears to 100 percent.

Spouse and:

No children	$100
1 child	169
2 children	222
3 children	275
each additional child	55

No spouse and:

1 child	$69
2 children	122
3 children	174
each additional child	53

Dependent parents
1 parent... $81
2 parents.. 162

PRISONERS OF WAR

Former prisoners of war who were incarcerated for at least 30 days are entitled to a presumption of service connection for disabilities resulting from certain diseases if manifested to a degree of 10 percent at any time after active service, including psychosis and anxiety states. These presumptions may be rebutted by proof of other intervening causes.

Other Disability Benefits

Specially Adapted Homes

ELIGIBILITY/BENEFIT

A disabled veteran may be entitled to a grant from VA for a home especially adapted to their needs.

FOR $38,000 GRANT

VA may approve a grant of not more than 50 percent of the cost of building, buying or remodeling adapted homes or paying indebtedness on those homes already acquired, up to a maximum of $38,000.

Veterans must be entitled to compensation for permanent and total service-connected disability due to:

(a) the loss or loss of use of both lower extremities, such as to preclude locomotion without the aid of braces, crutches, canes, or a wheelchair, or

(b) disability which includes (1) blindness in both eyes, having only light perception, plus (2) loss or loss of use of one lower extremity, or

(c) a loss or loss of use of one lower extremity together with (1) residuals of organic disease or injury, or (2) the loss or loss of use of one upper extremity, which so affects the functions of balance or propulsion as to preclude locomotion without using braces, canes, crutches or a wheelchair.

See Veterans Mortgage Life Insurance discussion on Page 49 for additional information.

FOR $6,500 GRANT

VA may approve a grant for the actual cost, up to a maximum of $6,500, for adaptations to a veteran's residence which are determined by VA to be reasonably necessary. Alternatively, the grant may be used to assist eligible veterans in acquiring a residence which has already been adapted with special features determined to be reasonably necessary for the veteran's disability. In the latter situation, the amount of the grant is based on the fair market value of the existing special features, and not their cost.

Veterans must be entitled to compensation for permanent and total service-connected disability due to:

(a) Blindness in both eyes with 5/200 visual acuity or less, or
(b) Anatomical loss or loss of use of both hands.
See Veterans Mortgage Life Insurance.

SUPPLEMENTAL FINANCING

Eligible veterans with available loan guaranty entitlement may also obtain a guaranteed loan or a direct loan from VA to supplement the grant to acquire a specially adapted home.

Automobiles or Other Conveyances

ELIGIBILITY

Veterans and current service personnel qualify for this benefit if they have service-connected loss of one or both hands or feet, or permanent loss of use, or permanent impairment of vision of both eyes.

For adaptive equipment eligibility only, veterans entitled to compensation for ankylosis of one or both knees, or one or both hips, also qualify.

BENEFIT

For the automobile or other conveyance there is a one-time payment by VA of not more than $5,500 toward the purchase of an automobile or other conveyance.

VA will pay for adaptive equipment, its repair, replacement, or re-installation required because of disability for the safe operation of a vehicle purchased with VA assistance or for a previously or subsequently acquired vehicle.

WHERE TO APPLY

Contact a VA regional office or the prosthetic office at a VA medical center.

Clothing Allowance

ELIGIBILITY

Any veteran who is entitled to receive compensation for a service-connected disability for which he or she uses prosthetic or orthopedic appliances, including a wheelchair, which VA determines tends to wear out or tear clothing, may receive a clothing allowance. Any veteran whose service-connected skin condition requires prescribed medication which irreparably damages the veteran's outer garments also may receive the allowance.

BENEFIT

Annual clothing allowance of $452.

WHERE TO APPLY

Contact the nearest regional office or VA medical center.

PENSION

ELIGIBILITY

This program furnishes support for veterans with limited income who had 90 days or more of active military service, at least one day of which was during a period of war. Their discharge from active duty must have been under conditions other than dishonorable. They must be permanently and totally disabled for reasons neither traceable to military service nor due to willful misconduct. Payments are made to qualified veterans to bring their total income, including other retirement or Social Security income, to an established support level. Countable income may be reduced by certain unreimbursed medical expenses. Pension is not payable to those who have assets that can be used to provide adequate maintenance. Veterans in receipt of pensions between Feb. 1, 1985, and Jan. 31, 1992, may elect to participate in a vocational training program if found eligible for services. Under this pilot program a veteran may receive up to 24 months or more of vocational training and related services as well as up to 18 months of placement and post-placement services. Work income will affect the receipt of pension.

To be eligible for non-service-connected (NSC) payments, an incompetent veteran who is unmarried and has no dependents may not have more than $25,000 in assets. To receive benefits, a competent veteran must be found by the VA to be 100 percent and permanently disabled or unable to work.

Pensions, interest payments, Social Security benefits and IRA accounts are considered assets and are counted toward the financial limit.

Some confusion may arise among some NSC recipients because of a change in the law in 1978, which brought about an "improved pension." Benefits and rules have changed, but anyone applying today falls under the improved plan, while provisions under the old plan remain in effect for those who signed up under its program.

Veterans should be aware that claims could take more than a year to be approved by the VA if records are not easily located or are missing. Total and permanent disability must be proved by a doctor's verification or by an examination at a VA hospital or medical center, but the VA may require an examination in addition to the doctor's statement.

Care for an NSC recipient at a VA medical center is based on need and space available. Prescription drugs for these veterans provided by the VA are charged at the rate of $2 for a 30-day supply.

VA regulations allow exceptions to eligibility rules to avoid hardship, because decisions may vary from official to official and some regulations are not clear-cut.

Veterans organization service officers can provide information on the NSC pension program.

AID AND ATTENDANCE OR HOUSEBOUND

A veteran who is a patient in a nursing home or otherwise determined by VA to be in need of the regular aid and attendance of another person, or is permanently housebound, may be entitled to higher income limitations or additional benefits, depending on the type of pension received.

IMPROVED PENSION

Effective Dec. 1, 1991, the improved pension program provides for the following annual rates, generally payable monthly. The annual payment is reduced by the amount of the annual countable income of the veteran and the income of any spouse or dependent children.

Veteran without dependent spouse or child $7,397
Veteran with one dependent (spouse or child) $9,689
Veteran in need of regular aid and attendance with
    no dependents $11,832
Veteran in need of regular aid and attendance with
    one dependent $14,124

Veteran permanently housebound with no dependents $9,041
Veteran permanently housebound with one dependent $11,333
Two veterans married to one another $9,689
Veterans of World War I and Mexican Border Period,
    add to the applicable annual rate $1,673
Increase for each additional dependent child $1,258

REDUCTION WHILE IN NURSING HOME OR DOMICILIARY

When a veteran without a spouse or a child is being furnished nursing home or domiciliary care by VA, the pension is reduced to an amount not in excess of $90 per month after three full calendar months of care. The reduction may be delayed if nursing home care is being continued for the primary purpose of providing the veteran with a prescribed program of rehabilitation services.

PROTECTED PENSION PROGRAMS

Pensioners entitled to benefits as of Dec. 31, 1978, who do not elect to receive pension under the improved pension program, will continue to receive pension benefits at the rate they were entitled to receive on Dec. 31, 1978, as long as they remain permanently and totally disabled, do not lose a dependent, or their incomes do not exceed the adjusted income limitation. The income limitation is increased yearly based on changes in the Consumer Price Index.

Education and Training

VA administers a number of education and training programs for veterans, servicepersons and eligible dependents.

Montgomery GI Bill (Active Duty)

ELIGIBILITY

The Montgomery GI Bill (Active Duty), also known as Chapter 30, is a program of education benefits generally for individuals who enter active duty for the first time after June 30, 1985. Active duty for benefit purposes now includes full-time National Guard duty performed after Nov. 29, 1989.

ENTITLEMENT

The participant generally must serve continuously on active duty for three years of a three-year or greater enlistment or, for a lesser benefit, two years of an initial active duty obligation of less than three years. An individual also may qualify for the full benefit by initially serving two continuous years on active duty, followed by four years of Selected Reserve service. In the latter case, the participant must enter the Selected Reserve within one year of release from active duty.

The participant must meet the requirements for a high school diploma or an equivalency certificate before the first period of active duty ends. Completing 12 credit-hours toward a college degree meets this requirement.

PARTICIPATION REQUIREMENTS

Participation in the Montgomery GI Bill requires that the service-person have his or her military pay reduced by $100 a month for the first 12 months of active duty. This money is not refundable. Generally, if an individual decides not to participate in this program, this decision cannot be changed at a later date.

An exception is made under specific conditions for servicepersons who are involuntarily separated from active duty with an honorable discharge after Feb. 2, 1991. If the serviceperson decides to participate before separation, military pay will be reduced before separation, and education or training may take place following separation.

VIETNAM ERA GI BILL CONVERSION

Also eligible for Montgomery GI Bill benefits are those individuals who had remaining entitlement under the Vietnam Era GI Bill on Dec. 31, 1989, and served on active duty without a break from Oct. 19, 1984. The individual must have served to June 30, 1988; or June 30, 1987, followed by four years in the Selected Reserve after release from active duty. The individual must have entered the Selected Reserve within one year of release from active duty. The individual who converts from the Vietnam Era GI Bill, must have met the requirements for a high school diploma or an equivalency certificate before Dec. 31, 1989. Completion of 12 credit hours toward a college degree meets the requirement.

DISCHARGES AND SEPARATIONS

For the Montgomery GI Bill program, the discharge must be "honorable." Discharges designated "under honorable conditions" and "general" do not establish eligibility for education benefits. A discharge for one of the following reasons could result in a reduction of the required length of active duty:

(a) convenience of the government;
(b) disability;
(c) hardship;

(d) a medical condition existing before service; or

(e) certain reductions in force (RIF).

EDUCATION AND TRAINING AVAILABLE

The following education and training opportunities are available under the Montgomery GI Bill:

(a) courses at colleges and universities leading to associate, bachelor or graduate degrees, and independent study or cooperative training programs.

(b) courses leading to a certificate or diploma from business, technical or vocational schools.

(c) apprenticeship or on-job-training programs.

(d) correspondence courses.

(e) flight training from Sept. 30, 1990, to Sept. 30, 1994. Before beginning officer training, the veteran must have a private pilot license and meet the physical requirements for a commercial license.

The individual may also receive tutorial assistance benefits if enrolled in school half time or more. Remedial, deficiency and refresher training may also be available.

PAYMENTS

Veterans who served on active duty for three years, or two years active duty plus four years in the Selected Reserve or National Guard will receive $350 a month in basic benefits for 36 months. Those who enlist for less than three years will receive $275 a month. VA pays an additional amount, commonly called a "kicker," if directed by the Department of Defense.

WORK-STUDY

To be eligible for work-study benefits, a person must train at the three-quarter or full-time rate. Veteran-students will be paid in advance 40 percent of the amount specified in the work-study agreement with VA. Under this program, they may perform outreach services under the supervision of a VA employee, prepare and process VA paperwork, work at a VA medical facility, or perform other approved activities.

PERIOD OF ELIGIBILITY

For the most part, benefits under Chapter 30 end 10 years from the date of the veteran's last discharge or release from active duty. VA can extend this 10-year period if the veteran was prevented from training during this period because of a disabilityor because he or she was held by a foreign government or power. The 10-year period can also be extended if an individual re-enters active duty for 90 days or more after becoming eligible. Under certain circumstances, periods of active duty of less than 90 days can qualify for extensions.

If the veteran's discharge is upgraded by the military, the 10-year period begins on the date of the upgrade.

If eligibility is based on both the Vietnam Era GI Bill and the Montgomery GI Bill, and discharge from active duty was before Dec. 31, 1989, the veteran will have until Jan. 1, 2000. In most cases, VA will subtract from the 10-year period those periods the veteran was not on active duty between Jan. 1, 1977, and Oct. 18, 1984.

If eligibility is based on two years of active duty and four years in the Selected Reserve, the veteran's eligibility will end the later of: (a) 10 years from release from active duty; or (b) 10 years from completion of the four-year Selected Reserve obligation.

Montgomery GI Bill (Selected Reserve)

ELIGIBILITY

The Montgomery GI Bill (Selected Reserve) is a program of education benefits for members of the reserve elements of the Army, Navy, Air Force, Marine Corps and Coast Guard, as well as the Army National Guard and the Air National Guard. This program is also referred to as Chapter 106.

To be eligible for the program, a reservist must:

(a) have a six-year obligation to serve in the Selected Reserve signed after June 30, 1985, or, if an officer, agree to serve six years in addition to the original obligation;
(b) complete Initial Active Duty for Training (IADT);
(c) meet the requirements for a high school diploma or equivalent certificate before completing IADT; and
(d) remain in good standing in a Selected Reserve unit.

EDUCATION AND TRAINING AVAILABLE

Reservists can receive benefits for undergraduate degrees or for technical courses leading to certificates of colleges and universities. A six-year commitment that begins after Sept. 30, 1990, is needed to receive benefits for pursuit of:

(a) courses leading to a certificate or diploma from business, technical or vocational schools.
(b) cooperative training.

(c) apprenticeship or on-job-training.

(d) correspondence training.

(e) independent study programs.

(f) flight training from Sept. 30, 1990, to Sept. 30, 1994. Before beginning training the reservist must have a private pilot license and meet the physical requirements for a commercial license.

Remedial, deficiency and refresher training may also be available to the reservist.

PAYMENTS

Payments are made monthly. The full-time rate is $170 a month for school attendance. Entitlement is for a maximum of 36 months of assistance.

WORK-STUDY

Reservists training at the three-quarter or full-time rate are eligible for the work-study program. Terms of participation are the same as under the Montgomery GI Bill (Active Duty), except that reservists can also work at a military facility if the work is related to the Chapter 106 program.

PERIOD OF ELIGIBILITY

If a reservist stays in the Selected Reserve, benefits end 10 years from the date the reservist became eligible for the program. VA may extend the 10-year period if the individual could not train due to a disability caused by Selected Reserve service. If a reservist leaves the Selected Reserve because of a disability, the individual may use the full 10 years.

In all other cases, benefits and on the day the reservist leaves the Selected Reserve. However, if the 10-year period ends while he or she is attending school, VA will pay benefits until the end of the term. If the training is not on a term basis, payments may continue for 12 weeks.

Veterans' Educational Assistance Program
(VEAP)

ELIGIBILITY

Under VEAP, active duty personnel voluntarily participate in a plan for education or training in which their savings are administered and added to by the federal government. Servicepersons were eligible to enroll in VEAP if they entered active duty for the first time after Dec. 31,

1976, and before July 1, 1985. Some contribution to VEAP must have been made prior to April 1, 1987. The maximum participant contribution is $2,700. While on active duty, participants may make a lump sum contribution to the training fund.

A serviceperson who participated in VEAP is eligible to receive benefits while on active duty if: (a) at least three months of contributions are available or one month for a high school or elementary school program; and (b) the first active duty commitment is completed.

If the individual's first term is for more than six years, benefits may be available after six years. For an elementary or high school program, the individual must be in the last six months of the first enlistment.

A veteran who participated in VEAP is eligible to receive benefits if:

(a) the first enlistment was prior to Sept. 8, 1980, or the participant entered active duty as an officer before Oct. 17, 1981, and served for a continuous period of 181 days or more or — if served for a shorter period — was discharged for a service-connected disability; or

(b) enlisted for the first time on or after Sept. 8, 1980, or entered active duty as an officer on or after Oct. 17, 1981, and completed 24 continuous months of active duty; and

(c) was discharged from service under conditions other than dishonorable.

A veteran who completes a shorter period of active duty to which called or ordered will meet the length-of-duty requirement. A veteran could also still be eligible even though the required continuous months of active duty were not completed if the veteran:

(a) receives VA disability compensation or military disability retirement.

(b) served a previous period of at least 24 continuous months of active duty before Oct. 17, 1981; or

(c) was discharged or released for early out, hardship or service-connected disability.

NOTE: An individual who contributed or who could have contributed to VEAP before being voluntarily separated from active duty with an honorable discharge after Feb. 2, 1991, may make an irrevocable election before such separation to receive Montgomery GI Bill (Active Duty) benefits.

EDUCATION AND TRAINING AVAILABLE

VEAP participants may pursue associate, bachelor or graduate degrees at colleges or universities. Courses leading to a certificate or diploma from business, technical or vocational schools may also be taken. Other opportunities include apprenticeship or on-job-training programs, cooperative courses and correspondence school courses. Flight training may be pursued from April 1, 1991, through Sept. 30, 1994. Before beginning training, the veteran must have a private pilot license and meet the physical requirements for a commercial license. A participant may also study abroad, but only in programs leading to a college degree. A participant with a deficiency in a subject may receive tutorial assistance benefits if enrolled half time or more. Remedial, deficiency and refresher training also may be available.

PAYMENTS

When the participant elects to use VEAP benefits to pursue an approved course of education or training, the Defense Department will match the participant's contribution at the rate of $2 for every $1 the individual put into the fund. Defense may make additional contributions to the fund.

A typical payment situation under VEAP might be as follows: A participant contributes $1,800 over a 36-month period and the government adds $3,600 (2 for 1 match); there is no additional benefit from the Defense Department. This results in a total entitlement amount of $5,400. This amount would be divided by 36 months, yielding a monthly benefit of $150 for full-time schooling for the veteran.

A veteran will receive monthly payments for the number of months contributed, or for 36 months, whichever is less. As indicated above, the amount of the payment is determined by dividing the number of months that contributions were made into the participant's training fund total.

PERIOD OF ELIGIBILITY

A veteran has 10 years from the date of last discharge or release from active duty in which to use VEAP benefits. This 10-year period can be extended by the amount of time the veteran could not train because of a disability or because of being held by a foreign government or power.

The 10-year period may also be extended if the veteran re-enters active duty for 90 continuous days or more after becoming eligible. The extension ends 10 years from the date of discharge or release from the later active duty period. For periods of less than 90 continuous days, the veteran may qualify for extensions under certain circumstances. A veteran with a discharge upgraded by the military will have 10 years from the date of the upgrade.

WORK-STUDY

Work-study benefits are available under the same terms as described under the Montgomery GI Bill (Active Duty) program.

Vocational and Educational Counseling

ELIGIBILITY

Servicemembers and veterans eligible to receive VA education or vocational rehabilitation benefits may receive a range of vocational and educational counseling services from VA Vocational Rehabilitation and Counseling. In addition, the following individuals may receive these services regardless of eligibility for any other VA educational benefits:

(1) Servicemembers within 180 days of their planned discharges or releases from active duty.

(2) Veterans within one year from the date they left active duty, provided the last discharge or release was other than dishonorable.

COUNSELING REQUIREMENTS FOR INDIVIDUALS RATED INCOMPETENT

If VA has rated a veteran or servicemember incompetent, VA must counsel the individual prior to his or her entrance into an educational or training program for which VA will pay benefits.

COUNSELING SERVICES

Counseling services include educational and vocational counseling and guidance; testing; analysis of and recommendations to improve job marketing skills; identification of employment, training, and financial aid resources; and referrals to other agencies providing these services.

VA does not pay for travel expenses for servicemembers or veterans receiving these counseling services.

Vocational Rehabilitation

ELIGIBILITY

Veterans and servicemembers who served in the Armed Forces on or after Sept. 16, 1940, are eligible for vocational rehabilitation if all three of the following conditions are met:

(a) They suffered a service-connected disability or disabilities in active service which entitle them to at least 20 percent compensation or would do so but for receipt of military retirement pay. Veterans may also be eligible if they have a compensable rating of less than 20 percent and first applied for vocational rehabilitation before Nov. 1, 1990.

(b) They were discharged or released under other than dishonorable conditions or are hospitalized awaiting separation for disability.

(c) VA determines that they need vocational rehabilitation to overcome an impairment to their ability to prepare for, obtain or retain employment consistent with their abilities, aptitudes and interests. Their service-connected disabilities must materially contribute to this employment handicap.

PERIOD OF ELIGIBILITY

Generally, the veteran must complete a rehabilitation program within 12 years from the date VA notifies him or her of entitlement to compensation. This period may be deferred or extended if a medical condition prevented the veteran from training or if the veteran has a serious employment handicap.

LENGTH OF REHABILITATION PROGRAM

Eligible disabled veterans may receive up to four years of rehabilitation services, including full-time training or its equivalent either in part-time training or in a combination of part-time and full-time training. In some cases, rehabilitation services may exceed four years. For example, if a veteran with a serious employment handicap receives services under an extended evaluation to improve his or her training potential, the total of the extended evaluation and the training phases of the rehabilitation program may exceed four years.

Following participation in the training portion of a rehabilitation program, a veteran may receive counseling, job search and work adjustment services for up to 18 months. Employment services may also be given if the veteran is eligible for vocational rehabilitation and these services are the only assistance needed to overcome the employment handicap and enable the veteran to become suitably employed.

BENEFITS

A disabled veteran will be given an evaluation to establish eligibility and entitlement and to determine whether the veteran needs extended evaluation, independent living services, educational or vocational training, employment services, or a combination of these benefits.

In the educational or vocational training phase of a rehabilitation program, veterans may: (a) enroll in trade, business or technical schools or in college-level institutions; (b) engage in training on the job or in an apprenticeship program; (c) take on-farm training; (d) enter programs which combine school and on-job-training; or (e) train in special rehabilitation facilities or at home when this is necessary because of serious disability. Veterans may also receive services and assistance to improve their ability to live more independently in their communities.

After completion of the training phase of a rehabilitation program, VA will assist the veteran to find and hold a suitable job.

SUBSISTENCE ALLOWANCES AND REHABILITATION PROGRAM COSTS

While in training and for two months after the completion of training, eligible veterans may receive subsistence allowances in addition to their disability compensation or retirement pay. Servicemembers cannot receive subsistence allowances until they leave active duty. VA pays the costs of tuition, fees, books, supplies and equipment. VA may also pay for special supportive services, such as tutorial assistance, prosthetic devices, lip-reading training and signing for the deaf. If during training or employment services the veteran's disabilities cause transportation expenses which would not be incurred by nondisabled persons, VA will help the veteran to pay for at least part of these expenses. If the veteran runs into financial difficulty during training, VA may provide an advance against future benefit payments.

WORK-STUDY

See Work-Study under Montgomery GI Bill (Active Duty).

RATES FOR VOCATIONAL REHABILITATION PROGRAM

Type of training	No dependents	One dependent	Two dependents	Each add'l. dependent
Institutional				
Full-time	$333	$413	$486	$35
Three-quarter-time	250	310	364	27
Half-time	167	207	244	18
Farm cooperative/ apprenticeship/OJT				
Full-time	291	352	405	26
Extended evaluation/ Independent living				
Full-time	333	413	486	35
Three-quarter-time	250	310	364	27
Half-time	167	207	244	18
Quarter-time	84	103	121	10

Special Program for Veterans Rated Unemployable

ELIGIBILITY/BENEFIT

A special program exists to rehabilitate veterans awarded 100 percent disability compensation based upon unemployability.

A veteran who has been granted an unemployability rating may request an evaluation and, if found entitled, may participate in a program of rehabilitation services and training and receive special assistance in securing employment which is available under the Vocational Rehabilitation Program.

If a veteran with an unemployability rating secures gainful employment during the special program period, the unemployability rating is protected from reduction until he or she has worked continuously for 12 months.

Special Program for Veterans Receiving Pension

ELIGIBILITY/BENEFIT

Veterans who are awarded VA pension through Jan. 31, 1992, may be eligible for up to 24 months — or more under certain circumstances —of vocational training. Program participants may also receive up to 18 months of employment counseling, job search and work adjustment services.

Every veteran under age 45 at the time pension is awarded, during the period Feb. 1, 1985 through Jan. 31, 1992, must participate in an evaluation by VA to determine the veteran's ability to benefit from vocational training and services. VA will suspend the pension award of any new pension recipient under age 45 who fails to participate in an evaluation unless the veteran's condition or other circumstances prevent completion of the evaluation.

Veterans aged 45 or older who are awarded pensions during this program period and veterans of any age who were awarded pensions prior to Feb. 1, 1985, may apply for an evaluation and participation in vocational training.

If the evaluation indicates the veteran could achieve a vocational goal and the veteran wants vocational training, VA will help develop a plan of training and supportive services needed to reach the goal. These veterans are not required to take part in a vocational training program.

A veteran will continue to receive a pension during training or employment services. If a veteran has begun to participate in this training program and subsequently loses entitlement to a pension, training under this program may be continued unless the pension termination was based upon a finding of fraud or administrative error in awarding the pension.

If a veteran participates in vocational training and the pension is terminated for excessive work or training income, the veteran may continue to receive VA health care and retain priority for treatment for three years after the date the pension is terminated.

Pension training program participants may work up to 12 months with no change in their evaluation as permanently and totally disabled. The employment must be within the scope of the vocational goal or a related field identified in the participant's VA rehabilitation plan and must be obtained within one year after eligibility for counseling expires. Earnings during this 12-month period count as income, however, for pension purposes.

VA HOME LOANS

The purpose of the VA home loan program is to help eligible veterans and their surviving spouses finance the purchase of homes with favorable loan terms and at a rate of interest which is usually lower than rates charged on similar mortgage loans. Such VA loans involve no downpayment unless (1) required by the lender, (2) the purchase price is more than the reasonable value of the property, as determined by the VA, or (3) the loan is made with graduated payment features.

The importance of the VA loan program is reflected by the fact that during fiscal year 1991, the VA guaranteed more than 181,000 home loans totaling more than $15.4 billion dollars.

PURPOSES OF VA HOME LOANS

VA home loans are available for the following purposes:

- To buy a home.
- To buy a residential unit in certain new or proposed, existing or converted condominium projects.
- To build a home.
- To repair, alter, or improve a home.
- To refinance an existing home loan.
- To buy a manufactured home with or without a lot.
- To buy and improve a manufactured home lot on which to place a unit owned and occupied by the veteran.
- To improve a home through installation of a solar heating and/or cooling system or other weatherization improvements.
- To purchase and improve simultaneously a home with energy conserving measures.

• To refinance an existing VA loan to reduce the interest rate.
• To refinance a manufactured home loan in order to acquire a lot.
• To simultaneously purchase and improve a home.

SERVICE ELIGIBILITY

Home loan eligibility requirements vary with regard to time and length of service.

A veteran is eligible for VA financing if his/her service falls within any of the following categories:

Wartime Service. If veteran served any time during
• World War II (September 16, 1940 to July 25, 1947).
• Korean Conflict (June 27, 1950 to January 31, 1955), or
• Vietnam Era (August 5, 1964 to May 7, 1975).
• Persian Gulf War (August 2, 1990 to present).

The veteran must have served at least 90 days on active duty and been discharged or released under other than dishonorable conditions. If less than 90 days were served, the veteran may be eligible if discharged because of a service-connected disability.

Peacetime Service. If service fell entirely within any one of the following periods:
• July 26, 1947 to June 26, 1950.
• February 1, 1955 to August 4, 1964, or
• May 8, 1975 to September 7, 1980 (if enlisted) or to October 16, 1981 (if officer).

The veteran must have served at least 181 days of continuous active duty and been discharged or released under conditions other than dishonorable. If less than 181 days were served, the veteran may be eligible if discharged because of a service-connected disability.

Service after September 7, 1980 (enlisted) or October 16, 1981 (officer). If the veteran was *separated* from service which began after these dates, he/she must have:
• Completed 24 months of continuous active duty or the full period (at least 181 days) for which you were called or ordered to active duty, and been discharged or released under conditions other than dishonorable; or
• Completed at least 181 days of active duty with a hardship discharge, a discharge for the convenience of the Government, or been determined to have a compensable service-connected disability; or
• Been discharged for a service-connected disability.

Active Duty Service Personnel. Veterans now on active duty are eligible after having served on continuous active status for at least 181 days, regardless of when service began.

OTHER TYPES OF SERVICE

- Certain United States citizens who served in the armed forces of a government allied with the United States in World War II.
- Unmarried surviving spouses of the above-described eligible persons who died as the result of service or service-connected injuries. (Children of deceased veterans are not eligible.)
- The spouse of any member of the Armed Forces serving on active duty who is listed as missing in action, or is a prisoner of war and has been so listed for a total of more than 90 days.
- Individuals with service as members in certain other organizations, services, programs and schools may also be eligible. Questions about whether this service qualifies for home loan benefits should be referred to the Loan Guaranty Division of the nearest VA regional office.

LOAN APPROVAL REQUIREMENTS

To get a VA loan, the law requires that:

- A person must be an eligible veteran who has available home loan entitlement;
- The loan must be for an eligible purpose;
- The veteran must occupy or intend to occupy the property as a home within a reasonable period of time after closing the loan;
- The veteran must have enough income to meet the new mortgage payments on the loan, cover the costs of owning a home, take care of other obligations and expenses, and still have enough income left over for family support (a spouse's income is considered in the same manner as the veteran's); and
- The veteran must have a good credit record.

THE LOAN GUARANTEE

VA-guaranteed loans are made by private lenders such as banks, savings and loan associations, or mortgage companies. To get a loan, a veteran must apply to the lender. If the loan is approved. VA guarantees the loan when it is closed. The guaranty means the lender is protected against loss if the veteran or a later owner fail to repay the loan.

VA will guarantee up to 50 percent of a home loan up to $45,000. For loans in excess of $45,000, up to 40 percent of the loan or a maximum of $36,000 can be guaranteed, with a minimum guaranty of $22,500, subject to the amount of entitlement a veteran has available. The veteran may generally borrow up to the reasonable value of the property or the purchase price, whichever is less, plus the funding fee, if required. For certain refinancing loans, the maximum loan is limited to 90 percent of the value of the property, plus the funding fee, if required. To determine the reasonable value, VA requires an appraisal of the property. The maximum amount of entitlement which may be used depends on the loan purpose and loan amount and will be the lesser of the percentage or dollar limits in the following table.

Loan Amount	Guaranty Percent	Dollar Amount
Up to $45,000	50%	$22,500
$45,001 to $56,250	40% - 50%	$22,500
$56,251 to $144,000	40%	$36,000
Over $144,000 (Purchase or construction loan only)	25%	$46,000
Manufactured home $20,000 and/or Lot loan*		40%

*A loan secured by a manufactured home which is permanently affixed to a lot and considered to be real property under the laws of the State where it is located may be eligible for a guaranty to the same extent as a home loan.

Veterans' maximum home loan entitlement was raised from $4,000 to $7,500 in 1950, to $12,500 in 1968, to $17,500 in 1974, to $25,000 in 1978, to $27,500 in 1980, to $36,000 in 1988, and up to $46,000 in 1989 for certain specific purposes. A veteran who previously obtained a VA loan can use the remaining entitlement for any eligible purpose, except that veterans who used their entitlement to purchase a manufactured home must first dispose of the manufactured home prior to the purchase of a second manufactured home with a VA guaranteed loan. The amount of remaining entitlement is the difference between $36,000 (or $46,000 for certain loans) and the amount of entitlement used on prior loans. Veterans refinancing an existing VA loan with a new VA loan at a lower interest rate need not have any entitlement available for use.

OBTAINING A CERTIFICATE OF ELIGIBILITY

VA determines a veteran's eligibility and, if qualified, the VA issues a certificate of eligibility to be used in applying for a VA loan.

Should a certificate from VA be needed, a veteran must complete VA Form 26-1880, Request for Determination of Eligibility and Available Loan Guaranty Entitlement (this form may be obtained from any VA office).

STEPS IN ARRANGING VA LOAN

- Find suitable property.
- Apply to lender for loan.
- Present discharge papers and/or Certificate of Eligibility.
- Have property appraised by an approved appraiser to determine reasonable value.
- Loan received when application is approved.

Lenders may be found by contacting the local chamber of commerce, examining the telephone directory under "Mortgages," or by inquiring at banks, savings and loan associations, mortgage companies, real estate brokers' offices, and other public and private lending agencies. The local VA regional office will also provide a list of lenders who are active in the program.

LOAN REPAYMENT TERMS

The maximum VA home loan term is 30 years and 32 days; however, the term may never be for more than the remaining economic life of the property as determined by the appraisal.

REPAYMENT PLAN

VA will guarantee loans to purchase homes made with the following repayment plans:

- **Traditional Fixed-Payment Mortgage**
- **GPM (Graduated Payment Mortgage)**
- **Buydowns**
  The builder of a new home or seller of an existing home may "buy down" the veteran's mortgage payments by making a large lump-sum payment up front at closing that will be used to supplement the monthly payments for a certain period, usually 1 to 3 years.
- **GEM (Growing Equity Mortgage)**

DOWNPAYMENT REQUIREMENTS

- **Traditional Fixed-Payment Mortgage, Buydown Loans, and Growing Equity Mortgage**
  VA does not require a downpayment if the purchase price or cost is not more than the reasonable value of the property as determined by VA, but the lender may require one. If the purchase price or cost is more than the reasonable value, the difference must be paid in cash by the veteran.
- **Graduated Payment Mortgage**
  The maximum loan amount may not be for more than the reasonable

value of the property or the purchase price, whichever is less. Because the loan balance will be increasing during the first years of the loan, a downpayment is required to keep the loan balance from exceeding the reasonable value or the purchase price.

INTEREST RATES

The maximum interest rate on VA loans varies from time to time based on changes in the mortgage market. Once a loan is made, the interest rate set in the note will stay the same for the life of the loan. However, if the VA interest rate goes down, and the veteran still owns and occupies the property, he/she may apply for a new VA loan to refinance the previous loan at a lower interest rate without using any additional entitlement.

In February 1992, the following maximum VA loan rates were in effect:

Home Loans — 8.5%
Graduated Payment Mortgages — 8.75%
Home Improvement Loans — 10%
Manufactured Home Loans — 11%
Manufactured Home Lots Only — 10.5%
Manufactured Home and Lot Loans — 10.5%

CLOSING COSTS

Payment in cash is required on all home loan closing costs, including title search and recording, hazard insurance premiums, prepaid taxes, and the 1 percent origination fee which may be required by lenders in lieu of certain other costs. In the case of refinancing loans, all such costs may be included in the loan, as long as the total loan does not exceed 90 percent of the reasonable value established by VA for the property. Loans, including refinancing loans, are charged a funding fee by the VA, with the exception of loans made to certain disabled veterans and unremarried surviving spouses of veterans who died as a result of service or service-connected disabilities. The funding fee is based on the loan amount and, at the lender's discretion, may be included in the loan. The amount of the funding fee will be in accordance with the following table.

Loan Category	Funding Fee
Purchase or construction loans with downpayments of less than 5 percent; Refinancing loans; Home improvement/repair loans.	1.25 percent of the loan
Purchase or construction loans with downpayments of at least 5 percent but less than 10 percent.	0.75 percent
Purchase or construction loans with downpayments of 10 percent or more.	0.50 percent
Manufactured home loans.	1.0 percent

DISCOUNT POINTS

Generally, veterans are not permitted to pay discounts or "points" in connection with VA financing, although these charges are usually paid by persons selling homes to VA buyers. The amount of discount to be paid is a matter of negotiation between the seller and the lender. VA has no direct control over the charging of discounts.

Veterans may pay discount points only in connection with the following types of VA loans:

• When refinancing an existing home loan on owned property.
• When repairing, altering, or improving a home.
• When building a home on land already owned or to be purchased from a source other than the builder.
• In some cases, when purchasing a home from a seller who VA determines is legally precluded from paying such a discount.

EQUAL HOUSING OPPORTUNITY

Discrimination in the sale of housing because of race, color, religion, sex or national origin **is prohibited** by federal laws. Veterans are protected from the following acts when they are based on discrimination on account of race, color, religion, sex or national origin:

• Refusal to deal,
• Discrimination in terms of sale,
• Discriminatory advertising,
• False representations that a dwelling is not available,
• Blockbusting,
• Discrimination in financing, and
• Discrimination in real estate services.

All VA program participants — builders, brokers and lenders offering housing for sale with VA financing — must comply with Executive Order 11063 banning discrimination in all federally assisted housing and the Civil Rights Act of 1968, as amended.

The local VA office will investigate any suspected discrimination by a builder or lender. To start a VA investigation, the veteran should submit a written complaint directly to the local VA office. VA has a form for complaints (VA Form 26-8827, Housing Discrimination Complaint) which may be requested from a local VA office. When the suspected discrimination concerns HUD/FHA (Department of Housing and Urban Development/Federal Housing Administration) home loans and other housing, complaint letters should be sent to the Department of Housing and Urban Development, Assistant Secretary for Fair Housing and Equal Opportunity, Washington, D.C. 20410.

AVAILABILITY OF HOMES

If a veteran is unable to find new homes available for sale with VA financing, or is unable to determine whether homes being built are available for sale with VA financing, the local VA regional office should be contacted. In addition, in many areas VA has repossessed homes which it will sell to qualified buyers.

CREDIT FOR FARMS AND HOMES

Advice can be provided by the Farmers Home Administration (FmHA) to qualified individuals to buy, improve or operate farms. Loans are available for housing in towns generally up to 10,000 population. In some circumstances the town population can be as large as 20,000.

For individual loans, applications from eligible veterans have preference for processing. For further information contact FmHA, U.S. Department of Agriculture, Washington, D.C. 20250, or apply at local FmHA offices, usually located in county seat towns.

FHA MORTGAGE INSURANCE

The Department of Housing and Urban Development (HUD) administers the Federal Housing Administration Home Mortgage Insurance Program for veterans. These home loans require less downpayment than under other FHA programs. Veterans on active duty are eligible who originally enlisted before Sept. 8, 1980, or who entered on active duty before Oct. 14, 1982, and who were discharged under other than dishonorable conditions with at least 90 days of service. Veterans with enlisted service after Sept. 7, 1980, or who entered on active duty after Oct. 16, 1981, must have served at least 24 months unless discharged for hardship or disability. Active duty for training is qualifying service. Submit VA Form 26-8261a, available at any VA office, to VA for a Certificate of Veteran Status. This certificate is submitted by the lender to FHA.

STATE PROGRAMS

Many states offer housing programs which are independent of federal programs. The programs and benefits, as well as the qualifying criteria, may differ from one state to the next. Information on state programs may be obtained from state officials or from the local VA regional office.

WHAT VA LOANS CAN DO

VA loans offer the following important advantages over most conventional loans:

- No downpayment is required in most cases;
- The interest rate usually is lower than conventional mortgage interest rates;
- The buyer is informed of the estimated reasonable value of the property;
- There is a limitation on closing costs;
- On an assumable mortgage (for loans closed on or after March 1, 1988), the assumption must be approved in advance by the lender or VA;
- Long amortization (repayment) terms;
- The right to prepay without penalty;
- For houses appraised by VA prior to construction, inspections during stages of construction assure compliance with the approved plans, and include a warranty to the buyer from the builder that the house has been built in conformity with approved plans and specifications; and
- Forbearance (leniency) is extended to worthy VA homeowners experiencing temporary financial difficulty.

WHAT VA CANNOT DO

VA does not have the legal authority to:
- Act as the veteran's architect. It does not supervise construction of the house to be purchased;
- Guarantee that the house is free of defects;
- Act as the veteran's attorney;
- Compel a builder to remedy defects in construction or otherwise compel the builder to live up to a contract;

- Guarantee a completely satisfactory house, or that it can be sold at a satisfactory price; and
- Guarantee that the veteran is making a good investment.

RELEASE OF LIABILITY

A release of liability to the Government means that the Government will not attempt to collect from the veteran in the event he/she defaults on the loan and VA pays a claim under the guaranty. The purchaser may be released of that liability to VA if the loan is current and if the purchase has been obligated by contract to purchase the property and assume the liability. In addition, the purchaser must satisfy VA that he/she is a good credit risk.

The purchaser does not have to sell the home to a veteran to obtain a release from liability to the Government. The proposed purchaser may be a veteran or a nonveteran. If the veteran purchased the home with a VA direct loan, he/she may be released from liability to the Government under the same conditions as a veteran with a guaranteed GI loan. A spouse is also liable to the Government if he/she signed the note when the GI loan was made. However, when the veteran is released from liability to the Government, the spouse will also be released from such liability.

A veteran may apply to VA for a release from liability by submitting a request to the VA regional office that processed the loan. If the loan closed on or after March 1, 1988, the first contact should be with the lender to see if they will handle the request as an authorized agent of VA. No special form is needed. However, the request should include the VA loan number if known (it is shown on the reverse of the certificate of eligibility), the address of the property, the name and address of the proposed purchaser, and the name and address of the holder of the mortgage.

Either the lender or the Loan Guaranty Officer at the VA regional office which processed the original loan determines whether the veteran will be released from liability to the Government. Upon request, the lender or VA will send all necessary information and forms for transferring the liability to the new purchaser and obtaining a release.

The holder of a mortgage may release the veteran from liability if VA does. However, VA has no authority to require the holder to do so. Further information concerning this should be obtained from the firm or agency to which payments are being made prior to the actual sale of the property. If the holder of the mortgage refuses to release the veteran from liability, he/she is still liable to the holder even though released from liability to the Government. What happens would depend on the facts of the case and local laws.

The cost of obtaining a release of liability will vary, depending on when the loan was obtained. Older loans involve only the cost of a credit report on the proposed purchaser and the cost of recording the assumption agreement and release, if recording is necessary. Such costs must be paid by either the veteran or the proposed purchaser.

For loans closed on or after March 1, 1988,the law allows a lender or VA to collect a processing charge for determining whether or not the proposed assumption may be approved. In addition, the law requires that an assumer of the GI loan pay to VA a funding fee equal to one-half of 1 percent of the loan balance. This is usually collected at loan closing, sent to the lender with the other information on the sale, and then forwarded to VA.

The veteran's entitlement cannot be restored after release from liability to the Government unless VA is also released from liability on the guaranty by the holder, and the veteran is otherwise eligible for restoration. Normally, VA is not relieved of its liability on the guaranty unless the loan is paid in full, as VA continues to be liable on the guaranty even though the veteran has been released from liability to the Government.

Additional information concerning the release of veterans from liability on GI loans may be obtained from the nearest VA office.

RESTORING ELIGIBILITY

If a veteran sold a home purchased with a VA loan, it is possible to have the home loan benefit restored to permit purchase of another home with a VA loan. To do this, the veteran must have disposed of the property which originally secured the loan, and the VA loan must be paid in full or the holder must relieve VA of liability. These events do not have to occur at the same time, but both requirements must be met before VA can reinstate the home loan benefit. To find out if the loan has been paid in full, the veteran should contact the lender or the VA office which guaranteed the loan.

THE FOLLOWING AMORTIZATION TABLE IS PRESENTED FOR COMPARISON PURPOSES.

AMORTIZATION TABLE
Monthly Principal and Interest Payments Over 30 Years*

Mortgage Amount	7½%	8%	8½%	9%	9½%	10%	10½%	11%	11½%	12%
$20,000	$140	$147	$154	$161	$168	$176	$183	$190	$198	$206
$30,000	210	220	231	241	252	263	274	286	297	309
$40,000	280	295	308	322	336	351	366	381	396	411
$50,000	350	370	385	402	420	439	457	476	495	514
$60,000	420	440	461	483	505	527	549	571	594	617
$70,000	490	514	536	563	589	614	640	667	693	720
$80,000	559	587	615	644	673	702	734	762	792	823
$90,000	629	660	692	724	757	790	823	857	891	926
$100,000	699	734	769	805	841	878	915	952	990	1,029
$120,000	839	881	923	966	1,008	1,050	1,098	1,143	1,188	1,234
$140,000	979	1,027	1,076	1,126	1,177	1,229	1,281	1,333	1,386	1,440
$160,000	1,119	1,174	1,230	1,287	1,345	1,414	1,464	1,524	1,584	1,646
$180,000	1,259	1,321	1,384	1,448	1,514	1,580	1,647	1,714	1,783	1,852
$200,000	1,398	1,468	1,538	1,609	1,682	1,755	1,829	1,905	1,981	2,057
$250,000	1,748	1,834	1,922	2,012	2,102	2,194	2,287	2,381	2,476	2,572

*Rounded to nearest dollar.

QUESTIONS AND ANSWERS

Q. Is a guaranteed loan a gift?

A. No. It must be repaid.

Q. Does VA home loan entitlement provide cash to the veteran?

A. No. The amount of entitlement relates only to the amount VA will guarantee the lender against loss.

Q. Does VA make any loan directly to eligible veterans?

A. Yes, but only to supplement a grant to get a specially adapted home for certain eligible veterans who have a permanent and total service-connected disability(ies). See VA Pamphlet 26-69-1 for information concerning specially adapted housing grants.

Q. How much entitlement does each veteran have?

A. Originally, the maximum entitlement available was $2,000; however, legislation enacted since that time has provided veterans with increases in entitlement up to the present $36,000, and up to $46,000 for certain specific purposes.

Q. Does a veteran's home loan entitlement expire?

A. No. Home loan entitlement is generally good until used. However, the eligibility of service personnel is only available so long as they remain on active duty. If they are discharged or released from active duty before using their entitlement, a new determination of their eligibility must be made, based on the length of service and the type of discharge received.

Q. What service is not eligible?

A. Veterans are not eligible for VA financing based on the following:
  • World War I service.
  • Active Duty for Training in the Reserves.
  • Active Duty for Training in the National Guard (unless "activated" under the authority of title 10, U.S. Code).

Q. Does it take longer to get a VA or FHA loan than a conventional loan?

A. No. Typically, from application to closing takes less than 45 days.

Q. May a lender require security from the veteran in addition to the property being purchased?

A. Yes. This is a matter between the veteran and the lender. While VA does not require that additional security be taken, it does not object if the veteran is willing.

Q. Does the issuance of a certificate of eligibility guarantee approval of a VA loan?

A. No. The veteran must still be found to be qualified for the loan from an income and credit standpoint.

Q. What is the maximum purchase with a VA loan, with a minimum down payment?

A. For a VA loan, which requires no down payment, the maximum is $184,000, all across the country.

Q. How are VA loans processed?

A. There are two ways a lender may process VA home loans — on a "prior approval" or "automatic" basis.

When the loan is processed on a prior approval basis, the lender takes the application, requests VA to appraise the property, and verifies the veteran's income and credit record. All this information is put together in a loan package and sent to VA for review. If VA approves the loan, a commitment by VA to guarantee the loan is sent to the lender. The lender then closes the loan and sends a report of the closing to VA. If the loan complies with VA requirements, VA issues the lender a certificate of guaranty.

In automatic processing, the lender (assuming the VA provides the authority) still orders an appraisal from VA, but has the authority to make the credit decision on the loan without VA's approval.

Q. If a lender is unwilling to accept a veteran's application for a loan, what should the veteran do?

A. The veteran should see another lender. The fact that one lender is not interested in making the loan the veteran wants does not mean that other lenders will not make the loan.

Q. What should a veteran do while waiting for loan approval?

A. sometimes it may take longer than anticipated for the lender or VA to process a loan application. Ordinarily, you should plan on an average of 4 to 6 weeks to obtain a decision on your application. No commitments should be made based upon the anticipated loan until it has been approved.

Q. May a veteran pay off a VA loan before it becomes due?

A. Yes. A VA loan may be partially or fully paid at any time without penalty.

Q. May the maturity on a VA loan be extended to reduce the monthly payments?

A. Yes, provided the veteran and the lender want to extend it and the extension provides for complete repayment of the loan within the maximum period permitted for loans of its type.

Q. Does the seller have to pay points on a VA mortgage?
A. Yes, the seller will have to pay points, but this can be negotiated at the time of the contract.

Q. Does having a VA loan limit a veteran's right or ability to sell the property?
A. No. A veteran may sell the property to a veteran or nonveteran at any time. However, if the loan was closed after March 1, 1988, and it will be assumed, the qualifications of the assumer must be reviewed and approved by the lender or VA.

Q. If a veteran dies before the loan is paid off, will the VA guaranty pay off the balance of the loan?
A. No. The surviving spouse, other coborrower, or the veteran's estate must continue to make the payments.

Q. May a veteran join with a nonveteran in obtaining a VA loan?
A. Yes, but the guaranty is based only on the veteran's portion of the loan.

Q. Can a veteran get a VA loan to buy or construct a residential property containing more than one family unit?
A. Yes, but the total number of separate units cannot be more than four if one veteran is buying. If the veteran must depend on rental income from the property to qualify for the loan, the veteran must: (a) show that he/she has the background or qualifications to be successful as a landlord, and (b) have enough cash reserves to make the loan payments for at least 6 months without help from the rental income.

Q. Can a veteran get a VA business loan?
A. No, but business loans may be obtained through the SBA (Small Business Administration).

Q. Can a veteran get a VA farm loan?
A. No, except for a farm on which there is a farm residence which will be personally occupied by the veteran as a home.

Q. Can a veteran obtain a VA loan for the purchase of property in a foreign country?
A. No. The property must be located in the United States, its territories,

or possessions. The latter consist of Puerto Rico, Guam, Virgin Islands, American Samoa, and Northern Mariana Islands.

Q. If both a husband and wife are eligible, may they acquire property jointly and so increase the amount which may be guaranteed?

A. They may acquire property jointly, but the amount of guaranty on the loan may not exceed the lesser of 40 percent of the loan amount or $36,000.

Q. How may a veteran obtain a release of liability from VA?

A. By having the buyer assume all of the veteran's liabilities on the VA loan, and by having VA or the loan holder approve the buyer and the assumption agreement.

Q. If a loan closed prior to March 1, 1988 can be assumed without VA's approval, why should a veteran be concerned about requesting and obtaining a release from personal liability?

A. If a veteran does not obtain a release of liability, and VA suffers a loss on account of a default by the assumer or some future assumer, a debt may be established against the veteran.

Q. When a veteran sells the property to someone who will assume the existing VA loan, is the veteran released automatically, from personal liability for repayment of the loan?

A. No. If the loan was closed after March 1, 1988, the lender or VA must be notified and requested to approve the assumer and grant the veteran release from liability. If the loan was closed prior to March 1, 1988, the loan may be assumed without approval from VA or the lender. However, the veteran is strongly urged to request a release of liability from VA.

Q. If a veteran obtains a release of liability, is restoration of entitlement automatic?

A. No, the entitlement can only be restored after the VA loan is paid in full.

Q. If a veteran plans to sell a home purchased with the assistance of a VA loan, what should be done to avoid future liability for the loan?

A. In planning to sell your home, you may take either of two steps to avoid future liability: (1) You can arrange for your VA loan to be paid in full which allows you to obtain restoration of your entitlement and reuse your benefit for another home loan, or (2) you can allow the purchaser to assume your VA loan and obtain a release of your liability on the loan from the holder of the mortgage and VA provided, of course, both agree. However, release of liability does not meet all the requirements for restoring your home loan benefit for a future purchase.

Q. Can a veteran get used entitlement back to use again?

A. If you have used all or part of your entitlement, you can get that entitlement back to purchase another home if the following conditions for "restoration" are met:

- The property has been sold *and* the loan has been paid in full, or
- A qualified veteran-transferee (buyer) must agree to assume the outstanding balance on the loan and agree to "substitute" his or her entitlement for the *same* amount of entitlement you originally used to get the loan. The buyer must also meet the occupancy and income and credit requirements of the law.

Restoration of entitlement is not automatic. You must apply for it by completing and returning VA Form 26-1880 to any VA regional office or center.

Application forms for substitution of entitlement may be requested from the VA office that guaranteed the loan.

Q. What recourse is available to a veteran recalled to active military duty and therefore unable to meet full payment on a VA home loan?

A. The Soldiers' and Sailors' Relief Act of 1940 makes it possible for the courts, upon proper application and showing, to provide relief while you are in service and for a period of time determined by the court after your discharge, provided your income is so reduced that you are unable to make the required payments.

LIFE INSURANCE

STATUS OF LIFE INSURANCE PROGRAMS

ENDING DATE FOR POLICY LETTER

Program	Beginning Date	Ending Date for New Issues	Policy Letter Prefix
U.S. Government (USGLI)	May 1919	April 24, 1951	K
National Service (NSLI)	Oct. 8, 1940	April 24, 1951	V, H
Veterans Special (VSLI)	April 25, 1951	Dec. 31, 1956	RS, W
Service Disabled (SDVI)	April 25, 1951	Still Open	RH
Veterans Reopened (VRI)	May 1, 1965	May 2, 1966	J, JR, JS
Servicemen's Group (SGLI)	Sept. 29, 1965	Still Open	
Veterans Mortgage (VMLI)	Aug. 11, 1971	Still Open	
Veterans Group (VGLI)	Aug. 1, 1974	Still Open	

Until July 1, 1972, the maximum amount of government life insurance, exclusive of SGLI, VGLI, and VMLI, that one could carry was $10,000. Effective that date, policyholders with WWII National Service Life Insurance (V) could elect to use their dividends to purchase additional paid-up coverage, which, for the first time, permitted these insureds to have more than $10,000 coverage. Policyholders with Veterans Special Life Insurance (RS, W) and Veterans Reopened Insurance (J, JR, JS) may now purchase these paid-up additions, as well. Effective Jan. 1, 1983, all United States Government Life Insurance (K) policies in a premium-paying status were declared to be paid up in full.

ELIGIBILITY FOR SERVICE-DISABLED VETERANS INSURANCE (RH)

Veterans separated from service on or after April 25, 1951, who are granted a service-connected disability but are otherwise in good health may apply to VA for up to $10,000 life insurance coverage at standard insurance rates within two years from the date VA notifies the veteran that the disability has been rated as service-connected.

REINSTATEMENT OF LAPSED INSURANCE

Lapsed term policies may be reinstated within five years from the date of lapse. However, NSLI on the Limited Convertible Term Plan (Policy prefix W) may not be reinstated if the term period which ends after the policyholder's 50th birthday has expired.

Lapsed permanent plan policies may be reinstated at any time except that J and JR policies must be ininstated within five years from date of lapse, and an endowment plan must be reinstated within the endowment period.

AUTOMATIC RENEWAL

A five-year term policy which is not lapsed at the end of the term period is automatically renewed for an additional five-year period. The exception is the NSLI Limited Convertible Term Plan (policy prefix W) which may be converted to a permanent plan, but cannot be renewed after the insured's 50th birthday. The premium rate for each renewal is based on the attained age of the insured, except "V" and "RS" prefixed policies renewed beyond age 70. The rate on these policies is based on the age 70 renewal rate, with no further increases occurring over the remaining life of the contract.

CONVERTIBILITY

Any term policy which is in force may be converted to a permanent plan if requirements are met. NSLI policyholders, however, are not eligible to convert to an endowment plan while totally disabled. Upon reaching renewal at age 70 or older, NSLI "V" and "RS" term policies on total disability premium waiver are automatically converted to a permanent plan of insurance which provides cash and loan value as well as higher annual dividends.

MODIFIED LIFE

A "modified life at age 65" plan of insurance is available to NSLI policyholders. The comparatively low premium rates for this plan remain the same throughout the premium-paying period, while the face value reduces by 50 percent at age 65. The reduced amount may be replaced with a "special ordinary life" plan, for an additional premium.

In 1972, a "modified life at age 70" plan became available, which is like the modified life at age 65 plan except that face value reduction does not occur until age 70. The premium rate is only slightly higher than for the modified life at age 65 plan.

DIVIDENDS

Dividends are paid to holders of "K," "V," "RS," "W," "J," "JR," and "JS" insurance on the policy anniversary date. Dividends currently are not paid to holders of "H" or "RH" policies, or to holders of the current policies, SGLI, VMLI and VGLI.

GUARANTEED PERMANENT PLAN POLICY VALUES

When a permanent plan policy has had premiums paid or waived for at least one year, and it is not lapsed, the guaranteed values include cash surrender, loan and reduced paid-up provisions. If a permanent plan policy lapses after being in force for at least three months, it will automatically be extended as term insurance. The period of this protection is determined by the net cash value of the policy. The amount of extended coverage is the face value less any indebtedness.

POLICY LOANS

Policyholders may borrow up to 94 percent of the cash surrender value of their permanent plan on insurance and continue the insurance in force by payment of premiums.

All NSLI policy loans applied for on and after Nov. 2, 1987, are charged interest at an adjustable rate which may increase or decrease annually each Oct. 1. Future changes to the adjustable loan interest rate will be tied to the 10-year U.S. Treasury securities index. The annual interest charged on adjustable-rate loans will not go higher than 12 percent or lower than 5 percent. The interest rates currently on United States Government Life Insurance (USGLI) policy loans and existing fixed rate NSLI policy loans will remain unchanged. Interest on policy loans is compounded annually. The current interest rate may be obtained at any VA office.

TOTAL OR PERMANENT DISABILITY

NSLI policyholders who become totally disabled before their 65th birthday and are likely to remain so for six or more months should consult VA about their entitlement to premium waiver. USGLI policyholders who become totally and permanently disabled should consult VA about their right to receive the proceeds of their policies in monthly payments.

TOTAL DISABILITY INCOME PROVISION (TDIP)

Full information about adding the TDIP rider to a policy is available from the VA Regional Office and Insurance Center which maintains the veteran's insurance records, or the nearest VA office. The provision currently provides that an NSLI policyholder will be paid $10 per month, per $1,000 insurance, after being totally disabled for six consecutive months. A few older riders pay $5 per month. In either instance, disability must have commenced before the insured reached his or her 60th or 65th birthday, depending on the type of rider. USGLI policies also carry a TDIP provision. The amount of the monthly payment, however, differs from that paid to NSLI policyholders. TDIP payments do not reduce the face value of the policy. TDIP is not available for any policy with the prefix RH, JR, or JS.

Servicemen's Group Life Insurance (SGLI)

All members of the uniformed services, including cadets and midshipmen of the four service academies, are automatically insured under Servicemen's Group Life Insurance (SGLI) for $100,000, unless they elect in writing to be covered for a lesser amount, or not to be covered at all. Full-time coverage is also provided, under certain conditions, for (1) persons who volunteer for assignment to the Ready Reserve of a uniformed service, and (2) persons assigned to or who, upon application, would be eligible for assignment to the Retired Reserve of a uniformed service and have completed at least 20 years of satisfactory service creditable for retirement purposes.

Part-time coverage is provided, under certain conditions, to eligible members of the reserves who do not qualify for full-time coverage.

Premiums are deducted automatically from a member's pay, or otherwise, collected from members on active duty or in the Ready Reserve by their uniformed service. Members of the Retired Reserve currently must submit premiums directly to the Office of Servicemen's Group Life Insurance (OSGLI).

Members performing full-time duty under calls or orders not limited to 30 days or less, and members of the Ready Reserve who qualify for full-time coverage, are covered for 120 days following separation from service with no additional premium during that period. Those members who are totally disabled at separation retain SGLI coverage up to one year or until the disability ceases to be total in degree, whichever occurs first, with no additional premium cost during this period.

Members of the reserve who qualify for full-time coverage and who, upon application, are eligible for assignment to or are assigned to the Retired Reserve may convert their coverage to an individual commercial policy with any of the participating companies. As an alternative, they may continue their SGLI coverage after separation or release from their reserve obligation, provided the initial premium with identifying information is submitted within 120 days of release, to the Office of Servicemen's Group Life Insurance, 213 Washington Street, Newark, N.J. 07102.

If the initial premium is not submitted within the 120 days, coverage may be granted, provided an application — SGLV 8713, Evidence of Insurability — and the initial premium are submitted to OSGLI within one year after the member's SGLI coverage is terminated.

Veterans Group Life Insurance (VGLI)

SGLI may be converted to five-year term coverage known as VGLI (Veterans' Group Life Insurance). This program is administered by OSGLI (Office of Servicemen's Group Life Insurance), 213 Washington Street, Newark, N.J., 07102, and is supervised by the Department of Veterans Affairs. Coverage may be obtained in increments of $10,000 up to a maximum of $100,000, but not more than the amount of SGLI that the member had in force at the time of separation from military service.

VGLI is available to:

(a) Individuals being released from active duty on or after Aug. 1, 1974.

(b) Reservists who, while performing active duty or inactive duty for training under a call or order specifying a period of less than 31 days, suffer an injury or disability which renders the reservists uninsurable at standard premium rates.

(c) Members of the Individual Ready Reserve (IRR) and Inactive National Guard (ING).

Members on active duty entitled to full-time SGLI coverage can convert to VGLI by submitting the premium before the end of 120 days following the date of separation from service. The insurance is effective on the 121st day. If the veteran, unless totally disabled, does not submit the premium within 120 days, the veteran may be granted VGLI, provided initial premium and evidence of insurability are submitted within one year after the veteran's SGLI coverage is terminated. Insurance will be effective on the date the premium is received in the office of SGLI.

Members with full-time SGLI coverage who are totally disabled at the time of separation and whose service makes them eligible for VGLI may purchase the insurance while remaining totally disabled up to one year following separation. The effective date of VGLI will be at the end of the one-year period following separation or the date the disability ends, whichever is earlier, but not prior to 120 days after separation.

Members insured under part-time SGLI coverage who incur a disability or aggravate a preexisting disability during a reserve active or inactive period can, within the 120-day period following the period during which the disability was incurred or aggravated, apply for VGLI with the insurance made effective on the 121st day.

Totally disabled members must submit proof of disability with an application and the first premium. As persons separate from active duty, reenlist and effect other changes in duty status, some persons will be eligible for both SGLI and VGLI. Any former member insured under VGLI who may again become eligible for SGLI is automatically insured under the SGLI program. Both plans can be participated in if it is advantageous to the individual, as long as the combined amount of SGLI and VGLI does not exceed $100,000 at any one time.

A VGLI policyholder has the right to convert to an individual commercial policy at standard premium rates, regardless of health, with any of the participating companies licensed to do business in the veteran's state. The individual policy will be effective the date after the insured's VGLI terminates at the end of the five-year period. The OSGLI will advise the insured of the impending date of termination and give additional information regarding the conversion of VGLI to an individual policy.

Individuals who remain in the IRR or ING throughout their period of VGLI coverage can renew their VGLI for additional five-year periods instead of converting to an individual policy. They can still convert at the end of subsequent periods of coverage. Veterans wanting further information may contact their nearest VA office, or write to or call the Office of Servicemen's Group Life Insurance at (201) 802-7676.

Veterans Mortgage Life Insurance (VMLI)

The maximum amount of mortgage life insurance available for those who have been granted or will be granted a specially adapted housing grant is $40,000. Protection is automatic unless eligible veterans decline in writing or fail to respond to a final request for information on which their premium can be based. Premiums are automatically deducted from VA benefit payments or paid direct, if the veteran does not draw compensation, and will continue until the mortgage, up to the maximum amount of insurance, has been liquidated, or the home is sold, or until the coverage terminates when the veteran reaches age 70, or dies. If a mortgage is disposed of through liquidation or sale of the property, VMLI may be obtained on the mortgage of a second or subsequent home.

Income Tax Ruling

The Internal Revenue Service has announced that interest on dividends left on deposit with the VA is not taxable. For details on this ruling contact the IRS.

BENEFIT PROGRAMS FOR SURVIVORS

Dependency and Indemnity Compensation (DIC)

ELIGIBILITY

Death Due to Service-Connected Disability — DIC payments are authorized for surviving spouses, unmarried children under 18 (as well as certain helpless children and those between 18 and 23 if attending a VA-approved school), and certain parents of service personnel or veterans who died from: (1) a disease or injury incurred or aggravated in line of duty while on active duty or active duty for training; or (2) an injury incurred or aggravated in line of duty while on inactive duty training; or (3) a disability otherwise compensable by VA. Death cannot be the result of willful misconduct.

Death Due to Nonservice-Connected Cause — DIC payments are also authorized for surviving spouses, unmarried children under 18 (as well as certain helpless children and those between 18 and 23 if attending a VA-approved school), of certain veterans who were totally service-connected disabled at time of death and whose deaths were not the result of their service-connected disability, if: (1) the veteran was continuously rated totally disabled for a period of 10 or more years or (2) if so rated for less than 10 years, was so rated for a period of not less than five years from the date of discharge from military service. Payments under this provision are subject to offset by the amount received from judicial proceedings brought on account of the veteran's death.

If death occurred after service, the veteran's discharge must have been under conditions other than dishonorable.

DEFINITION OF SURVIVING SPOUSE

Date of Marriage — To qualify, a surviving spouse generally must have been married to the veteran one year or more, or for any period of time if a child was born of or before the marriage. Other conditions apply in certain cases.

Residence With Veteran — The surviving spouse must have lived continuously with the veteran from the time of marriage until the veteran's death, except where there was a separation not due to the fault of the surviving spouse.

Surviving Spouse Remarriage — Remarriage makes a surviving spouse ineligible based on the death of that veteran unless the remarriage was void or annulled by a court. A surviving spouse may also be ineligible if after the death of the veteran, she or he has lived with another man or woman and held herself or himself out openly to the public to be the spouse.

Deemed-Valid Marriage — If she or he meets the other qualifications, a spouse who married a veteran without knowing that a legal impediment to the marriage existed may be eligible for compensation under certain conditions.

BENEFITS

DIC SURVIVING SPOUSE

Pay grade	Monthly rate	Pay grade	Monthly rate
E-1	$616	W-4	$884
E-2	635	O-1	780
E-3	652	O-2	805
E-4	693	O-3	862
E-5	711	O-4	912
E-6	727	O-5	1,005
E-7	762	O-6	1,134
E-8	805	O-7	1,225
E-9*	841	O-8	1,343
W-1	780	O-9	1,440
W-2	811	O-10*	1,580
W-3	835		

*There are special rates for certain individuals in these categories.

There are additional payments for children.

The monthly rates of DIC for parents depend upon the income of the parents and whether there is only one parent, two parents not living together or two parents together or remarried with spouse. The income limit for two parents together or remarried and with spouse is $11,313; that for one parent or two parents not together is $8,414.

AID AND ATTENDANCE

Surviving spouses, and parents receiving DIC may be granted a special allowance for aid and attendance if they are patients in a nursing home or require the regular aid and attendance of another person. The allowance is $184 monthly, payable in addition to the DIC rate for a surviving spouse and $185 monthly additional for a parent receiving DIC.

HOUSEBOUND

Surviving spouses qualified for DIC who are not so disabled as to require the regular aid and attendance of another person but who, due to disability, are permanently housebound may be granted a special allowance of $90 monthly, in addition to the DIC rate otherwise payable.

Reinstated Entitlement Program for Survivors (REPS)

ELIGIBILITY/BENEFIT

Certain survivors of veterans who died of service-connected causes incurred or aggravated prior to August 13, 1981 are eligible for benefits. The benefits are similar to the benefits for students and surviving spouses with children between ages 16 and 18 which were eliminated from the Social Security Act. The benefits are payable in addition to any other benefits to which the family may also be entitled. The amount of benefits is based on information obtained from the Social Security Administration.

Death Compensation Relating to Deaths Before January 1, 1957

ELIGIBILITY

Death compensation payments are authorized for surviving spouses, certain helpless children, and dependent parents of servicepersons or veterans who died before Jan. 1, 1957, from a service-connected cause not the result of willful misconduct.

Survivors with eligibility for death compensation benefits may elect to receive DIC benefits. Generally the DIC benefits will pay greater rates, especially for surviving spouses and children. More specific information about death compensation benefits may be obtained from the nearest VA regional office. If a survivor has eligibility for both death compensation and DIC, the VA office processing the claim will notify the survivor about the dual entitlement and will explain how to elect payments under the DIC program.

Nonservice-Connected Death Pension

INTRODUCTION/ELIGIBILITY

Certain surviving spouses and children of deceased wartime veterans may qualify for nonservice-connected death pensions.

The veteran must have had 90 days wartime service, unless discharged or retired for service-connected disability, and been discharged under conditions other than dishonorable. If the veteran died in service not in line of duty, benefits may be payable if the veteran had completed at least two years of honorable active service.

Surviving spouses and unmarried children under age 18 — or until 23 if attending a VA-approved school — of deceased veterans with wartime service may be eligible for pension based on need if they meet the applicable income standards.

Otherwise qualified children who became permanently incapable of self-support because of a mental or physical defect before reaching age 18 may receive a pension as long as the condition exists or until they marry.

Pension is not payable to those whose estates are so large that it is reasonable they look to the estates for maintenance.

A surviving spouse who is a patient in a nursing home or is otherwise determined to be in need of the regular aid and attendance of another person, or is permanently housebound, may be entitled to higher income limitations or additional benefits, depending on the type of pension received.

DEFINITION OF SURVIVING SPOUSE

Date of Marriage — To qualify as a surviving spouse, an individual must have married the veteran at least one year prior to his or her death unless a child resulted from the union.

Residence with Veteran — A surviving spouse must have lived continuously with the veteran from the time of marriage until the veteran's death, except where there was a separation not due to the fault of the surviving spouse.

Remarriage — Remarriage following the death of the veteran makes the surviving spouse ineligible for pension based on the death of that veteran unless the remarriage was void or annulled by a court. A surviving spouse may also be ineligible if after the death of the veteran she or he has lived with another man or woman and held herself or himself out openly to the public to be the spouse.

Deemed-Valid Marriages — If she or he meets the other qualifications, a person who married a veteran without knowing that a legal impediment to the marriage existed may be eligible for pension in certain cases.

BENEFITS

The improved pension program provides monthly payment to bring an eligible person's income to a support level that has been established by law. This support level is reduced by the annual income from other sources such as Social Security that may be payable to the surviving spouse or dependent children. Countable income may be reduced by certain unreimbursed medical expenses. Pension is not payable to those who have assets that can be used to provide adequate maintenance.

Improved Pension   **Annual Income**

Surviving spouse without dependent children $4,957
Surviving spouse with one dependent child $6,494
Surviving spouse in need of regular aid and attendance
    without dependent child $7,929
Surviving spouse in need of regular aid and attendance
    with one dependent child $9,462
Surviving spouse permanently housebound
    without dependent child $6,061
Surviving spouse permanently housebound
    with one dependent child $7,594
Increase for each additional dependent child $1,258
Pension rates for surviving children:
    For each child $1,258

Montgomery G.I. Bill (Active Duty) Death Benefit

VA will pay a death benefit to a designated survivor if the service-person's death is in service and is service-connected, and if the serviceperson was participating under the Montgomery G.I. Bill at time of death.

The death benefit also will be paid if the serviceperson would have been eligible to participate but for the high school diploma requirement and the length-of-service requirement. The amount paid will be equal to the participant's actual military pay reduction less any education benefits paid or any accrued benefits.

Survivors' and Dependents' Education

ELIGIBILITY

Educational assistance benefits are available to spouses and children of:

(a) veterans who died, or are permanently and totally disabled, as the result of a disability arising from active service in the Armed Forces.
(b) veterans who died from any cause while rated permanently and totally disabled from service-connected disability.
(c) servicepersons presently missing in action or captured in line of duty by a hostile force.
(d) servicepersons presently detained or interned in line of duty by a foreign government or power.

EDUCATION AND TRAINING AVAILABLE

Benefits may be awarded for pursuit of associate, bachelor or graduate degrees at colleges and universities (including independent study, cooperative training and study abroad programs). Courses leading to a certificate or diploma from business, technical, or vocational schools may also be taken. Other opportunities include apprenticeship or on-job-training programs and farm cooperative courses. Benefits for correspondence courses are available to spouses only. Secondary school programs may be pursued if the individual is not a high school graduate.

The individual may also receive tutorial assistance benefits if he or she is enrolled half-time or more and has a deficiency in a subject. Remedial, deficiency and refresher training may also be available.

SPECIAL BENEFITS

An eligible child who is handicapped by a physical or mental disability that prevents pursuit of an educational program may receive special restorative training. This may involve speech and voice correction, language retraining, lip reading, auditory training, Braille reading and writing, and similar programs. Specialized vocational training is available to an eligible spouse or child over age 14 who is handicapped by a physical or mental disability that prevents pursuit of an educational program.

On request, VA will provide counseling services, including testing, to help an eligible dependent select an educational or vocational objective, develop a plan to achieve it, and overcome any problems which might interfere with its successful achievement.

PAYMENTS

Payments are made monthly. The full-time rate is $404 a month for full-time school attendance, with lesser amounts for part-time training. A person may be entitled to receive educaitonal assistance up to a total of 45 months or the equivalent in part-time training.

PERIOD OF ELIGIBILITY

Benefits to a spouse end 10 years from the date VA first finds the individual eligible. VA may grant an extension of this period if a physical or mental disability prevents the individual from using some portion of his or her education benefits. The disability must occur during the individual's 10-year period of eligibility.

Generally, children must be between the ages of 18 and 23 to receive benefits. Certain extensions may be granted, including for the period of time equal to the time the child spends on active duty. No extension can go beyond the individual's 31st birthday.

WORK-STUDY

Work-study benefits are available under the same terms described under Montgomery GI Bill (Active Duty).

LIMITED LOAN PROGRAM

A limited loan program is available to dependents who qualify for Survivor's and Dependents' Educational Assistance benefits.

Survivors and dependents who have passed their 10-year period of eligibility and who have remaining entitlement may be eligible for an educational loan. During the first two years after the end of their eligibility period they may borrow up to $2,500 per academic year to continue a full-time course leading to a college degree or to a professional or vocational objective which requires at least six months to complete. VA may waive the six-month requirement under certain circumstances. The loan program is based on financial need.

Spouses' Eligibility for Home Loans

Unmarried surviving spouses of veterans, including service personnel, who served during a period which occurred between September 16, 1940, and the present and who died as a result of service-connected disabilities, and spouses of service personnel on active duty who have been officially listed as missing in action or prisoners of war for more than 90 days, are eligible for GI loans to acquire a home. Spouses of those listed as POW or MIA are limited to one loan, and official notice to the spouse that the serviceperson is no longer listed as missing or captured ends entitlement.

BURIAL BENEFITS AND CEMETERIES

Eligibility for burial under the National Cemetery System is based upon past or present service in the U.S. armed forces or in the armed forces of any government allied with the U.S. in a war. Veterans discharged or separated from active duty under conditions other than dishonorable who have completed the required period of service and U.S. Armed Forces members who die on active duty are eligible for burial in one of VA's 114 national cemeteries. Spouses and dependent children of eligible living and deceased veterans and of current and deceased armed forces members also may be buried in a national cemetery.

The surviving spouse of an eligible veteran who remarried a non-veteran prior to Oct. 31, 1990, and whose remarriage was terminated by death or divorce prior to or on that date is eligible for burial in a national cemetery. A surviving spouse of an eligible veteran who remarried a non-veteran prior to Oct. 31, 1990, and whose remarriage was still intact on or after that date, however, is not eligible for burial in a national cemetery. A surviving spouse who remarries a non-veteran after Oct. 31, 1990, is not eligible for burial in a national cemetery.

Similar eligibility criteria apply to the two active national cemeteries administered by the Department of the Interior — Andersonville National Cemetery in Georgia and Andrew Johnson National Cemetery in Tennessee. Many states operate state veterans cemeteries under eligibility criteria that may differ from that of the VA.

Burial in a VA national cemetery includes the gravesite, opening and closing of the grave, and perpetual care. Many national cemeteries have columbaria for the inurnment of cremated remains or special sections for the burial of cremated remains. Headstones and markers are provided and placed to mark the grave at the government's expense.

NATIONAL CEMETERIES

The National Cemetery System comprises 114 national cemeteries distributed across the country. Of these 114 VA national cemeteries (see list following), 49 are closed, having reached capacity for casket burials. Most of these cemeteries can accept cremation burials, however, and all of them can inter the spouse or eligible children of a family member already buried. Another 24 national cemeteries may close by the year 2000 but efforts are under way to forestall some of these closures by acquiring adjacent properties. A new national cemetery, the San Joaquin Valley National Cemetery, is under construction in Northern California. In addition, environmental studies are under way for possible cemetery development in seven locations: Chicago, Seattle, Albany (N.Y.), Cleveland, Dallas, Oklahoma City and Pittsburgh.

Since 1973, 20 national cemeteries have been expanded, mainly through donations of lands adjoining the cemeteries. Total national cemetery acreage has more than doubled since 1973, from 4,000 to 10,000 acres, and gravesites also have more than doubled, increasing from 2 million in 1973 to 4.5 million. Annual interments in national cemeteries have increased from 36,400 to 61,372 since 1973. The increase is expected to continue until the year 2010 as the veteran population ages.

Burial in a national cemetery is open to all members of the armed forces and veterans discharged under conditions other than dishonorable, as well as their spouses, unremarried widow or widower, minor children and, under certain conditions, unmarried children. The first person to be buried need not be the veteran. Also eligible for burial are members of the reserve components of the armed forces, the Army and Air National Guard, and the Reserve Officers Training Corps who die while on active duty for training or performing full-time service.

The government does not arrange funerals for veterans or their dependents. No graves are reserved prior to death. Military honors are not provided by national cemeteries; however, cemetery directors assist family members in contacting military bases or veterans groups that may provide these services.

The National Cemetery System does not normally conduct burials on weekends and most cemetery offices are closed. A weekend caller, however, will be directed to one of three strategically located offices which remain open to schedule burials at the cemetery of the caller's choice during the upcoming week.

HEADSTONES AND MARKERS

The VA provides headstones and markers for the graves of veterans and eligible dependents anywhere in the world which are not already marked. In 1990, 292,103 headstones and markers were provided by the National Cemetery System. Flat bronze, flat granite, flat marble and upright marble types are available to mark the grave of a veteran or dependent in the style consistent with existing monuments at the place of burial. Bronze niche markers are also available to mark columbaria in VA national cemeteries used for the inurnment of cremated remains.

When burial is in a national cemetery, the headstone or marker is ordered by the national cemetery staff, who will place it on the grave. Information regarding style, inscription, shipping and placement can be obtained from the director of the national cemetery.

When burial takes place in a cemetery other than a national cemetery or a state veterans cemetery, the headstone or marker must be applied for separately. It is shipped at government expense to the consignee designated on the application. VA, however, does not pay the cost of placing the headstone or marker on the grave.

VA will provide a plot in a national cemetery upon which a headstone or marker is placed to memorialize an eligible veteran whose remains are not available for burial. The headstone or marker is the same as that used to identify a grave except that the phrase "In Memory of" is mandatory and precedes the authorized inscription. The plot and headstone or marker are available to memorialize eligible veterans (and deceased active duty members) whose remains were not recovered or identified, were buried at sea, donated to science, or cremated and scattered.

Eligibility requirements for a VA headstone or marker are identical to those for burials in a national cemetery.

PRESIDENTIAL MEMORIAL CERTIFICATES

A Presidential Memorial Certificate is a parchment certificate with a calligraphic inscription expressing the nation's grateful recognition of the veteran's service. The veteran's name is inscribed, and the certificate bears the signature of the President and the presidential seal in gold foil. Certificates are issued in the name of honorably discharged deceased veterans. Eligible recipients include next of kin, other relatives and friends. Other family members and friends may request a certificate in the name of an eligible veteran.

BURIAL FLAGS

An American flag is available to drape the casket of a veteran who was discharged under conditions other than dishonorable. After the funeral service, the flag may be given to the next of kin or a close associate of the deceased. The VA also will issue a flag on behalf of a service member who was missing in action and later presumed dead. Flags are issued at any VA regional office, VA national cemetery and most local post offices.

BURIAL EXPENSE REIMBURSEMENT

The VA makes a $300 burial and funeral expense payment for veterans who, at the time of death, were entitled to receive pension or compensation or would have been entitled to compensation but for receipt of military retirement pay. Eligibility is also established when death occurs in a VA facility or a nursing home with which VA contracted, and additional costs of transportation of the remains may be reimbursed in those cases. Claims must be filed within two years after permanent burial or cremation.

VA will pay an additional $150 plot or interment allowance if the requirements for the basic allowance are met or the veteran was discharged from active duty because of disability incurred or aggravated in line of duty and is not buried in a cemetery that is under U.S. government jurisdiction.

If the veteran is buried without charge for the cost of a plot or interment in a state-owned cemetery reserved solely for veteran burials, the $150 plot allowance may be paid to the state. To the extent that burial expenses were paid by the deceased's employer or a state agency, they will not be reimbursed to those making interment arrangements.

If the veteran's cause of death is service-related, the VA will pay a burial allowance up to $1,500 instead of the $300 basic allowance and the $150 plot allowance. The VA also pays the cost of transporting the remains of a service-disabled veteran to the national cemetery with available grave space nearest his or her home.

The person who bore the veteran's burial expenses may claim reimbursement. Any claim for the burial allowance must be supported by a verifiable statement of account showing the name of person for whom services were performed; the nature and cost of the service rendered; all credits; and the person or persons by whom payment in whole or in part was made.

OTHER NATIONAL AND STATE VETERANS CEMETERIES

Many states operate veterans cemeteries (see listing following). All of them except Nevada, Wyoming and Utah restrict burial eligibility to state residents. Eligibility for burial in Department of Army national cemeteries, such as Arlington National Cemetery, is more restrictive than VA national cemeteries. Department of the Interior national cemeteries follow VA eligibility criteria.

ARLINGTON NATIONAL CEMETERY

Arlington National Cemetery, located in Arlington, Virginia, across the Potomac River from Washington, D.C., is the most famous of all U.S. national cemeteries. Its origins extend back to pre-Civil War days although the federal government did not take over the cemetery until May 1964. The 612-acre cemetery is the burial site of more than 200,000 veterans (including many prominent military and civilian figures) and their dependents. At the current rate of approximately 15 funerals per weekday, it is projected that Arlington National Cemetery will not be filled until the year 2020.

Burial at Arlington National Cemetery is one of the nation's highest honors for the country's servicemen and women. The following are those servicemembers and family members who are eligible for burial there:

- Those who have died on active duty
- Those having at least 20 years active duty or active reserve service which qualifies them for retired pay either upon retirement or at age 60, and those retired for disability
- Veterans honorably discharged for 30 percent (or more) disability before October 1, 1949
- Holders of the nation's highest military decorations (Medal of Honor; Distinguished Service Cross; Air Force Cross or Navy Cross; Distinguished Service Medal, and Silver Star or the Purple Heart)
- Those with honorable military discharges who held elective office in the U.S. government or a high nonelective government position, served on the Supreme Court, or served in the Cabinet
- The spouse or unmarried minor (under 21) child of any of the above.

In addition to ground burial, Arlington also has a columbarium for cremated remains. Any veteran whose last discharge was honorable or his spouse or dependent children can be unurned in the columbarium.

For more information, write to Superintendent, Arlington National Cemetery, Arlington, VA 22211, or telephone 703-695-3250.

MATCHING FUNDS PROGRAM

The National Cemetery System administers a program of grants to states to assist them in establishing or improving state-operated veterans cemeteries. The matching funds program helps to provide additional burial space for veterans in locations where there are no nearby national cemeteries. As of August 1991, more than $26 million in 56 grants had been awarded to 16 states and the Territory of Guam.

List of VA National Cemeteries and State Veterans Cemeteries

ALABAMA
National Cemeteries:
Fort Mitchell, 553 Highway 165, 36875 (205-855-4731)
Mobile, 1202 Virginia St., Mobile 36604 (404-428-5631)
ALASKA
National Cemeteries:
Fort Richardson, P.O. Box 5-498, Fort Richardson 99505 (907 863-5146)
Sitka, P.O. Box 1065, Sitka 99835 (907-863-5146)
ARIZONA
National Cemeteries:
National Memorial Cemetery of Arizona, 23029 N. Cave Creek Rd., Phoenix
    85022 (602-261-4615)
Prescott, VA Medical Center, Prescott 86301 (602-445-4860, ext. 242)
ARKANSAS
National Cemeteries:
Fayetteville, 700 Government Ave., Fayetteville 72701 (501-444-5051)
Fort Smith, 2522 Garland Ave. and So. 6th St., Fort Smith 72901
    (501-783-5345)
Little Rock, 523 Confederate Blvd., Little Rock 72206 (501-374-8011)
CALIFORNIA
National Cemeteries:
Fort Rosecrans, Point Loma, P.O. Box 6237, San Diego 92106 (619-553-2084)
Golden Gate, 1300 Sneath Lane, San Bruno 94066 (415-761-1646)
Los Angeles, 950 So. Sepulveda Blvd., Los Angeles 90049 (213-824-4311)
Riverside, 22495 Van Buren Blvd., Riverside 92508 (714-653-8417)
San Francisco, P.O. Box 29012, Presidio of San Francisco, San Francisco
    94129 (415-561-2008)
San Joaquin Valley, Sustine 95322 (209-854-2276)
State Cemeteries:
Veterans Memorial Grove, Veterans Home of California, Yountville 94599
    (closed) (707-944-4000)
COLORADO
National Cemeteries:
Fort Logan, 3698 S. Sheridan Blvd., Denver 80235 (303-761-0117)
Fort Lyon, VA Medical Center, Fort Lyon 81038 (303-456-1260, ext. 231)
State Cemeteries:
Colorado State Veterans, Colorado State Veterans Center, Box 97, Homelake
    81135 (719-852-5118)
CONNECTICUT
State Cemeteries:
Colonel Raymond F. Gates Memorial, Veterans Home and Hospital, 287 West
    Street, Rocky Hill 06067 (203-529-2571)
Spring Grove Veterans, Darien, c/o Veterans Home and Hospital, Rocky Hill
    06067 (closed)
Middletown Veterans, c/o Veterans Home and Hospital, Rocky Hill 06067
    (203-344-1961)
DELAWARE
State Cemeteries:
Delaware Veterans Memorial, 2465 Chesapeake City Rd., Bear 19701 (302-
    834-8046)

FLORIDA
National Cemeteries:
Barrancas, Naval Air Station, Pensacola 32508 (904-452-3357)
Bay Pines, P.O. Box 477, Bay Pines 33504 (813-398-9426)
Florida, P.O. Box 337, Bushnell 33513 (904-793-7740)
St. Augustine, 104 Marine St., St. Augustine 32084 (904-793-7740)
GEORGIA
National Cemeteries:
Marietta, 500 Washington Ave., Marietta 30060 (404-428-5631)
State Cemeteries:
Milledgeville, c/o Department of Veterans Services, Floyd Veterans Memorial
   Bldg., Suite E-970, Atlanta 30334 (404-656-2300)
HAWAII
National Cemeteries:
National Memorial Cemetery of the Pacific, 2177 Puowaina Dr., Honolulu
   96813 (808-541-1427)
State Cemeteries:
Oahu, c/o Office of Veterans Services, PRI Tower, 733 Bishop St., Suite 1270,
   Honolulu 96813 (808-548-8150)
Hawaii Veterans, County of Hawaii, 25 Aupuni St., Hilo 96720 (808-961-8311)
Kauai Veterans, County of Kauai Public Works, 4396 Rice St., Lihue 96766
   (808-245-3318)
Makawao Veterans, 1295 Makawao Ave., Makawao 96768 (808-572-7272)
Hoolehua Veterans (Molokai), P.O. Box 526, Kauna Kakai 96748 (808-243-
   7845)
ILLINOIS
National Cemeteries:
Alton, 600 Pearl St., Alton 62003 (314-263-8691)
Camp Butler, R.R. #1, Springfield 62707 (217-522-5764)
Danville, 1900 East Main St., Danville 61832 (217-442-8000, ext. 391)
Mound City, Junction Hwy. 37 & 51, Mound City 62963 (314-263-8691)
Quincy, 36th & Maine Sts., Quincy 62301 (319-524-1304)
Rock Island, Rock Island Arsenal, Rock Island 61299 (309-782-2094)
State Cemeteries:
Sunset, Illinois Veterans Home, 1707 N. 12th St., Quincy 62301 (217-222-
   8641)
INDIANA
National Cemeteries:
Crown Hill, 700 W. 38th St., Indianapolis 46208 (317-674-0284)
Marion, VA Medical Center, Marion 46952 (317-674-0284)
New Albany, 1943 Ekin Ave., New Albany 47150 (502-893-3852)
IOWA
National Cemeteries:
Keokuk, 1701 J St., Keokuk 52632 (319-524-1304)
State Cemeteries:
Iowa Veterans Home & Cemetery, 13th & Summit Sts., Marshalltown 50158
   (515-752-1501)
KANSAS
National Cemeteries:
Fort Leavenworth, P.O. Box 1694, Fort Leavenworth 66027 (913-682-1748)
Fort Scott, P.O. Box 917, Fort Scott 66701 (316-223-2840)
Leavenworth, Veterans Administration Center, P.O. Box 1694, Fort
   Leavenworth 66027 (913-682-1748)

State Cemeteries:
KSH Cemetery, Kansas Soldiers Home, Fort Dodge 67843 (316-227-2121)

KENTUCKY
National Cemeteries:
Camp Nelson, 6980 Danville Rd., Nicholasville 40356 (606-885-5727)
Cave Hill, 701 Baxter Ave., Louisville 40204 (502-893-3852)
Danville, 377 North First St., Danville 40442 (606-885-5727)
Lebanon, R.R. #1, Box 616, Lebanon 40033 (502-692-3390)
Lexington, 833 W. Main St., Lexington 40508 (606-885-5727)
Mill Springs, R.R. #2, Nancy 42544 (606-636-6470)
Zachary Taylor, 4701 Brownsboro Rd., Louisville 40207 (502-893-3852)

LOUISIANA
National Cemeteries:
Alexandria, 209 Shamrock Ave., Pineville 71360 (318-473-7588)
Baton Rouge, 220 North 19th St., Baton Rouge 70806 (504-389-0788)
Port Hudson, 20978 Port Hickey Rd., Port Hudson 70791 (504-389-0788)

MAINE
National Cemeteries:
Togus, VA Medical & Regional Office Center, Togus 04330 (207-623-8411)
State Cemeteries:
Maine Veterans Memorial, Bureau of Veterans Services, State Office
Building, State #117, Augusta 04333 (207-289-4068)

MARYLAND
National Cemeteries:
Annapolis, 800 West St., Annapolis 21401 (301-644-9696)
Baltimore, 5501 Frederick Ave., Baltimore 21228 (301-644-9696)
Loudon Park, 3445 Frederick Ave., Baltimore 21229 (410-644-9696)
State Cemeteries:
Cheltenham Veterans, 11301 Crain Hwy., P.O. Box 10, Cheltenham 20623
(301-372-6398)
Crownsville, Veterans, 1080 Sunrise Beach Rd., Crownsville 21032
(301-987-6320)
Eastern Shore Veterans, 6827 E. New Market Ellwood Rd., Hurlock 21643
(301-943-3420)
Garrison Forest Veterans, P.O. Box 409, Owings Mills 21117 (301-363-6090)
Rocky Gap Veterans, Route #1, Box 82, Flintstone 21530 (301-777-2185)

MASSACHUSETTS
National Cemeteries:
Massachusetts, Bourne 02532 (508-563-7113)

MICHIGAN
National Cemeteries:
Fort Custer, 15501 Dickman Rd., Augusta 49012 (616-731-4164)

MINNESOTA
National Cemeteries:
Fort Snelling, 7601 34th Ave. So., Minneapolis 55450 (612-726-1127)

MISSISSIPPI
National Cemeteries:
Biloxi, P.O. Box 4968, Biloxi 39535 (601-388-6668)
Corinth, 1551 Horton St., Corinth 38834 (601-286-5782)
Natchez, 41 Cemetery Rd., Natchez 39120 (601-445-4981)

MISSOURI
National Cemeteries:
Jefferson Barracks, 101 Memorial Dr., St. Louis 63125 (314-263-8691)
Jefferson City, 1024 East McCarty St., Jefferson City 65101 (314-263-8691)

Springfield, 1702 E. Seminole St., Springfield 65804 (417-881-9499)
State Cemeteries:
Missouri Veterans Home, 620 N. Jefferson, St. James 65559 (314-265-3271)
MONTANA
State Cemeteries:
State Veterans, Fort William H. Harrison, Helena (406-444-6926)
Montana Veterans Home, P.O. Box 250, Columbia Falls 59912 (406-892-3256)
NEBRASKA
National Cemeteries:
Fort McPherson, HCO 1, Box 67, Maxwell 69151 (308-582-4433)
State Cemeteries:
Nebraska Veterans Home, Burkett Station, Grand Island 68803 (308-382-9420)
NEVADA
State Cemeteries:
Northern Nevada Veterans Memorial, 1201 Terminal Way #108, Reno 89520 (702-575-4441)
Southern Nevada Veterans Memorial, 1900 Buchanan Blvd., P.O. Box 878, Boulder City 89005 (702-486-5920)
NEW JERSEY
National Cemeteries:
Beverly, R.D. #1, Bridgeboro Rd., Beverly 08010 (609-877-5460)
Finn's Point, R.F.D. #3, Fort Mott Rd., Box 542, Salem 08079 (609-877-5460)
State Cemeteries:
Veterans Memorial, RR #1, Provenceline Rd., Wrightstown 08562 (609-758-7250)
New Jersey Memorial Home, 524 N.W. Blvd., Vineland 08360 (closed) (609-696-6400)
NEW MEXICO
National Cemeteries:
Fort Bayard, P.O. Box 189, Fort Bayard 88036 (915-540-6182)
Santa Fe, 501 N. Guadalupe St., P.O. Box 88, Sante Fe 87504 (505-988-6400)
NEW YORK
National Cemeteries:
Bath, VA Medical Center, Bath 14810 (607-776-2111, ext. 293)
Calverton, 210 Princeton Blvd., Calverton 11933 (516-727-5410)
Cypress Hills, 625 Jamaica Ave., Brooklyn 11208 (516-454-4949)
Long Island, Farmingdale 11735 (516-454-4949)
Woodlawn, 1825 Davis St., Elmira 14901 (607-776-2111, ext. 293)
NORTH CAROLINA
National Cemeteries:
New Bern, 1711 National Ave., New Bern 28560 (919-637-2912)
Raleigh, 501 Rock Quarry Rd., Raleigh 27610 (919-832-0144)
Salisbury, 202 Government Rd., Salisbury 28144 (704-636-2661)
Wilmington, 2011 Market St., Wilmington 28403 (919-343-4877)
OHIO
National Cemeteries:
Dayton, VA Medical Center, 4100 W. Third St., Dayton 45428 (513-262-2115)
OKLAHOMA
National Cemeteries:
Fort Gibson, Rt. 2, Box 47, Fort Gibson 74434 (918-478-2334)

State Cemeteries:
Oklahoma Veterans, Military Dept., 3501 Military Circle N.E., Oklahoma City 73111-4398 (405-425-8643)

OREGON
National Cemeteries:
Eagle Point, 2763 Riley Rd., Eagle Point 97524 (503-826-2511)
Roseburg, VA Medical Center, Roseburg 97470 (503-440-1000)
Willamette, 11800 S.E. Mt. Scott Blvd., P.O. Box 66147, Portland 97266 (503-273-5250)

PENNSYLVANIA
National Cemeteries:
Indiantown Gap, P.O. Box 187, Annville 17003 (717-865-5254)
Philadelphia, Haines St. & Limekiln Pike, Philadelphia 19138 (609-877-5460)
State Cemeteries:
Pennsylvania Soldiers and Sailors, P.O. Box 6239, 560 East Third St., Erie 16512-6239 (814-871-4531)

PUERTO RICO
National Cemeteries:
Bayamon, P.O. Box 1298, Bayamon 00621 (809-785-7281)

RHODE ISLAND
State Cemeteries:
Rhode Island Veterans, 301 S. County Trail, Exeter 02822-9712 (401-884-7482)

SOUTH CAROLINA
National Cemeteries:
Beaufort, 1601 Boundary St., Beaufort 29902 (803-524-3925)
Florence, 803 E. National Cemetery Rd., Florence 29501 (803-669-8783)

SOUTH DAKOTA
National Cemeteries:
Black Hills, P.O. Box 640, Sturgis 57785 (605-347-3830)
Fort Meade, VA Medical Center, Fort Meade 57785 (605-347-3830)
Hot Springs, VA Medical Center, Hot Springs 57747 (605-745-4101)
State Cemeteries:
South Dakota Veterans Home, 2500 Minnekahta Ave., Hot Springs 57747 (605-745-5127)

TENNESSEE
National Cemeteries:
Chattanooga, 1200 Bailey Ave., Chattanooga 37404 (615-855-6590)
Knoxville, 939 Tyson St., N.W., Knoxville 37917 (615-929-5360)
Memphis, 3568 Townes Ave., Memphis 38122 (901-386-8311)
Mountain Home, P.O. Box 8, Mountain Home 37684 (615-929-7891)
Nashville, 1420 Gallatin Rd. South, Madison 37115 (615-327-5360)
State Cemeteries:
Knoxville State Veterans, 5901 Lyons View Pike, Knoxville 37919 (615-558-6081)

TEXAS
National Cemeteries:
Fort Bliss, P.O. Box 6342, Fort Bliss 79906 (915-540-6182)
Fort Sam Houston, 1520 Harry Wurzbach Rd., San Antonio 78209 (512-820-3891)
Houston, 10410 Veterans Memorial Dr., Houston 77038 (713-653-3112)
Kerrville, VA Medical Center 3600 Memorial Blvd., Kerrville 78028 (404-347-2121, ext. 227)
San Antonio, 517 Paso Hondo St., San Antonio 78202 (512-820-3891)

UTAH
State Cemeteries:
Utah State Veterans, P.O. Box 446, Riverton 84065 (801-254-9036)
VERMONT
State Cemeteries:
Vermont Veterans Home War Memorial, 325 North St., Bennington 05201 (802-442-6353)
VIRGINIA
National Cemeteries:
Alexandria, 1450 Wilkes St., Alexandria 22314 (703-690-2217)
Balls Bluff, Leesburg 22075 (703-825-0027)
City Point, 10th Ave. & Davis St., Hopewell 23860 (804-222-1490)
Cold Harbor, Rt. 156 North, Mechanicsville 23111 (804-222-1490)
Culpeper, 305 U.S. Ave., Culpeper 22701 (703-825-0027)
Danville, 721 Lee St., Danville 24541 (704-636-2661)
Fort Harrison, 8620 Varina Rd., Richmond 23231 (804-222-1490)
Glendale, 8301 Willis Church Rd., Richmond 23231 (804-222-1490)
Hampton, Cemetery Rd. at Marshall Ave., Hampton 23669 (804-723-7104)
Hampton, VA Medical Center, Hampton 23669 (804-723-7104)
Quantico, P.O. Box 10, Triangle 22172 (703-690-2217)
Richmond, 1701 Williamsburg Rd., Richmond 23231 (804-222-1490)
Seven Pines, 400 E. Williamsburg Rd., Sandston 23150 (804-222-1490)
Staunton, 901 Richmond Ave., Staunton 24401 (703-825-0027)
Winchester, 401 National Ave., Winchester 22601 (703-825-0027)
WASHINGTON
State Cemeteries:
Washington Veterans Home, P.O. Box 698, Retsil 98378 (206-895-4705)
WEST VIRGINIA
National Cemeteries:
Grafton, 431 Walnut St., Grafton 26354 (304-265-2044)
West Virginia, Grafton 26354 (304-265-2044)
WISCONSIN
National Cemeteries:
Wood, 5000 W. National Ave., Milwaukee 53295 (414-382-5300)
State Cemeteries:
Wisconsin Veterans Memorial, Wisconsin Veterans Home, King 54946 (715-258-5586)
WYOMING
State Cemeteries:
Oregon Trail Veterans Cemetery, Box 669, Evansville 82636 (307-235-6673)
GUAM
State Cemeteries:
Veterans Cemetery of Guam, Dept. of Parks & Recreation, Agana 96910 (671-477-9620)

PASSPORTS TO VISIT OVERSEAS CEMETERIES

When traveling overseas primarily to visit the place of burial or memorialization, immediate members of the family (widows, parents, children, sisters, brothers, and guardians) of veterans buried in or commemorated on the Tablets of the Missing of the permanent American military cemeteries on foreign soil may be eligible for "Non-fee or Fee-free" passports. For additional information, please write to the American Battle Monuments Commission, Room 5127, Pulaski Building, 20 Massachusetts Ave., N.W., Washington, D.C. 20314.

HEALTH CARE

Hospitalization

Eligibility for VA hospitalization and nursing home care is divided into two categories: "mandatory" and "discretionary." (See Outpatient Medical Care for eligibility.) Within these two categories, eligibility assessment procedures based on income levels are used for determining whether nonservice-connected veterans are eligible for cost-free VA medical care. These income levels are adjusted on Jan. 1 of each year by the percentage that the improved pension benefits are increased.

VA must provide hospital care and may provide nursing home care to veterans in the mandatory category, and may provide hospital and nursing home care to veterans in the discretionary category if space and resources are available in VA facilities.

The law requires VA to provide hospital care to veterans in the mandatory category at the nearest VA facility capable of furnishing the care in a timely fashion. If no VA facility is available, care must be furnished in a Defense Department facility or another facility with which VA has a sharing or contractual relationship. If space and resources are available after caring for mandatory category veterans, VA may furnish care to those in the discretionary category. Veterans in the discretionary category must agree to pay VA for their care.

Veterans in the mandatory category not subject to the eligibility assessment are service-connected veterans; veterans who were exposed to herbicides while serving in Vietnam or to ionizing radiation during atmospheric testing and in the occupation of Hiroshima and Nagasaki, and need treatment for a condition that might be related to the exposure; former prisoners of war; veterans receiving a VA pension; or World War II veterans eligible for Medicaid.

The following eligibility assessment applies to all other nonservice-connected veterans, regardless of age:

MANDATORY: Hospital care is considered mandatory if the patient is among the groups just listed or if the patient is a nonservice-connected veteran with income of $18,844 or less if single with no dependents, or $22,613 or less if married or single with one dependent, plus $1,258 for each additional dependent. Hospital care in VA facilities must be provided to veterans in the mandatory category. Nursing home care may be provided in VA facilities, if space and resources are available.

DISCRETIONARY: Hospital care is considered discretionary if the patient is a nonservice-connected veteran and income is above $18,844 if single with no dependents, or $22,613 if married or single with one dependent, plus $1,258 for each additional dependent. The patient must agree to pay an amount for care equal to what would have been paid under Medicare. The Medicare deductible currently is $652 and is adjusted annually. VA may provide hospital, outpatient and nursing home care in VA facilities to veterans in the discretionary category, if space and resources are available.

If the patient's medical care is considered discretionary, the VA holds the patient responsible for the cost of care or $652 for the first 90 days of care during any 365-day period. For each additional 90 days of hospital care, the patient is charged half the Medicare deductible. For each 90 days of nursing home care, an amount equal to the Medicare deductible is charged.

In addition to the charges enumerated, the patient will be charged $10 per day for inpatient hospital care and $5 a day for nursing home care.

The payment is based on the Medicare deductible and is adjusted annually.

HOW INCOME IS ASSESSED

The patient's total income under the eligibility assessment includes: Social Security, U.S. Civil Service retirement, U.S. Railroad Retirement, military retirement, unemployment insurance, any other retirement income, total wages from all employers, interest and dividends, workers' compensation, black lung benefits, and any other gross income for the calendar year prior to application for care. The income of spouse and dependents as well as the market value of stocks, bonds, notes, individual retirement accounts, bank deposits, savings accounts and cash also are used. Debts are subtracted from the patient's assets to determine net worth. The patient's primary residence and personal property, however, are excluded. The patient is not required to provide proof of income or net worth beyond filling out VA Form 10-10f, Financial Worksheet, at the time care is requested. VA has the authority to compare information provided with information obtained from the Department of Health and Human Services and the Internal Revenue Service.

MEDICAL CARE COST RECOVERY

All veterans applying for medical care at a VA facility will be asked if they have medical insurance. VA is authorized by law to bill insurance companies for the cost of medical care furnished to veterans, including service-connected veterans, for nonservice-connected conditions covered by health insurance policies. VA is required to determine if the cost of the medical care can be recovered from companies providing group or individual health insurance. A veteran may be covered by such a policy or be covered as an eligible dependent on a spouse's policy. VA is no different than other health-care providers who need insurance information. To collect benefits covered by health insurance, VA must obtain the information that appears on the health insurance identification card. Veterans are not responsible and will not be charged by VA for any charge required by their health insurance policies.

Nursing Home Care

BENEFIT

To provide skilled nursing care and related medical care in VA or private nursing homes for convalescents or persons who are not acutely ill and not in need of hospital care.

ELIGIBILITY

Admission or transfer to VA nursing home care units is essentially the same as for hospitalization. Direct admission to private nursing homes at VA expense is limited to: (1) a veteran who requires nursing care for a service-connected disability after medical determination by VA, (2) any person in an Armed Forces hospital who requires a protracted period of nursing care and who will become a veteran upon discharge from the Armed Forces, or (3) a veteran who had been discharged from a VA medical center and is receiving home health services from a VA medical center. VA may transfer veterans who need nursing home care to private nursing homes at VA expense from VA medical centers, nursing homes, or domiciliaries. VA-authorized care normally may not be provided in excess of six months except for veterans whose need for nursing home care is for a service-connected disability or for veterans who were hospitalized primarily for treatment of a service-connected disability. Nursing home care for nonservice-connected veterans whose income exceeds the income threshold amount applicable to hospital care eligibility may be authorized only if the veteran agrees to pay the applicable copayment. Veterans who have a service-connected disability are given first priority for VA nursing home care.

Domiciliary Care

BENEFIT

To provide care on an ambulatory self-care basis for veterans disabled by age or disease who are not in need of acute hospitalization and who do not need the skilled nursing services provided in nursing homes. (See Domiciliaries—page 168).

ELIGIBILITY

VA provides domiciliary care to veterans whose annual income does not exceed the maximum annual rate of VA pension, and to veterans the Secretary of Veterans Affairs determines have no adequate means of support.

Outpatient Medical Treatment

BENEFIT

To provide necessary medical services on an outpatient basis within the limits of VA facilities. Outpatient medical treatment may include medical examination and related medical services, including drugs and medicines, rehabilitation, consultation, professional counseling, training and mental health services to treat physical and mental disabilities. As part of outpatient medical treatment, certain veterans may be eligible for home health services necessary or appropriate for the effective and economical treatment of disabilities, including such home improvements and structural alterations as are determined necessary to assure the continuation of treatment or to provide access to the home or to essential sanitary facilities. Cost limitations apply to these improvements and alterations.

ELIGIBILITY

VA must furnish outpatient care without limitation, for any disability:

- to veterans for service-connected disabilities.
- to veterans with a 50 percent or more service-connected disability.
- to veterans who have suffered an injury as a result of VA hospitalization.
- to veterans in a VA-approved vocational rehabilitation program.

VA must furnish outpatient care for any condition to eliminate the need for hospitalization, to prepare for hospitalization or to prepare for short-term treatment of a condition for which the veteran was hospitalized to:

- any 30-40 percent service-connected disabled veteran.
- any veteran whose annual income is not greater than the maximum pension rate of a veteran in need of regular aid and attendance.

VA may furnish outpatient care without limitation to:

- veterans in a VA-approved vocational rehabilitation program.
- former prisoners of war.
- World War I or Mexican Border Period veterans.
- veterans who receive increased pension or compensation based on the need for regular aid and attendance of another person, or who are permanently housebound.

VA may furnish outpatient care to eliminate the need for hospitalization, to prepare for hospitalization, or for a condition for which the veteran was hospitalized to:

- any 0-20 percent service-connected disabled veteran.
- any mandatory category veteran whose income is more than the pension rate of a veteran in need of regular aid and attendance.
- discretionary category veterans, subject to a copayment of $26 per outpatient visit.
- allied beneficiaries, beneficiaries of other federal agencies and certain other nonveterans.

Veterans receiving medication on an outpatient basis from VA facilities for the treatment of nonservice-connected disabilities or conditions are charged $2 for each 30-day or less supply of medication provided. Veterans receiving medication for treatment of service-connected conditions and veterans rated 50 percent or more service-connected are not charged.

Outpatient Dental Treatment

Outpatient dental treatment begins with an examination and may include the full spectrum of diagnostic, surgical, restorative and preventive techniques.

ELIGIBILITY

Dental care will be provided under the following conditions:

(a) Dental conditions or disabilities that are service-connected and compensable in degree will be treated.

(b) Service-connected dental conditions or disabilities that are not compensable in degree may receive one-time treatment if the conditions can be shown to have existed at discharge or within 180 days from active service. Veterans must apply to VA for care for the service-connected dental condition within 90 days following separation. Veterans will not be considered eligible if their separation document indicates that necessary treatment was completed by military dentists during the 90 days prior to separation. Veterans who served on active duty for 90 days or more during the Persian Gulf War are included in this category.

(c) Service-connected, noncompensable dental conditions resulting from combat wounds or service injuries, and service-connected non-compensable dental conditions of former prisoners of war who were incarcerated less than 90 days may be treated.

(d) Veterans who were prisoners of war for more than 90 days may receive complete dental care.

(e) Veterans also may receive complete dental care if they are receiving disability compensation at the 100-percent rate for service-connected conditions or are eligible to receive it by reason of individual unemployability.

(f) Nonservice-connected dental conditions that are determined by VA to be associated with and aggravating service-connected medical problems may be treated.

(g) Disabled veterans participating in a vocational rehabilitation program may be treated.

(h) Veterans may be treated for nonservice-connected dental conditions or disabilities for which treatment was begun while in a VA medical center, when it is professionally determined to be reasonably necessary to complete such dental treatment on an outpatient basis.

(i) Veterans scheduled for admission to inpatient services or who are receiving medical services may be provided outpatient dental care if the dental condition is professionally determined to be complicating a medical condition currently under treatment by V A.

Nonservice-connected veterans whose incomes exceed the income threshold amount applicable to hospital care eligibility may be authorized dental treatment only if they agree to pay the applicable copayment.

NONAPPLICABLE CONDITIONS

Eligibility for dental care is generally more limited than for medical services. Among the categories not eligible for dental care are:

(a) Veterans in receipt of aid and attendance or housebound benefits, unless such treatment was started during a period of inpatient care of if they are otherwise eligible.

(b) Veterans whose eligibility for medical services is based solely on need of ambulatory care in preparation for, or to obviate the need of, hospitalization.

Agent Orange and Ionizing Radiation Examinations

Under the auspices of VA's Agent Orange and Ionizing Radiation Registries, veterans claiming exposure to Agent Orange or atomic radiation are provided with a free, comprehensive medical examination, including base-line laboratory tests and other tests determined necessary by the examining physician to determine their current health status. Results of the examination, which includes completion of a questionnaire about the veteran's service/exposure history, are entered into a special, computerized program maintained by VA. This database assists VA in analyzing the types of health conditions being reported by veterans regardless of origin. Registry participants are advised of the results of their examination in personal consultation. The Agent Orange Registry and the Ionizing Radiation Registry serve as outreach mechanisms which assist VA in providing participants with significant information of concern to them. Veterans wishing to participate in either of VA's registry programs should contact the nearest VA health-care facility to request an examination. Appointments generally can be arranged within two to three weeks.

Medical

POST TRAUMATIC STRESS DISORDER (PTSD)

The Veterans Administration maintains 23 specialized inpatient and 56 clinical teams for treating **post traumatic stress disorder (PTSD)**, an ailment caused by a psychological reaction to traumatic experience of war. Its symptoms may include anxiety, depression, irritability, isolation and rage. Because of an increasing public awareness of the problem, more veterans are seeking help, where earlier they may have been reluctant to do so because of the perceived stigma.

A study has found that 15.2 percent (479,000) of the 3.14 million men who served in Vietnam suffer from PTSD, and 8.5 percent (610) of the 7,200 women who served there have the ailment. The VA reports that 40,800 veterans have experienced service-connected PTSD. Veterans may get treatment or counseling at one of the 196 Vet Centers around the country simply by walking in. Vet Centers provide an initial assessment that may include referral to a clinical team at a VA hospital. There also is help for PTSD sufferers through special clinical teams based at VA medical centers.

- Outpatient services are offered in mental health clinics, day-treatment centers, hospital programs, alcohol- and drug-dependence treatment programs

- Contract care in community-based facilities for those with substance abuse disorders

- In the Compensated Work Therapy Program, VA contracts with private industry to secure work for disabled veterans to be used as a therapeutic tool to improve functional levels and mental and physical health.

Beneficiary Travel

ELIGIBILITY/BENEFIT

Payment or reimbursement for travel costs to receive VA medical care, called beneficiary travel payment, may be made to the following veterans:

- (a) Veterans rated at 30 percent or more service-connected.
- (b) Veterans rated below 30 percent and traveling in connection with treatment of a service-connected condition.
- (c) Veterans who are in receipt of VA pension.
- (d) Veterans traveling in connection with a compensation and pension examination.
- (e) Veterans whose income is less than or equal to the maximum base VA pension rate.
- (f) Veterans whose medical condition requires use of a special mode of transportation if the veteran is unable to defray the costs and travel is preauthorized, or the medical condition is a medical emergency.

All travel is subject to a deductible of $3 for each one-way trip — with an $18 per month cap — except travel for a compensation and pension examination or travel by special modes of transportation.

Counseling for Persian Gulf Veterans

Beginning in 1992, Congress has authorized marital and family counseling for veterans of the Persian Gulf War and their spouses and children. The counseling is being administered at VA medical centers and vet centers.

Agent Orange and Nuclear Radiation Treatment

VA provides priority treatment to any Vietnam-Era veteran who, while serving in Vietnam, may have been exposed to dioxin or to a toxic substance in a herbicide or defoliant used for military purposes. Priority health-care services also are available for any veteran exposed to ionizing radiation from the detonation of a nuclear device in connection with nuclear tests or with the American occupation of Hiroshima and Nagasaki, Japan, during the period beginning on Sept. 11, 1945, and ending on July 1, 1946. Treatment currently is authorized through Dec. 31, 1993, for veterans exposed to Agent Orange or nuclear radiation.

Alcohol and Drug Dependence Treatment

Nonservice-connected veterans whose incomes exceed the threshold amount may be authorized treatment only if the veteran agrees to pay the applicable copayment. After hospitalization for alcohol or drug treatment, veterans may be eligible for outpatient care, or may be authorized to continue treatment or rehabilitation in facilities such as halfway houses at VA expense.

Prosthetic Appliances

ELIGIBILITY

Veterans may be provided prosthetic appliances necessary for treatment of any condition when receiving hospital, domiciliary, or nursing home care in a facility under the direct jurisdiction of VA. Veterans who meet the basic requirements for outpatient medical treatment may be provided needed prosthetic services if the appliance is required: (1) for a service-connected disability or adjunct condition, (2) for a disability for which a veteran was discharged or released from active service, (3) for a veteran participating in a rehabilitation program under 38 USC Chapter 31, (4) as part of outpatient care to complete treatment of a disability for which hospital, nursing home or domiciliary care was provided, (5) for any medical condition for a veteran with a service-connected disability rated at 50 percent or more or for a veteran receiving compensation as a result of treatment in a VA facility, (6) for a veteran in receipt of increased pension or allowance based on needing aid and attendance or being permanently housebound, (7) for a veteran of World War I or the Mexican Border period, or (8) for a former prisoner of war.

WHERE TO APPLY

To apply for these services, veterans may contact the prosthetic activity at a VA medical center.

Blind Aids and Services

ELIGIBILITY

Veterans are eligible to receive authorized aids for the blind if they are service-connected for blindness, if they are entitled to compensation from VA for any service-connected disability, or if they are eligible for medical services.

Veterans with best-corrected vision of 20/200 or less in the better eye or field defect of 20 degrees or less are considered to be blind.

Blind veterans need not be receiving compensation or pension to be eligible for admission to a VA blind rehabilitation center or clinic.

BENEFIT

(a) Annual Visual Impairment Services Team (VIST) provides a total health and benefits review for eligible blind veterans.

(b) Adjustment to blindness training.

(c) Home improvements and structural alterations to homes (HISA Program).

(d) Low-vision aids and training in their use.

(e) Approved electronic and mechanical aids for the blind, and their necessary repair and replacement.

(f) Guide dogs, including the expense of training the veteran to use the dog, and the cost of the dog's medical care.

(g) Talking books, tapes and Braille literature are available from the Library of Congress.

WHERE TO APPLY

To apply for these services, veterans may contact the coordinator for the blind at any VA medical center. For talking books, veterans may contact either the medical center librarian or the coordinator for the blind. For equipment, veterans may contact the facility's Prosthetics and Sensory Aids office.

Readjustment Counseling (Vet Centers)

ELIGIBILITY

Veterans who served on active duty during the Vietnam Era or served in the war or conflict zones of Lebanon, Grenada, Panama and the Persian Gulf theaters during periods of hostilities or war are entitled to counseling to assist in readjustment to civilian life. Application may be made at any time.

BENEFIT

To provide outreach and counseling to help veterans resolve war-related psychological difficulties and to help them achieve a successful post-war readjustment to civilian life. One common readjustment problem is post-traumatic stress disorder, or PTSD. This refers to such symptoms as nightmares, intrusive recollections or memories, flashbacks, anxiety or sudden reactions after exposure to traumatic conditions. Other readjustment difficulties may affect functioning in school, family or work.

Readjustment Counseling Service assistance includes group, individual and family counseling, community outreach and education. Vet center staff help veterans find services from VA and non-VA sources if needed.

Vet centers are situated in downtown or suburban locations. The nearest location can usually be found in the U.S. Government section of the phone book under Department of Veterans Affairs. In areas which are distant from vet centers or VA medical facilities, veterans may obtain readjustment counseling from community, private sector counselors, psychologists, social workers, or other professionals who are on contract with VA. To locate a contract provider, contact the nearest vet center.

Medical Care for Merchant Seamen

ELIGIBILITY/BENEFITS

Those Merchant Marine seamen whose World War II service qualifies them for veterans' benefits must present their DD-214, discharge certificate, when applying for medical care benefits at VA medical centers. VA regional offices can provide information on obtaining a certificate.

Medical Care for Allied Beneficiaries

ELIGIBILITY/BENEFITS

VA is authorized by law to provide reciprocal medical care to veterans of nations allied or associated with the United States during World War I or World War II. Such treatment must be authorized and reimbursed by the foreign government. Apply at any VA medical facility.

The law also authorizes VA to provide hospitalization, outpatient and domiciliary care to certain former members of the armed forces of the governments of Czechoslovakia or Poland who participated during World Wars I and II in armed conflict against an enemy of the United

States if they have been citizens of the United States for at least 10 years. Benefits are the same as those provided to U.S. veterans. Apply at any VA medical facility.

CHAMPVA

The Civilian Health and Medical Program of the Department of Veterans Affairs (CHAMPVA) is a cost-sharing program wherein the Veterans Administration shares the cost of covered medical services and supplies. Eligibility and authorization for CHAMPVA benefits are handled by the CHAMPVA Center in Denver, while the processing and payment of claims are handled by private companies under contract with the Department of Defense.

The following are eligible for benefits, providing they are not eligible for Medicare Part A or medical benefits administered by the Department of Defense's Civilian Health and Medical Program of the Uniformed Services (CHAMPUS):

• The spouse or child of a veteran who has been judged by the VA as having a permanent and total service-connected disability;
• The surviving spouse or child of a veteran who died as a result of a service-connected condition, or who, at the time of death was judged permanently and totally disabled from a service-connected condition;
• The surviving spouse or child of a person who died while on active military service and in the line of duty. (Includes the surviving spouse who remarries and whose subsequent marriage(s) terminates.)

To request CHAMPVA benefits, a veteran must complete an Application for Medical Benefits for Dependents or Survivors — CHAMPVA VAF 10-10d and submit it to the CHAMPVA Center, 4500 Cherry Creek Drive South, Box 64, Denver, CO 80222. The form may be obtained by writing to the above address or phoning toll free 1-800-733-8387. It will take approximately 60 days to verify eligibility.

CHAMPVA covers most health care that is medically necessary. If there is other insurance, except for Medicare, the claim must be filed before filing with CHAMPVA. When CHAMPVA beneficiaries become entitled to Medicare hospital insurance (Part A), eligibility ceases for all CHAMPVA benefits. If an individual is not entitled to Medicare Part A, but chooses to enroll for Part B at their own expense, he or she continues to be eligible for CHAMPVA.

CHAMPVA pays 75 percent of the allowable amount for covered services after a deductible for outpatient care. For all types of medical care, the remainder of charges after the CHAMPVA payment is the patient's cost-share, or copayment.

The beneficiary propulation receiving CHAMPVA benefits has approximated 86,000 per year in recent years.

Overseas Medical Benefits

ELIGIBILITY/BENEFITS

Reimbursed fee-basis medical care is available to veterans outside of the United States for treatment of adjudicated, service-connected disabilities and conditions related to those disabilities. Prior to treatment, an authorization must be obtained from the nearest American embassy or consulate. In Canada, veterans should contact the local office of Veterans Affairs Canada. In emergency situations, treatment should be reported within 72 hours. Nursing home care is not available in foreign jurisdictions.

Other Overseas Benefits

ELIGIBILITY/BENEFITS

Virtually all monetary benefits — compensation, pension, educational assistance, burial allowances — are payable regardless of place of residence or nationality. There are, however, some program limitations in foreign jurisdictions: home loan guaranty benefits are available only in the United States and selected territories and possessions, and educational benefits are limited to approved degree-granting programs in institutions of higher learning. Beneficiaries residing in foreign countries should contact the nearest American embassy or consulate for information and claims assistance. In Canada, the local office of Veterans Affairs Canada should be contacted.

Homeless Veterans

Veterans comprise about one-third of the estimated 500,000 to 700,000 homeless persons in the United States. The VA does not have any programs designed specifically to assist the homeless; however, some VA programs, by their nature, have served homeless veterans and provided help to other disadvantaged veterans who otherwise would be homeless. Some of these programs and initiatives include the following:

• Home retention services to assist veterans who are in danger of losing their homes

• Outreach programs to ensure that veterans are aware of benefits and services available to them

• A staff member in each VA medical center who coordinates activities for homeless veterans and works with community groups that assist the homeless

- A program designed to help disabled veterans make the transition from homeless and/or prolonged hospital care to independent living

- A joint Housing and Urban Development/VA initiative to provide housing and treatment services to homeless, mentally ill veterans and those suffering from substance abuse disorders who are living in the streets or in shelters

- A network of 196 Vietnam veteran outreach centers offering counseling, each with a coordinator who works with VA regional offices and other concerned public and private sector homeless groups

- A project in cooperation with Social Security to locate homeless veterans and facilitate their access to Social Security benefits to which they are entitled. SSA outreach workers will also join VA teams to meet with veterans in shelters, soup kitchens and on the streets

- Vocational rehabilitation and counseling to assist those with service-connected disabilities to achieve independence in daily living and become employable

- A fiduciary or guardianship program manages benefits of veterans who are incapable of managing their funds

- 35 VA domiciliaries provide treatment for eligible ambulatory veterans disabled by medical or psychiatric disorders, injury or age who do not need hospitalization or nursing home care. 22,000 psychiatric beds provide inpatient care

APPEALS

The Congress has recognized the right of those eligible to receive VA benefits to contest VA's determinations on their claims. This recognition is embodied in the following statement (U.S. Code: Title 38, Section 3.103(a)):

"Every claimant has the right to written notice of the decision made on his or her claim, the right to a hearing, and right of representation. Proceedings before VA are from one side only in nature, and it is the obligation of VA to assist a claimant in developing the facts pertinent to the claim and to render a decision which grants every benefit that can be supported in law while protecting the interests of the Government."

Most all field determinations are appealable; however, those of medical content such as the appropriateness of specific types of medical care or drugs to be prescribed are not. These are judgmental decisions for the physician. Ratings, compensation, pension and education benefits, and waiver of recovery of overpayments are the typical issues which may be appealed to the Board of Veterans Appeals.

Theoretically, there are five successive steps of appeal which the review can follow: (1) VA Regional Office, (2) Board of Veterans Appeals, (3) U.S. Court of Veterans Appeals, (4) U.S. Court of Appeals for the Federal District, and (5) U.S. Supreme Court. However, as practical matter, the last two judicial levels are only rarely involved; for the most part reconsiderations and actions if pursued end with the U.S. Court of Veterans Appeals.

Of considerable importance and highly recommended, service organizations such as Disabled American Veterans, American Legion, Veterans of Foreign Wars and some 29 other organizations have experienced, VA-accredited representatives who will assist an appellant through the entire filing and appeal procedures. There also is a network of assistance available through state and county veteran service officers. All of these services are free, but the claimant should consider carefully the quality of expertise available from one source as compared to another.

SEQUENCE OF PROCEDURES

1. Veteran files claim for benefit with VA field office.

2. If claim is not approved, the VA field office informs the veteran of the decision and any procedure for further action. The VA is responsible for notifying the claimant of: (a) the right to initiate an appeal and the time limit to do so, (b) the right to a personal hearing, and (c) the right to representation. This information will be included in each notification of a determination of entitlement or non-entitlement to VA benefits.

3. Veteran files Notice of Disagreement with VA field office within one year. A written statement by a claimant or representative expressing disagreement with a factual or legal conclusion is acceptable as a Notice of Disagreement. The statement should state the belief that a claim for benefits was improperly disallowed by reason of an error of fact or law. The claimant should outline where he/she believes the decision to be in error. Notice of Disagreement must be filed within one year from the date of mailing of notification of the initial decision being appealed; otherwise that decision will become final.

4. Unless the issues are resolved by granting the appeal or the Notice of Disagreement is withdrawn the VA field office provides a Statement

of the Case. The purpose of the Statement of the Case is to give the claimant notice of the pertinent facts and the action taken. Information will also be provided regarding the claimant's right to file a Substative Appeal to the BVA and the time limits to do so. The Statement of the Case will contain:

- A summary of the evidence in the case relating to the issue(s) the appellant or representative disagrees with;
- A summary of the applicable laws and regulations, with appropriate citations; and
- The decision of the agency of original jurisdiction on each issue and the reasons for such decision.

5. The veteran files a Substantive Appeal (VA Form 1-9) within 60 days or within the remaining time frame of 1 year of the Notice of Disagreement. This document should clearly identify the benefit sought and point out errors of fact or law believed to have been made in the determination. All statements should relate to specific items in the Statement of the Case identifying any facts the claimant disagrees with.

A claimant or representative may request a personal hearing at the VA field station of jurisdiction, or a hearing can be requested at any stage of the procedure, depending on whether it is a pre- or post-decisional hearing or a hearing on appeal. In either case, a hearing must be provided at whichever level requested, which could be by a hearing officer in the field, or by a Board of Veterans Appeals officer in the field or in Washington, D.C. If, however, a hearing is requested prior to an initial decision by the field station, it will be conducted by the field officer's rating board. If the hearing is requested after an initial decision, it will be conducted by the field office hearing officer who has the power to overturn the prior decision.

6. If the field officer decision at this point is unfavorable, the case is automatically forwarded to the Board of Veterans Appeals. Hearings conducted by the Board are non-adversarial and the proceedings are not limited by strict rules of evidence presentation. If the Board of Veterans Appeals disallows the appeal, the VA decision is final unless new and material evidence is presented or a motion for reconsideration is granted, or the decision is overturned by the Court.

7. The adverse decision may be appealed to the U.S. Court of Appeals. To obtain a review of a Board decision by the U.S. Court of Veterans Appeals, a person adversely affected must file a Notice of Appeal within 120 days after the date on which notice of the adverse decision is mailed by the Board of Veteran Appeals. There is a $50 filing fee on the appeal to the Court. However, the fee may be waived if the

claimant can demonstrate that it will cause financial hardship. Unlike the Board of Veterans Appeals, there are strict standards for evidence representation at the Court of Appeals. The appeal may be presented by the claimant, a privately employed attorney or non-attorneys who have been recognized by the Court may also represent the claimant.

A SKETCH OF PROCEDURES

1. Veteran files claim for benefit to field office.
2. If claim not approved, field office informs veteran of decision and of procedure for further action.
3. Veteran files notice of disagreement to field office. He has one year to file this.
4. Field Station sends to veteran Statement of the Case. This covers complete detail.
5. Veteran files Form 1-9, Substantive Appeal. Hearing can be requested at field station — in person or by representative.
6. If not favorable, the case is automatically forwarded to Board of Veterans Appeals.
7. If adverse decision at Board of Veterans Appeals, file appeal within 120 days to the U.S. Court of Appeals.

A word of caution: The system of appeals, from start to finish, is thought to be within the understanding of most veterans; however, the guidance of a service officer or other experienced person is absolutely essential through every phase of this procedure to achieve the desired results.

U.S. BOARD OF VETERANS APPEALS

On July 28, 1933, President Franklin D. Roosevelt created the Board of Veterans Appeals by Executive Order 6230. The Board is directly responsible to the DVA Secretary, and it provides review on appeal to the Secretary, as well as every possible assistance to claimants. It also affords an opportunity for full consideration of claims to permit final action equitable both to the veteran and the government.

The Board is located in Washington, D.C., and has 21 appellate Sections each at the present time, but subject to change is generally comprised of three Board members. Issues of a medical nature are reviewed by a Board Section which includes a physician as one of its members. Claims involving legal questions are reviewed by Board Sections where all members are attorneys. Each Section has staff attorneys who initially review the appeals and draft proposed decisions.

The Board has a heavy workload. For example, a total of 65,000 World War II cases were heard in 1950, and in 1955 the Korean War produced 49,000 cases. Post Vietnam cases amounted to about 44,000 each year. Of almost 45,000 cases heard in Fiscal Year 1991, 14 percent were allowed, 30 percent were remanded, and 56 percent were denied. More than 80 percent of the claimants before the Board were represented by accredited service organizations.

U.S. COURT OF VETERANS APPEALS

The Veterans Judicial Review Act, Public Law 100-687 of November 18, 1988, established the U.S. Court of Veterans Appeals. The Court is authorized seven judges and has jurisdiction to review decisions of the Board of Veterans Appeals in cases in which a Notice of Disagreement has been filed with the Board of Veterans Appeals after November 18, 1988, the date the Court came into being. The decisions of the Court are final and must be followed by the Board of Veterans Appeals as well as the Department of Veteran Affairs.

The Court is a court of review, not a trial court. The claimant is not entitled to a personal hearing before the Court, nor is the claimant permitted to furnish additional evidence. The Court limits its review of a case to the Board of Veterans Appeals decisions only, plus evidence included in the file at the time of the Board's decision. The Court is empowered to review all legal and Constitutional issues including the validity of VA adjudication procedures and operations. It also hears a full range of cases on veterans benefits, including those involving disability benefits, loan eligibility, and educational benefits. Its workload included 1,621 cases filed in 1990 and an increase in 1991 to 1,904 cases through October 1991. However, only 737 cases were processed in 1991, leaving a backlog of 2,539 cases.

The judicial review process by the Court is distinctly adversarial. The VA, which earlier provided assistance to a veteran and gave him/her the benefit of the doubt, opposes the veteran before the Court and argues that the Board of Veterans Appeals decision should be upheld. The cases often involve complex legal questions and may well evolve on the way issues are framed and argued. An attorney or qualified representative is a necessity, as a veteran without training and experience would be at a distinct disadvantage in trying to present his/her case in a most favorable way.

Prior to the Veterans Judicial Review Act of 1988 there was a limitation of a $10 fee that could be charged for legal assistance, an unattractive return to an attorney. However, the 1988 law allows attorneys to set and collect fees which are "not excessive or unreasonable" for services rendered. Fee agreements are subject to review by both the Board of Veterans Appeals and the Court. The fee may be paid directly by the Secretary out of an award of past benefits, but with a 20 percent limitation imposed.

CRITICISM OF PRESENT SYSTEM

There has been discussion between the Federal Bar Association and the VA regarding the regional office rating boards. The role and qualifications of the board members as to legal training and skills to perform this very important function have been a matter of contention for some time. The Bar Association would like to see a lawyer as a member of that board. There remains concern that no lawyer has any input into a claimant's case until the Board of Veterans Appeals has first rendered a final decision.

There are two other areas of criticism: First, the Court of Veterans Appeals, a court independent of the VA, has been critical of the VA's slow compliance with decisions rendered by the Court. On the other hand, the VA has complained that the Court too often refers cases back to VA for further review instead of directly ordering the change, thus extending the time it takes for VA to issue benefits and resolve cases.

OTHER FEDERAL BENEFITS

INTRODUCTION

There are various benefits available to veterans and their dependents which are not administered by the Department of Veterans Affairs. The benefits that follow are summarized with information on how to contact the proper agency.

Employment Assistance

JOB-FINDING ASSISTANCE

Assistance in finding jobs is provided to veterans through state employment offices throughout the country. Local veterans employment representatives provide functional supervision of job counseling, testing, and employment referral and placement services provided to veterans. Priority in referral to job openings and training opportunities is given to eligible veterans, with preferential treatment for disabled veterans. Employment offices also assist veterans by providing information about job marts and on-the-job and apprenticeship training opportunities, in cooperation with VA regional offices and vet centers. Veterans should apply for this kind of help at their nearest state employment office, not at VA.

Reemployment Rights

Under the Veterans' Reemployment Rights (VRR) law (Chapter 43, Title 38, U.S. Code), a person who left a civilian job to enter active duty in the Armed Forces, either voluntarily or involuntarily, may be entitled to return to his or her civilian job after discharge or release from active duty. This law covers reemployment rights under certain conditions for those who rendered active duty service, initial active duty for training, active duty for training, and inactive duty for training.

There are four basic eligibility criteria that must be met under the Veterans' Reemployment Rights law:

1. The person must have been employed in an "other than temporary" civilian job.

2. The person must have left the civilian job for the purposes of entering military service.

3. The person must not remain on active duty longer than four years, unless the period beyond four years is at the request and for the convenience of the federal government and the military discharge form carries this statement. Active duty during a period of declared national emergency, if at the request of and for the convenience of the federal government, does not count toward this four-year limitation. In some cases, the limitation may be extended to five years.

4. The person must be discharged or released from active duty under honorable conditions.

The VRR law places the returning veteran in the job that would have been attained if he or she had remained continuously employed instead of going on active duty. This means that the person may be entitled to benefits that are generally based on seniority, such as pensions, pay increases, missed promotions and missed transfers.

The law also protects a veteran from discharge without just cause for one year from the date of reemployment, and a Reservist or National Guard member from discharge without just cause for six months after returning from initial active duty for training. In addition, the law also prohibits discrimination in hiring, promotion or other advantage of employment because of one's obligation as a member of a reserve component of the armed forces, including the National Guard.

Applications for reemployment should be given verbally or in writing to a person who is authorized to represent the company for hiring purposes. A record of when and to whom the application was given should be kept. If there are problems in attaining reemployment, the applicant may be eligible for representation by the Department of Labor.

Questions on the VRR law, or requests for assistance in attaining reemployment if there are problems with private employers or state or local governments, should be directed to the Department of Labor's director for Veterans Employment and Training (DVET) for the state in which the employer is located. Consult telephone directories under U.S. Department of Labor for the telephone number of the DVET or call 1-800-442-2838 for the appropriate DVET telephone number.

When the federal government is the employer of members of the National Guard or reserve, the Office of Personnel Management (OPM) is specifically charged with enforcing the VRR law within the executive branch of the federal government. For additional information, consult the telephone directory under U.S. Government, or contact the Office of Personnel Management, Veterans' Coordinator, Room 6504, 1900 E Street, N.W., Washington, DC 20415, telephone (202) 606-0960.

Postal employees are covered by Section 517 of the Employee and Labor Relations Manual of the U.S. Postal Service. This section is entitled "Military Leave" and covers all aspects of military leave procedures for enlistees and reservists. For additional information, consult the local telephone directory under U.S. Government, or contact the Program Manager, Employee Relations Department, U.S. Postal Service, Washington, D.C. 20260-4256, telephone (202) 268-3970.

APPLYING FOR REEMPLOYMENT

A veteran must apply to the pre-service employer within 90 days after separation from active duty. If the veteran is hospitalized or recuperating when discharged, the 90-day application period begins upon release from the hospital or completion of recuperation, which may last up to one year. For reservists and National Guard members returning from initial active duty for training, the application period is 31 days instead of 90.

Affirmative Action in Employment

Federal legislation prohibits employers with federal contracts or subcontracts of $10,000 or more from discriminating in employment against Vietnam-Era and "special disabled" veterans. Special disabled veterans, covered throughout their working lives, are those veterans entitled to compensation — or veterans who but for the receipt of military retired pay would be entitled to compensation — who are rated under laws administered by VA for disability at 30 percent or more, or rated at 10 or 20 percent in the case of a veteran who has been determined under Section 1506 of Title 38, USC, to have a serious employment handicap, or a person who was discharged or released from active duty because of a service-connected disability. Federal legislation requires these contractors to take affirmative action to employ and advance in employment Vietnam-Era and special disabled veterans. Vietnam-Era veterans are covered by this program through 1994.

Legislative requirements are administered by the U.S. Labor Department's Office of Federal Contract Compliance Programs (OFCCP). Complaints may be filed with any OFCCP regional office, not VA.

Job Training and Reemployment

By law, the U.S. Department of Labor's Office of Veterans' Employment and Training offers several programs for job training and assistance.

The Disabled Veterans Outreach Program — Its purpose is to provide job and training opportunities for disabled and other veterans through contacts with employers; develop on-the-job training opportunities; provide outreach to veterans through community agencies; provide assistance to local employment service offices; develop linkages with other agencies to promote maximum employment opportunities for veterans; to provide job placement, counseling, testing, and job referral to eligible veterans, especially disabled Vietnam veterans. For information, veterans should contact the regional or state director for Veterans Employment and Training Service of the U.S. Department of Labor.

Job Training Partnership Act — Develops programs to meet the employment and training needs of service-connected disabled veterans, Vietnam-era veterans and veterans recently separated from military service. Programs include enhancement of services provided to eligible veterans by other providers of employment and training services funded by federal, state, or local governments; providing employment and training services not adequately provided by other public employment and training services providers; and outreach and public information activities to develop and promote maximum job and training opportunities for eligible veterans.

VETS

The U.S. Department of Labor's Veterans Employment and Training Services (VETS) have offices in every state and in 10 cities that provide the following services:

- Monitor veterans employment and training programs
- Administer veterans training programs under the Job Training and Partnership Act
- Protect the reemployment rights of veterans, including those on

temporary active duty with the National Guard or Reserves
- Department of Labor state directors provide technical assistance to state job service offices, which offer referrals for job training, counseling, job search and other help to veterans. Veterans also may get information at state offices concerning unemployment compensation, reemployment rights and tax credits available to employers of veterans.

Also, there is a professionally trained person in each state employment or Job Service Office to work directly with veterans on job assistance.

The VETS program administers a Disabled Veterans Outreach Program, providing specialists in state employment offices and other locations to develop employer and community support for hiring disabled and other veterans.

For more information about any of these programs, veterans should contact any office of the Veterans Employment and Training Service listed under U.S. Government in phone books where VETS offices are located.

In addition to at least one VETS office in every state, there are regional offices in Boston, New York, Philadelphia, Chicago, Atlanta, Dallas, San Francisco and Seattle.

TRANSITION ASSISTANCE PROGRAM

In anticipation of downsizing the military forces, the Department of Labor has established the Transition Assistance Program (TAP) to meet the job search needs of service people scheduled for separation. The program was authorized under Public Law 101-510 to establish a partnership between the Department of Defense, the VA and the Department of Labor to provide employment and training information to armed forces personnel who are within 180 days of separating or retiring.

Three-day workshops to assist in this transition to civilian jobs are conducted at military installations throughout the nation. In addition, service personnel being separated with a service-connected disability are offered the Disabled Transition Assistance Program in addition to the three-day TAP workshops.

In 1992, TAP plans to operate at 168 sites in 44 states serving 97 percent of all separating veterans in the continental U.S.

For further information, contact VETS, U.S. Department of Labor, 200 Constitution Ave., N.W., Room S1313, Washington, D.C. 20210, or call (202) 523-5573.

STATE EMPLOYMENT SERVICES

The U.S. Department of Labor works with states to provide employment and training services to eligible veterans through the local veterans employment representative program and the disabled veterans outreach program.

Local veterans employment representatives (LVERs) are state employees in state job service offices. They perform the following functions:

• Supervise services to veterans, including counseling, testing and help in identifying training or employment opportunities;
• Monitor job listings from federal contractors and see that eligible veterans receive preference in referrals;
• Promote and monitor participation of veterans in federally-funded employment and training programs;
• Cooperate with the VA in identifying and assisting veterans who need work-specific prosthetic devices, sensory aids or other special equipment to improve their employability; and
• Contact community leaders, employers, unions, training programs and veterans organizations to ensure that eligible veterans receive the services they are entitled to.

There is one full-time LVER in each local job service office which had 1,100 or veteran applicants the preceding year, one additional LVER for every 1,500 additional veteran applicants and one part-time LVER in other offices with at least 350 veteran applicants.

State Job Services (also known as state employment service or employment security agencies) receive grants from the U.S. Department of Labor to fund and support the LVER positions.

LVERs are appointed in the following order: (1) qualified service-connected disabled veterans; (2) qualified eligible veterans and (3) other qualified eligible persons.

Disabled Veterans' Outreach Programs (DVOP) specialists develop job and training opportunities for disabled veterans and coordinate the necessary employability services required to allow disabled veterans to be competitive in the labor market, and build community support for hiring veterans with disabilities.

DVOP specialists receive lists of all service-connected disabled veterans in their state from the Department of Veterans Affairs, and inform veterans of opportunities open to them and also provide vocational guidance and employment counseling. Specialists also serve as case managers for veterans taking part in federally funded job training programs as well as for veterans placed in jobs. They keep in monthly contact with these veterans and their employers to ensure that training is completed successfully. They also assist the trainee with job-related problems.

Under the DVOP program, the U.S. Department of Labor provides grants to the state jobs services to pay for one specialist for each 5,300 Vietnam-era or disabled veteran in the state. One quarter of the specialists must be placed in locations other than the job service office. DVOP specialists also work at Department of Veterans Affairs regional offices and vet centers, state or county veterans service offices, and community-based organizations serving veterans and military installations.

For more information about U.S. Department of Labor employment and training programs for veterans, contact: VETS, U.S. Department of Labor, Washington, D.C. 20210.

NATIONAL VETERANS TRAINING INSTITUTE

Job placement and training services for veterans are enhanced through the program of the National Veterans Training Institute, designed to develop professional skills for persons who provide job training assistance for veterans. The program is funded by the U.S. Department of Labor's Veterans Employment and Training Service, which provides direction and oversight. The program is administered by the University of Colorado, where week-long courses include professional skills development, veterans benefits, and case management. Participants in the program are selected from among professionals in the VA, state employment agencies, and other sources of persons providing service for veterans.

The goal of the Institute is to train service workers to build veteran job readiness by developing networks of community services available to veteran job-seekers. The training includes special emphasis on skills that will ensure that veterans with disabilities receive priority in employment and training services.

The Institute also has a Resource and Technical Assistance Center offering a network for information-sharing essential to veterans employment and training efforts.

Information on the Institute can be obtained from the National Veterans Training Institute, University of Colorado, 1250 14th St., Denver, Colorado 80202, (303) 892-1712.

FEDERAL CONTRACTING - JOBS

Qualified Vietnam-era and special disabled veterans get priority referral for jobs with federal contractors and subcontractors. A business with a federal contract of $10,000 or more must take affirmative action to hire and promote these veterans, and must list certain job openings with the nearest Job Service or Employment Service Office.

While contractors are not required to hire all those who are referred, they must have affirmative action plans and show that they have followed them and that they have not discriminated against veterans or other covered groups. This requirement applies to all jobs with a salary starting under $25,000 at all levels of employment, including executives. Federal contractors must show that they have conducted outreach programs to recruit Vietnam-era and special disabled veterans, and that they have disseminated information about promotion activities internally.

Companies with federal contracts must file an annual VETS-100 report. Information may be obtained from the Office of Veterans Employment and Training, U.S. Department of Labor, Washington, D.C. 20210, or from the local veterans employment representative in any job service office.

Copies of "Affirmative Action Obligations of Contractors and Sub-contractors for Disabled Veterans and Veterans of the Vietnam Era, Rules and Regulations" may be obtained from the Office of Federal Contract Compliance Programs, Employment Standards Administration, U.S. Department of Labor, Washington, D.C. 20210.

UNEMPLOYMENT COMPENSATION

The purpose of unemployment compensation for ex-service members is to provide a weekly income for a limited period of time to help them meet basic needs while searching for employment. The amount and duration of payments are governed by federal and state laws and vary considerably. Benefits are paid from federal funds.

Ex-service members should apply immediately after leaving military service at their nearest state employment office, not VA, and present copy 4 of their military discharge form (DD-214) to determine their elibility for benefits.

A federal and state unemployment compensation program provides weekly financial assistance to veterans and recently discharged service personel while they seek employment. Benefits and other provisions follow requirements of state employment agencies, but benefits are financed by federal funds. Veterans and newly separated persons must meet eligibility requirements of the unemployment insurance laws of the state where they apply.

STATE UNEMPLOYMENT COMPENSATION TABLE

STATE	Initial Waiting Week	Weekly Benefit amount for total unemployment		Benefit weeks for total unemployment*	
		Minimum	Maximum	Minimum	Maximum
ALA	0	$22	$150	15+	26
ALASKA	1	44-68	212-284	*16	*26
ARIZ	1	40	175	12	26
ARK	1	41	230	9	26
CALIF	1	40	230	*14+	*26
COLO	1	25	239	13+	26
CONN	0	15-22	288-338	*26	*26
DEL	0	20	245	24	26
D.C.	1	13	*335	*26	*26
FLA	1	10	225	10	26
GA	*0	37	*185	9+	26
HAWAII	1	5	308	*26	*26
IDAHO	1	44	215	10	26
ILL	1	51	214-279	26	26
IND	1	50	116-171	14	26
IOWA	0	29-35	194-238	11+	26
KANS	1	57	231	10	26
KY	0	22	209	15	26
LA	1	10	181	8	26
MAINE	1	35-52	198-297	21+22	26
MD	0	25-33	*223	26	26
MASS	1	14-21	282-423	10+30	30
MICH	0	60	283	15	26
MINN	*1	38	265	10+	26
MISS	1	30	165	13+	26
MO	*1	45	170	11+	26
MONT	*1	50	201	8	26
NEB	1	20	154	20	26
NEV	0	16	211	12+	26
N.H.	0	34	179	26	26
N.J.	*1	66	*308	15	26
N. MEX	1	37	185	19	26
N.Y.	*1	40	*280	26	26
N.C.	1	22	258	13-26	26
N. DAK	1	43	206	12	26
OHIO	1	42	211-234	20	26
OKLA	1	16	*212	*20+	*26
OREG	1	60	259	*5+	*26
PENN	1	35-40	*304-312	16	26
P.R.	1	7	120	*26	*26
R.I.	1	41-51	285-356	15+	26
S.C.	1	20	186	15	26
S. DAK	1	28	154	18+	26
TENN	1	30	170	12+	26
TEX	*1	38	231	9+	26
UTAH	1	14	230	10	26
VT	1	26	192	26	26
VI	1	32	191	13+	26
VA	1	65	208	12	26
WASH	1	64	258	16+30	26
W.VA	1	24	263	26	26
WIS	0	43	230	13+	26
WYO	1	38	200	11-26	26

*Certain qualifying variations.

Benefits are based on the rate of pay from previous employment, and all states require that an applicant have qualified earnings during a period specified by law. An applicant must register for work, and be ready and able to work. Each state sets the amount of the benefit and the duration of the benefit period, which is the same as for non-veterans. In the case of a newly separated service person applying for benefits, the previous employer is the military service, thus providing the veteran with a work record he otherwise would not have under the program of Unemployment Compensation for Ex-servicemembers (UCX). A veteran to be eligible for UCX must have been released under honorable conditions, and have completed a full term of active service. State benefits and requirements are the same for all applicants. Amendments to the UCX law provide for coverage for Desert Shield/Storm veterans.

Military retirement pay is deducted from UCX benefits, and severance pay and unused leave upon discharge may be deducted as well.

When applying for UCX benefits, a veteran should register immediately at any state employment office. He then may become eligible for benefits if he meets the state requirements and if a suitable job is not available.

(See accompanying table showing amount and duration of benefits for each state.)

Federal jobless benefits have been extended for two 13-week periods. The first was Public Law 102-64, signed by the president on Nov. 15, 1991, and the second was Public Law 244, signed on Feb. 7, 1992.

GOVERNMENT CIVILIAN EMPLOYMENT

Job possibilities for veterans applying for work with the federal government in the near future are likely to continue to be more favorable than job possibilities in the private market place. This is not to say that government jobs will be plentiful, primarily because of the anticipated downsizing of many government-related activities (especially those involving the Department of Defense). Nevertheless, there are a number of federal veterans preference benefits which will provide many veterans (with a minimum length of service and/or disability rating) with a hiring advantage over competing non-veterans. The following discussion provides information on numbers of veterans in federal government service, veterans preference for federal employment, reemployment rights, and service credit where a military veteran also served in non-military service.

Recent figures illustrate the importance of military veterans in the non-military government sector. In the executive branch of the federal government — excluding postal workers — there are 2,240,000 employees of which 640,000 are veterans. A further breakdown indicates that 90,000 of the veterans have disabled ratings, and some 29,000 of these disabled veterans have a 30 percent or greater disability rating. Postal service employment totals 760,000 of which 290,000 are veterans. Of these veterans, 17,250 have disabilities rated at 30 percent or more.

An interesting profile of government workers of Reserve and Guard units called up to active duty during Desert Storm involved a total of over 17,500 persons. These federal workers are now classified as veterans whether or not they were of that classification before. Their average age was 38 years, with an average of 11.9 years of government service. Included were 43 percent representing wage board (blue collar) employees, 16 percent women, and 77 percent of those called up were Defense Department civilians. About 1,500 clerks and letter carriers were Postal Service employees.

Blue collar workers in the executive branch (excluding the Postal Service) account for 380,000 of the 2,240,000 civil service employees. These blue collar jobs are in such work categories as crafts, machinists, maintenance and repair shop workers, painters, custodial, and other hourly-paid, full-time occupations. Differing blue collar job hourly wage rates are set by wage boards in some 150 wage areas. For example, the wage level in a high cost area such as San Francisco exceeds that in a lower cost area such as Oklahoma City.

Through the last several years the federal government has experienced a turnover level in excess of 300,000 persons per year. The present turnover is somewhat lower because of the recent recession, but the federal government remains a relatively good source of veterans employment. Similar to the private sector, increasing automation in government operations has put a higher premium on analytical and computer-related skills.

VETERANS' READJUSTMENT APPOINTMENTS (VRA)

The Veterans' Readjustments (VRA) Act, which took effect on March 23, 1991, is the most recent special veterans job opportunity law. It facilitates federal agency efforts to hire veterans who served during and after the Vietnam era. Under this law, federal agencies may hire certain qualified veterans *directly* under the VRA authority. These appointees are hired for a probationary 2-year period. Successful completion of the

2-year VRA appointment leads to a permanent civil service appointment.

When agencies have vacancies to fill, they can choose eligibles from civil service examination lists, agency employees, or current and former federal employees with civil service status. The VRA authority gives agencies an alternative source for selecting quality candidates.

Who is eligible under the law for a VRA appointment? — *Post-Vietnam*-era veterans are those who *first* entered on active duty as (or first became) members of the Armed Forces after May 7, 1975. To be eligible, they must have served for a period of more than 180 days active duty and have other than a dishonorable discharge. The 180-day service requirement does not apply to: (1) veterans separated from active duty because of a service-connected disability, or (2) Reserve and Guard members who served on active duty during a period of war, such as the Persian Gulf War, or in a military operation for which a campaign or expeditionary medal is authorized.

Vietnam-era veterans are those who served on active duty any time during the period August 5, 1964 to May 7, 1975, whether or not they served after May 7, 1975. To be eligible, they must meet the same 180-day service and discharge requirements as post-Vietnam-era veterans, *and* also: (1) have a compensable service-connected disability, (2) have been separated for a disability incurred or aggravated in the line of duty, *or* for service during the Vietnam-era only, have a campaign or expeditionary medal, such as the Vietnam Service Medal or an Armed Forces Expeditionary Medal.

How long are veterans eligible for VRA appointments after they leave the service? — Eligible post-Vietnam-era veterans qualify for 10 years after the date of their last separation or until December 17, 1999, whichever date is later. Eligible Vietnam-era veterans qualify for a VRA appointment until 10 years after separation or until December 31, 1993, whichever is later. Eligible veterans with a service-connected disability of 30% or more can be hired without time limit.

What jobs can be filled under VRA authority? — Agencies can use the VRA authority to fill white collar positions up through GS-11 and equivalent jobs under other pay systems. Each agency decides whether a veteran meets the basic experience or education requirements for a job. Agencies may require the applicant to pass a test for some jobs.

How do veterans apply for VRA appointments? — Veterans should contact the agency personnel office where they want to work to find out about job openings. Agencies recruit candidates and make VRA appointments directly. For a list of local agency personnel offices or information about the civil service employment system, veterans should contact the Veterans's Representative at the OPM offices listed below (Table 1). Veterans seeking career development help should contact their local state employment service or VA office.

Agencies must give preference to disabled veterans and others with veterans preference over veterans who are not eligible for preference. Also, in some cases, agencies provide special training programs for VRA appointees. A program could include on-the-job assignments or classroom training.

VETERANS PREFERENCE FOR FEDERAL JOBS

Candidates who pass an examination are ranked by their scores. Veterans eligible for preference are entitled to have 5 or 10 extra points (see below) included in their scores if they pass an examination. A passing score is 70 or higher. Regardless of their scores, qualified veterans with a compensable service-connected disability of 10 percent or more are placed at the top of most civil service examination lists of eligibles, except for scientific and professional jobs at GS-9 or higher.

Federal agencies hiring candidates from an examination list must consider the top three available candidates for each vacancy. An agency may not pass over a candidate with preference and select an individual without preference who has the same or lower score unless the Office of Personnel Management (OPM) approves the agency's decision. Veterans may apply within 120 days after service discharge for any examination open during their military service.

Five points are added to the passing examination score of a veteran who served during the period December 7, 1941, to July 1, 1955; or for more than 180 consecutive days, any part of which occurred after January 31, 1955, and before 1976; or in a campaign or expedition for which a campaign medal has been authorized, including Lebanon, Grenada, Panama, and Southwest Asia (Desert Shield/Storm). Medal holders who enlisted after September 7, 1980, or who entered on active duty on or after October 14, 1982, must have served continuously for 24 months, or for the full period called, or ordered to active duty. The service requirement does not apply to veterans with compensable service-connected disabilities, or to veterans separated for disability in the line of duty, or for hardship.

Ten points are added to the passing examination score of a veteran who served at any time and who: (1) has a service-connected disability or (2) is receiving compensation, disability retirement benefits, or pension from the military or the VA. Individuals who received a Purple Heart qualify as disabled veterans. An unmarried spouse of certain deceased veterans also qualifies for the 10 point hiring preference. The category also includes the spouse of a veteran unable to work because of a service-connected disability, and a mother of a veteran who died in service or who is permanently and totally disabled. Ten-point preference eligibles may apply for any job for which: (1) a list of

Table 1.
U.S. Office of Personnel Management
Local Veterans Representatives for General Employment Inquiries

Alabama
Lee Hockenberry
Huntsville Area Office
(205) 544-5130

Alaska
John Busteed
Anchorage Service Center
(907) 271-5823

Arizona
Jack Mallin
Phoenix Area Office
(602) 640-5809

Arkansas
(See Oklahoma)

California
John Andre
Los Angeles Service Center
(818) 575-6507

Susan Fong-Young
San Francisco Service Center
(916) 551-3270

Marc Gunby
San Francisco Service Center
(415) 744-7217

Colorado
Doris Veden
Denver Area Office
(303) 969-7036

Connecticut
A.J. Dubois
Hartford Area Office
(203) 240-3607

Delaware
(See Philadelphia, PA)

District of Columbia
William Robinson
Washington Area Service Center
(202) 606-1848

Florida
Georgia Deal or Claudia Griffin
Orlando Area Office
(407) 648-6148

Georgia
Nick Barone
Atlanta Area Office
(404) 331-4531

Hawaii
Arleen Gates
Honolulu Service Center
(808) 541-2781

Idaho
(See Washington State)

Illinois
Henry Kranz
Chicago Area Office
(312) 353-6234

Indiana
Lisa Phelps
Indianapolis Area Office
(317) 226-6245

Iowa
(See Kansas City, MO)

Kansas
Laura Toth
Wichita Area Office
(316) 269-6797

Kentucky
(See Ohio)

Louisiana
(See San Antonio, TX)

Maine
(See New Hampshire)

Maryland
Thomas Platt
Baltimore Area Office
(301) 962-3222

Massachusetts
Donald MacGee
Boston Area Office
(617) 565-5922

Michigan
Taddy Johnstone
Detroit Area Office
(313) 226-2095

Minnesota
Paul McMahon
Twin Cities Area Office
(612) 725-3633

Mississippi
(See Alabama)

Missouri
Richard Krueger
Kansas City Area Office
(816) 426-5705
Kirk Hawkins
St. Louis Area Office
(314) 539-2341

Montana
(See Colorado)

Nebraska
(See Kansas)

Nevada
(Contact Los Angeles Service
Center for counties of Clark,
Lincoln, and Nye. Remaining
counties should contact Susan
Fong-Young in San Francisco
Service Center.)

New Hampshire
Gloria Dunn
Portsmouth Area Office
(603) 433-0744

New Jersey
Don Hodge
Newark Area Office
(201) 645-2376

New Mexico
Janice Lybarger
Albuquerque Area Office
(505) 766-2906

New York
Larry Burkett
Syracuse Service Center
(315) 423-5650

North Carolina
Ayn Clayborne
Raleigh Area Office
(919) 790-2817

North Dakota
(See Minnesota)

Ohio
(For Southern Ohio)
George Helm
Dayton Area Office
(513) 225-2529

(For Northern Ohio area
see Michigan)

Oklahoma
Iva Brown
Oklahoma City Area Office
(405) 231-4613

Oregon
(See Washington State)

Pennsylvania
Ellie Smith
Harrisburg Field Office
(717) 782-4495

Gene Hyden
Philadelphia Service Center
(215) 597-7670
Nathan Singletary
Pittsburgh Representative Office
(412) 644-4358

Puerto Rico
Vivien Fernandez
San Juan Area Office
(809) 766-5620

Rhode Island
(See Connecticut)

South Carolina
(See North Carolina)

South Dakota
(See Minnesota)

Tennessee
(See Alabama)

Texas
Frank McLemore
Dallas Area Office
(214) 767-9135

Jose Borrero
San Antonio Area Office
(512) 229-6613

Utah
(See Colorado)

Vermont
(See New Hampshire)

Virgin Islands
(See Puerto Rico)

Virginia
Valerie DeMeis
Norfolk Area Office
(804) 441-3362

Washington (State)
Robert Coleman
Seattle Service Center
(206) 553-4691

West Virginia
(See Ohio)

Wisconsin
(For Northern Wisconsin, see
Minnesota; for Southern
Wisconsin, see Illinois)

Wyoming
(See Colorado)

examination eligibles is established, or (2) a non-temporary appointment was made in the last 3 years.

GENERAL REQUIREMENTS FOR VETERANS PREFERENCE

When applying for federal jobs, eligible veterans should claim preference on their job applications. Preference applies in hiring from civil service examinations for most excepted service jobs, and when agencies make temporary appointments, or use direct hire and OPM-delegated examining authority. An honorable or general discharge is necessary to obtain veterans preference. Military retirees with the rank of major or higher rank are not eligible for veterans preference unless they are disabled veterans. Guard or Reserve active duty for training purposes does *not* qualify an ex-serviceman for preference.

Veterans with 30 percent or higher compensable service-connected disability ratings are eligible for direct appointments to jobs without examination. Such jobs may lead to conversions to career appointments. If rejected for employment or retention because of disability or if passed over for hiring, veterans are entitled: (1) to be notified by the agency; (2) to respond to the agency's action; and, (3) to receive a copy of OPM's final determination. Once hired, disabled veterans can participate in the Disabled Veterans Affirmative Action Program and receive assistance in development and advancement opportunities.

When a candidate's work experience is evaluated in an examination, full credit is given for military service. Such service is either considered as an extension of the work the veteran did before entering the Armed Forces, or is rated on the basis of the actual duties performed in the Armed Forces, whichever is more beneficial to the veteran. Also, military time may count toward civil service retirement and vacations.

Generally, employees who have preference in examinations and appointments also have preference over other employees in retaining their jobs in the event of a reduction-in-force (RIF). However, certain employees who *retired* from military service are not eligible for preference for job retention purposes. When layoffs are necessary, each non-temporary employee competes for retention with other employees who perform similar work at the same grade of pay and who serve under similar conditions. Among competing employees, the order of separation is determined by type of appointment, length of service, and performance ratings.

To review, veterans have preference in retention over non-veterans. Veterans with disability ratings of 30 percent or higher, and whose performance has been rated acceptable, have preference over non-veterans and other veterans. However, the definition of preference eligibility for RIF protection purposes, as applied to *military retirees*, has not been amended. The dual compensation provisions are still in effect; therefore, most *military retirees*, even those with disability ratings of 30 percent or higher, do not qualify for retention purposes.

There are other veterans preference benefits. All physical requirements are waived for veterans who are found to be physically able to discharge the duties of the position in question without danger to themselves or to others. There also is a Disabled Veterans Affirmative Action Program (DVAAP) developed to promote recruitment, employment, and job advancement opportunities within the federal government for qualified disabled veterans. Agencies have primary responsibility for establishing and overseeing DVAAP.

THE DUAL COMPENSATION ACT — GOVERNMENT EMPLOYMENT OF MILITARY RETIREES

The Dual Compensation Act of 1964 specifically limits the conditions under which a retired member of the armed forces is entitled to veterans preference in hiring and RIF protection in government jobs. All retired officers are allowed to take civilian jobs, and all retired military personnel who take government civilian jobs received the full pay of the position except that retired regular officers and warrant officers may receive only a portion of their retired pay plus 50% of the remainder. The exempt amount of retired pay, effective December 1, 1991, is $8,809.94. Retired reserve officers and all enlisted personnel and regular officers retired for combat disability retain all retired pay in civilian jobs unless they retired after January 1979 and their combined pay of military and civilian salary exceeds $104,800, which is the salary of Level I of the Executive Schedule pay.

Credit for military service for annual leave purposes for military retirees is limited to a war or campaign expedition for which a badge has been issued, unless the veteran is retired for a combat disability. Also, a credit for military service of retirees for Civil Service retirement purposes is proper. However, since such military service also is creditable for post-1956 Social Security benefits, retirees who combine military service with civil service in a single annuity have their civil service retirement annuity recomputed at age 62 when they become eligible for Social Security.

Public Law 97-253 in 1982 established new requirements for *crediting post-1956 military service for Civil Service Retirement System (CSRS)* purposes. For those who first became employed in a civil service position *before October 1, 1982* there is the option of either: (1) making a deposit for post-1956 military service or (2) receiving credit as in the past, without making a deposit, and then having their annuity recomputed at age 62 to eliminate post-1956 military service if they are eligible for Social Security benefits. For those who first became employed under CSRS *after October 1, 1982*, credit will be applied for their post-1956 military service only if a deposit for the military service is made. Individuals hired after *January 1, 1984* who are subject to civil service will receive credit for their post-1956 military service only if a deposit is made under the Federal Employees Retirement System (FERS). For advice on various requirements that apply in this situation consult with the personnel officer.

The deposit under CSRS will be 7 percent of basic military pay, plus interest. (The interest-free grace period ended September 30, 1986.) For individuals subject to FERS social security, the deposit is 3% of basic military pay. The interest-free grace period is extended to 2 years after the initial appointment.

The Dual Compensation Law denies military retirees entitlement to veterans preference for RIF protection purposes. This reflects the theory that it would be unfair to give military retirees a retention advantage in a "second career" over other veterans and other employees whose only career was in the civil service. To further restate, Congress provided that an armed forces retiree *would not* retain veterans preference in RIF competition after beginning a second career in the federal service unless the employee's military retirement is based on a disabiliity incurred in the military service, or his military retired pay is not based on 20 years or more of active service.

JOB FAIRS

The federal government is making every effort to help veterans seeking jobs to make contact with private and public employers for both local and nationwide job opportunities. Joint sponsorship by OPM, VA, the U.S. Department of Labor, and the Department of Defense has resulted in successful job fairs in a number of major cities, and it is expected that more job fairs will be scheduled in the near future. In addition to the private firms using this format for hiring, the federal government is taking steps to make federal agencies aware of the new provisions of the Veterans Readjustment Appointment Authority (VRA) program for hiring veterans in light of the effectiveness of the program. Veterans should contact the nearest federal job information office in the area in which they desire employment to learn of any job fairs which are planned.

AUTOMATED JOB LISTING

A new OPM initiative for publicizing the availability of federal employment opportunities involves an automated listing of federal job openings in most U.S. areas. The number to call is 1-900-990-9200. The total cost of such calls, at 40 cents a minute, is expected to average about $2.50 and the caller can request an employment application. This new program was expected to be in place by April 1992.

The Federal Research Service, Inc. (P.O. Box 1059, Vienna, VA 22183) is a private company which sells a bi-weekly listing of some 3500-4000 federal jobs nationally. The Federal Personnel Guide, available from Key Publications at P.O. Box 42578, Washington, D.C. 20015, price $8.00, provides approximately 160 pages of material on a full range of federal employment subjects.

PAY TABLES

Two major pay tables list pay levels for most federal positions. Table 1 covers essentially all of the white collar positions in the federal government, and Table 2 lists salaries paid to U.S. Postal Service clerks and mail carriers. Blue collar, wage grade, employees are paid on an hourly rate ranging from about $6 to $20 an hour. Supervisory personnel are paid from 10 to 20 percent higher. However, actual wage scales differ among the 150 wage areas in the U.S.

JOB INFORMATION

Job information is available from all the U.S. Office of Personnel Management (OPM) regional offices at the following locations in addition to the locations presented in Table 1.

Office of Personnel Management
HEADQUARTERS OFFICE
   1900 E Street, NW, Washington, DC 20415
   FTS/632-9594 Comm/202-606-2424
REGIONAL OFFICES
Atlanta
   Richard B. Russell Fed. Bldg.
   75 Spring Street, SW, Atlanta, GA 30303-3019
   FTS/841-3459 Comm/404-331-3459
Chicago
   John C. Kluczynski Fed. Bldg.
   230 S. Dearborn Street, Chicago, IL 60604
   FTS/353-2901 Comm/312-353-2901
Dallas
   1100 Commerce Street, Dallas, TX 75242
   FTS/729-8227 Comm/214-767-8227
Philadelphia
   William J. Green Jr. Fed. Bldg.
   600 Arch Street, Philadelphia, PA 19106-1596
   FTS/597-4543 Comm/215-597-4543
San Francisco
   211 Main St., 7th Floor, San Francisco, CA 94105
   FTS/454-9662 Comm/415-974-9662

   OPM also offers federal employment information through a network
of Federal Job Information Centers (FJICs) and OPM's Area Offices in
several major metropolitan areas across the country. Specialists in the
FJICs and Area Offices can mail appropriate job announcements,
application form, and pamphlets. In addition, federal job opportunities
are posted in State Job Service-State Employment Offices.

All full-time federal employees annual salaries are based on 2080 hours per year, with allowance of 13 days sick leave, and annual leave of a minimum of 13 days and a maximum of 26 days per year. Employees also receive liberally subsidized life insurance and health insurance.

Table 1

GENERAL SCHEDULE
Annual Salaries — January 1992
(Step increases from 1 to 3 years in each step of grade)

Longevity Steps	1	2	3	4	5	6	7	8	9	10
Grade GS 1	$11,478	$11,861	$12,242	$12,623	$13,006	$13,230	$13,606	$13,986	$14,003	$14,356
2	12,905	13,212	13,640	14,003	14,157	14,573	14,989	15,405	15,821	16,237
3	14,082	14,551	15,020	15,489	15,958	16,427	16,896	17,365	17,834	18,303
4	15,808	16,335	16,862	17,389	17,916	18,443	18,970	19,497	20,024	20,551
5	17,686	18,276	18,866	19,456	20,046	20,636	21,226	21,816	22,406	22,996
6	19,713	20,370	21,027	21,684	22,341	22,998	23,655	24,312	24,969	25,626
7	21,906	22,636	23,366	24,096	24,826	25,556	26,286	27,016	27,746	28,476
8	24,262	25,071	25,880	26,689	27,498	28,307	29,116	29,925	30,734	31,543
9	26,798	27,691	28,584	29,477	30,370	31,263	32,156	33,049	33,942	34,835
10	29,511	30,495	31,479	32,463	33,447	34,431	35,415	36,399	37,383	38,367
11	32,423	33,504	34,585	35,666	36,747	37,828	38,909	39,990	41,071	42,152
12	38,861	40,156	41,451	42,746	44,041	45,336	46,631	47,926	49,221	50,516
13	46,210	47,750	49,290	50,830	52,370	53,910	55,450	56,990	58,530	60,070
14	54,607	56,427	58,247	60,067	61,887	63,707	65,527	67,347	69,167	70,987
15	64,233	66,374	68,515	70,656	72,797	74,938	77,079	79,220	81,361	83,502

Table 2

POSTAL PAY TABLE
Postal clerks and mail carriers
Current 1992 average Postal Clerk and Carrier salary is $33,000

There are other federal salary schedules: Executive salaries, Level 1 through 5, salaries range from $104,800 to $143,800; Foreign Service salaries from $17,686 to $83,502; VA Health Service Professionals salaries from $32,423 to $109,086; Postal Executive and Administrative salaries from $20,342 to $70,751; and Postal Career Executive salaries from $102,000 to $138,900.

POSTAL SERVICE SCHEDULE (PS)—FULL-TIME ANNUAL RATES*—EFFECTIVE NOVEMBER 16, 1991

PS GRADE	AA	A	B	C	D	E	F	G	H	I	J	K	L	M	N	O
1	$18,489	$20,707	$22,684	$24,664	$27,608	$27,811	$28,013	$28,215	$28,415	$28,617	$28,818	$29,021	$29,223	$29,422	$29,625	$29,827
2	18,786	21,040	23,067	25,090	28,096	28,314	28,532	28,749	28,970	29,188	29,406	29,625	29,842	30,063	30,280	30,498
3	19,103	21,398	23,476	25,554	28,623	28,859	29,097	29,329	29,567	29,800	30,038	30,273	30,508	30,744	30,981	31,214
4		21,351	23,923	26,057	29,196	29,450	29,705	29,960	30,214	30,469	30,724	30,981	31,236	31,490	31,744	31,998
5		22,756	25,504	27,698	29,816	30,089	30,364	30,637	30,912	31,185	31,460	31,735	32,008	32,284	32,556	32,831
6		24,249	27,183	28,314	30,483	30,781	31,079	31,375	31,674	31,971	32,268	32,566	32,864	33,163	33,462	33,759
7		24,816	27,820	28,984	31,207	31,528	31,847	32,168	32,491	32,809	33,131	33,449	33,770	34,092	34,411	34,731
8				29,528	31,982	32,331	32,678	33,025	33,375	33,722	34,070	34,416	34,766	35,113	35,459	35,809
9				30,311	32,829	33,206	33,581	33,958	34,331	34,707	35,082	35,459	35,834	36,212	36,587	36,963
10				31,135	33,722	34,128	34,531	34,938	35,345	35,748	36,154	36,561	36,964	37,371	37,777	38,181

*2080 hours per year. (Hourly rate regular employees computed on this basis.) This is the BASE salary which includes COLA.

STEP INCREASE WAITING PERIOD (IN WEEKS)

Steps (from/to)	AA-A	A-B	B-C	C-D	D-E	E-F	F-G	G-H	H-I	I-J	J-K	K-L	L-M	M-N	N-O	YRS.
Grades 1-3	96	96	88	88	44	44	44	44	44	44	34	34	26	26	24	14.9
Grades 4-7	—	96	96	44	44	44	44	44	44	44	34	34	26	26	24	12.4
Grades 8-10	—	—	—	52	44	44	44	44	44	44	34	34	26	26	24	8.8

MILITARY

Medals

Medals that were awarded while in active service will be issued upon individual request to the appropriate service. All requests for medals pertaining to service in the Navy, Marine Corps, and Coast Guard should be sent to the Navy Liaison Office, Room 3475, N-314, 9700 Page Blvd., St. Louis, MO 63132-5100. All requests for medals pertaining to service in the Air Force should be sent to the National Personnel Records Center (Military Personnel Records), 9700 Page Blvd., St. Louis, MO 63132-5100. Requests for medals pertaining to service in the Army should be sent to Army Commander, U.S. Army Reserve Personnel Center, ATTN: DARP-PAS-EAW, 9700 Page Blvd., St. Louis, MO 63132-5100. All requests for medals pertaining to service in the Air Force should be sent to the National Personnel Records Center (Military Personnel Records), 9700 Page Blvd., St. Louis, MO 63132-5100.

The veteran's full name should be printed or typed, so that it can be read clearly, but the request must also contain the signature of the veteran or the signature of the next of kin if the veteran is deceased. Include the veteran's branch of service, service number or Social Security number, whichever is appropriate, and dates of service, or at least the approximate years. If a copy of the discharge/separation document is available (WDAGO Form 53-55 or DD Form 214), please include it for veterans in the following categories: (1) discharged from the Army prior to 1960, or (2) discharged from the Air Force between Sept. 25, 1947, and Dec. 31, 1963, with a name that falls alphabetically between Hubbard, James E., and the end of the alphabet. If possible, send the request on Standard Form 180, "Request Pertaining To Military Records." These forms are generally available from VA offices or veterans organizations.

Commissary and Exchange Privileges

Honorably discharged veterans with a service-connected disability rated at 100 percent, unremarried surviving spouses of members or retired members of the Armed Forces, recipients of the Medal of Honor, eligible dependents of the foregoing categories, and eligible orphans are entitled to unlimited exchange and commissary store privileges in the United States. Certain reservists and dependents also are eligible. Entitlement to these privileges overseas is governed by international law, and privileges are available only to the extent agreed upon by the foreign governments concerned. Certification of total disability will be given by VA. Assistance in completing DD Form 1172 (Application for Uniformed Services Identification and Privilege Card) may be provided by VA.

Review of Discharges

Each of the military services maintains a Discharge Review Board with authority to change, correct, or modify discharges or dismissals that are NOT issued by a sentence of a general court martial. The board has NO authority to address medical discharges.

The veteran or, if deceased or incompetent, the surviving spouse, next of kin or legal representative may apply for a review of discharge by writing to the military department concerned using Department of Defense Form 293 (DD-293), which may be obtained at any VA office. If more than 15 years have passed since discharge, DD Form 149 should be used for applications to the Board for the Correction of Military Records.

Service discharge review boards conduct hearings by established boards in Washington, D.C. Traveling review boards also visit selected cities to hear cases based on demand as evidence by the number of applicants who have submitted DD Forms 293. In addition, the Army sends teams to other locations to videotape an applicant's testimony. This tape is reviewed by a regularly constituted board in Wash., D.C.

Under Public Law 95-126, discharges awarded as a result of unauthorized absence in excess of 180 days make persons ineligible for receipt of VA benefits regardless of action taken by discharge review boards unless VA determines there were compelling circumstances for the absences. In addition, boards for the correction of military records may consider such cases. Applications to these boards are made on DD Form 149.

Veterans with disabilities incurred or aggravated during active military service in line of duty may qualify for medical or related benefits regardless of the type of administrative separation and characterization of service.

Veterans separated administratively under other than honorable conditions may request that their discharges be reviewed for possible recharacterization, provided they file their appeal within 15 years from the date of separation.

Questions regarding discharge review may be addressed to the appropriate discharge review board at the following addresses:

Army — Army Discharge Review Board, Attention: SFMR-RBB, Room 200A, 1941 Jefferson Davis Highway, Arlington, VA 22202-4504.

Navy and USMC — Navy Discharge Review Board, 801 N. Randolph St., Suite 905, Arlington, VA 22203.

Coast Guard — Coast Guard, Attention: GPE1, Washington, DC 20593.

Send completed application to the address indicated on the form.

Discharges (Copies of)

A veteran and his or her spouse should be aware of the location of the veteran's discharge and separation papers. If the veteran cannot locate discharge and separation papers, duplicate copies may be obtained by contacting the National Personnel Records Center, Military Personnel Records, 9700 Page Blvd., St. Louis, MO 63132-5100. Specify that a duplicate separation document or discharge is needed. The veteran's full name should be printed or typed, so that it can be read clearly, but the request must also contain the signature of the veteran or the signature of the next of kin, if the veteran is deceased. Include the veteran's branch of service, service number or social security number, whichever is appropriate, and exact dates or approximate years of service. If possible, use the Standard Form 180, Request Pertaining To Military Records. These forms are available from VA offices and veterans organizations.

In case of a medical emergency, information from a veteran's record may be obtained by phoning the National Personnel Records Center: Air Force (314) 263-7243; Army (314) 263-7261; Navy/Marine Corps/Coast Guard (314) 263-7141.

If the spouse of a deceased veteran cannot locate a copy of the spouse's discharge or separation papers, the spouse is advised to contact the nearest VA Regional Office. VA Regional Office addresses and phone numbers are listed in the "VA Facilities" section in this book.

Correction of Military Records

The secretary of a military department, acting through a Board for Correction of Military Records, has authority to correct any military record when necessary to correct an error or remove an injustice. Applications for correction of a military record, including review of discharges issued by courts martial, may be considered by a correction board.

Generally, a request for correction must be filed by the veteran, survivor or legal representative within three years after discovery of the alleged error or injustice. The board may excuse failure to file within the prescribed time, however, if it finds it would be in the interest of justice to do so. It is the responsibility of the applicant to show why the filing of the application was delayed and why it would be in the interest of justice for the board to consider the application in spite of the delay.

To justify any correction, it is necessary to show to the satisfaction of the board that the alleged entry or omission in the records was in error or unjust. Applications should include all evidence which may be available, such as signed statements of witnesses or a brief of arguments supporting the requested correction. Application must be made on DD Form 149, which may be obtained at any VA office. Send completed application to the address indicated on the form.

Death Gratuity

Military services provide death gratuities of $6,000 to a deceased serviceperson's spouse or children. If designated by the deceased, parents, brothers or sisters may be provided the gratuity. This is paid as soon as possible by the last military command unit of the deceased. If not received within a reasonable time, application may be made to the service concerned.

The death gratuity is payable in case of any death in active service, or any death within 120 days thereafter from causes related to active service. The gratuity reverts to $3,000 by law 180 days after the Persian Gulf Conflict is declared officially ended.

Naturalization Preference

Some aliens with honorable service in the U.S. Armed Forces during periods in which the United States was engaged in conflicts or hostilities may be naturalized without having to comply with the general requirements for naturalization. Such aliens must have either been lawfully admitted to the United States for permanent residence or been inducted, enlisted, re-enlisted or extended an enlistment in the Armed Forces while within the United States, Puerto Rico, Guam, the Virgin Islands of the United States, the Canal Zone or American Samoa. Hostilities must be periods declared by the President.

Aliens with honorable service in the U.S. Armed Forces for three years or more during periods not considered a conflict or hostility by Executive Order may be naturalized provided they have been lawfully admitted to the United States for permanent residence. Applications must be made within six months of discharge for eligibility.

Aliens who have served honorably for at least 12 years may also be granted special immigrant status. To be eligible for this benefit the person must have enlisted outside the United States pursuant to a treaty or agreement between the United States and the Philippines, the

Federated States of Micronesia or the Republic of the Marshall Islands. The service must have occurred after Oct. 15, 1978.

In addition, Filipinos with active duty service during World War II in the Philippine Scouts, Commonwealth Army of the Philippines or a recognized guerrilla unit may be naturalized without having been admitted for lawful permanent residence or having enlisted or reenlisted in the United States. Such persons must submit their applications to the Immigration and Naturalization Service by Nov. 30, 1992.

Aliens who died as a result of wounds incurred or disease contracted during periods of hostilities may receive recognition as U.S. citizens. An application may be submitted by the person's next-of-kin, or other authorized representative. This posthumous citizenship is honorary only and does not confer any other benefits to the person's surviving relatives.

Contact the nearest office of the Immigration and Naturalization Service, Justice Department, for assistance.

BUSINESS ASSISTANCE
Small Business Administration

The U.S. Small Business Administration (SBA) offers veterans special consideration in the following areas:

- Management training programs
- Priority processing of veterans loan applications
- Coordinating training and counseling activities for veterans with other departments, and
- Allocating a portion of direct loan funds for veterans.

Each SBA local office has a veterans affairs officer who serves as the initial contact for information on SBA programs, while the SBA staff works closely with national veterans service organizations and other federal agencies to develop and monitor business-related services to veterans.

SBA also conducts special business training conferences for veterans across the country. They are announced in the local media and through veterans service organizations.

While most SBA loans are made by financial institutions and are guaranteed by SBA, regular business loans are made available to veterans on a special consideration basis. They usually do not exceed $350,000, have a maturity rate of up to 25 years, and have a competitive interest rate.

There is a program of direct SBA loans to Vietnam-era and disabled veterans. To be eligible, these veterans must have been discharged other than dishonorably, and served on active duty for more than 180 days between Aug. 5, 1964, and May 7, 1975, or have a VA-compensated disability of at least 30 percent, or have been discharged due to disability. Veterans who apply for this special program must meet the criteria for a regular business loan.

SBA loan requirements are the same for veterans as for other applicants, such as showing the ability to repay the loan from earnings, that financing is not otherwise available, and that there is substantial equity in the business.

SBA veterans affairs officers are listed in the phone book under U.S. Small Business Administration. A national toll-free number is: 1-800-827-5722. The SBA maintains an Office of Veterans Affairs under the Associate Deputy Administrator for Special Programs, Washington, D.C. 20416. This office does not make loans or provide counseling, but monitors the agency's service to veterans.

VA OFFICE OF SMALL AND DISADVANTAGED BUSINESS UTILIZATION

VA has an Office of Small and Disadvantaged Business Utilization (OSDBU) to assist small businesses to contract with and sell to the department. OSDBU provides information to large and small firms interested in doing business with VA. Like other federal purchasers, however, VA is required to place a fair portion of its contracts and purchases with small and disdavantaged businesses. VA also promotes business with veterans by requiring VA contracting offices to include veteran-owned contractors in mailings to solicit bids. These businesses are identified from the Procurement Automated Source System (PASS) maintained by the SBA. For more information, write to OSDBU (005SB) at the Department of Veterans Affairs, 810 Vermont Ave., N.W., Washington, D.C. 20420.

SPECIAL FRANCHISE INITIATIVE

The Veterans Transition Franchise Initiative (VETFRAN) is a combined Small Business Administration and International Franchise Association program, allowing veterans to purchase start-up franchised businesses with SBA assistance in the form of accelerated loan guarantees and management counseling. More than 100 franchisors have agreed to discount their franchise fee and/or to finance up to 50 percent of the franchise fee for veterans.

VETFRAN is available to all active duty service personnel and veterans. Active duty personnel have 24 months after discharge to take advantage of the program. An applicant must show proof of veterans status and must have been discharged other than dishonorably. Non-active duty veterans have until August 1993 to participate in the program.

Veterans can get information about VETFRAN by sending one dollar and a self-addressed, stamped business envelope to VETFRAN, P.O. Box 3146, Waco, Texas 76707. They will receive a newsletter, a fact sheet, and an updated list of franchisors and contact persons. The veteran then will contact the franchisor he chooses and will be prequalified by the franchisor, who will counsel the veteran about financing and other aspects of the business.

The SBA may make a direct loan if the applicant is a Vietnam-era veteran, or has a 30 percent or more compensable disability, and has been turned down by a bank for a commercial loan or for an SBA loan guarantee.

Most franchisors have agreed to finance half or more of the franchise fee. A typical arrangement under VETFRAN might be for a franchisor to finance 50 percent of the fee (for example, $20,000 on a $40,000 fee) forgive 30 percent ($12,000) and for the veteran to provide the remaining 20 percent ($8,000).

The SBA's 115 field offices and over 20 veterans' organizations have VETFRAN information.

SCORE

The Service Corps of Retired Executives (SCORE), an affiliate of the U.S. Small Business Administration, is comprised of 13,000 volunteers nationwide who use their business skills and experience to assist veterans and others in managing small business enterprises.

Workshops and seminars for pre-business management training, held at the local level are sponsored by 400 chapter affiliates. Programs are held at military installations for service personnel prior to separation as part of the veterans transition training program.

The program is making a special effort to reach women veterans for assistance, since women are going into business at double the rate of men. SCORE also is intensifying its outreach program to assist those who operated businesses of personnel called up for Operation Desert Storm as well as to returning troops. SCORE also is extending its outreach training program to assist both civilian and military personnel affected by the downsizing of the military establishment.

The program reaches out to the veteran either by seeing the client on site or having the client visit the SCORE representative in his office. Information on SCORE services reaches the veteran through service organizations, at military installations or through other agencies. The organization is listed in telephone books as well.

NATIONAL VETERANS BUSINESS CENTER

Veterans who are starting their own business can get help from the National Veterans Business Center, Golden, Colorado.

The center assists veterans with all phases of business startup and operation, including how to write a business plan and secure financing. In an effort to make veterans' business competitive, the center is establishing a database of information on contracts, government agencies and client businesses.

Veterans, by law, can secure government procurement contracts, business loans and management assistance through the Small Business Administration's Office of Veterans Affairs.

Information on these programs can be obtained by calling the National Veterans Business Center (303) 278-1998.

Questions and Answers

Q. How do I qualify for a direct loan? Am I eligible?

A. To be eligible, a Vietnam-era veteran (served between August 5, 1964 and May 7, 1975) must have been discharged from the Armed Forces under other than a dishonorable discharge. To qualify for a direct loan, the veteran must have been declined twice in writing by two different banks. He will need copies of the two decline letters.

Q. How much is the minimum or maximum loan that I can get?

A. There is no minimum amount; but, the maximum amount presently considered is $150,000.

Q. What documents do I need to submit to the bank or to SBA?

A. In addition to the two bank decline letters, and Certificate of Discharge (DD 214), SBA will need the loan documents previously submitted to the bank, which usually consist of the following:
   a. Business plan and market survey
   b. Sales and profit projections for 12 months
   c. Job resume (copy)
   d. Personal Financial Statement, which must not be more than 90 days old
   e. Application for Business Loan, which is obtained from your local SBA office
   f. Tax returns (copy) for the past year
   g. Lease agreement (copy) if you are in business. If you are establishing a business, data on the proposed location, such as rent cost, deposit requirements, etc.

Q. **What is the interest rate?**

A. The rate of interest on direct loans is published quarterly. Beginning January 1 thru March 31, 1989, the direct loan interest rate is 9 7/8%.

Q. **How much time do I have to repay the loan?**

A. Maturities of the loan depend upon use of proceeds.
   a. Working capital and inventory — usually 7 years.
   b. Machinery and equipment, furniture and fixtures — up to the prudent economic life of the items to be purchased but not more than 10 years.
   c. Real estate — usually 25 years.

Q. **How much money am I required to put into the business?**

A. The borrower is usually required to put up 30% to 50% of the total cost of establishing the business with the proposed loan not to exceed 50% to 70% of the total cost to establish the business.

Q. **Is there anything else I need to know?**

A. Yes. As a veteran your application will be given priority in processing; however, your application will be subject to meeting credit requirements required of all business applicants.

SOCIAL SECURITY

Social Security is one of the major sources of benefits available to veterans. Such benefits usually are independent of military retirement benefits. However, if in addition to a military benefit, one is in receipt of a government civil service pension for employment in which social security tax was not paid, the social security benefit may be affected. Also, social security survivors' benefits may affect benefits payable under the optional Department of Defense survivors benefit (SBP). There are no offsets by Social Security due to receipt of VA benefits.

The Social Security Administration (SSA) has about 1,300 offices across the country, but information can easily be obtained by calling the toll-free number — 1-800-772-1213 — between 7:00 a.m. and 7:00 p.m. any business day. The telephone service representative can also refer callers to the appropriate local office staff member. All calls are treated confidentially.

Under the Social Security system, an individual pays taxes into the system during the working years, both during and since the service years, and is eligible for monthly benefits upon retirement or disablement. Or, in the event of death, survivors collect benefits. Social Security is not intended to be an individual's sole source of income; it is expected to supplement pensions, insurance, savings and other investments accumulated during one's working years.

EARNING SOCIAL SECURITY

For someone to receive monthly cash payments after retirement, credit must be earned for a certain amount of work under Social Security. A maximum of 4 credits per year can be earned. These credits may have been earned at any time after 1936. Earnings under the Railroad Retirement Act may also be creditable, but generally only if the worker has less than 120 months of railroad service.

All employees and self-employed people earn Social Security credits the same way. The amount needed to earn a credit will increase automatically in future years as average wages increase. If an individual stops working under Social Security before becoming insured, credits for the earnings already reported will remain on the person's Social Security record. Additional credits can be added with subsequent work. No benefits based on earnings can be paid until enough credits have been earned to become insured.

No one can be fully insured with less than 6 credits (1 and 1/2 years of work), as was the case of being 65 years old prior to 1958. A person who has credit for 10 years of work can be sure of being fully insured for retirement benefits.

Having enough credits to be insured means only that certain kinds of Social Security benefits can be paid — it does not determine the amount. Table 1 shows how much credit for work covered by Social Security is needed to be fully insured.

Table 1.
CREDIT NEEDED TO BE FULLY INSURED—FOR WORKERS REACHING

62 In	Credits (Quarters) Needed
1984	33
1985	34
1986	35
1987	36
1988	37
1989	38
1990	39
1991 or later	40

Basic pay received while on active duty (or active duty for training) in the military service has been covered by Social Security since 1957. Basic pay received by uniformed members of the armed forces reserve components while on inactive duty training (such as weekend drills) has been covered by Social Security since 1988.

A veteran may receive additional credits for earnings in military service. These credits are granted for periods of active duty or active duty for training. No additional credits are given for inactive duty training.

Additional earnings credits are granted as follows:

Service in 1978 and later — An additional credit of $100 for each $300 of earnings is given for active duty basic pay. The maximum credit is $1,200 a year.

If a veteran enlisted in a regular armed forces component after September 7, 1980 and didn't complete at least 24 months of the first enlistment, credits can not be granted unless certain conditions are met. Also, credits are not allowed if active duty began after October 13, 1982, and at least 24 months of service was not completed, or the full obligated tour was not completed unless certain conditions are met. A local Social Security office should be contacted to obtain specific details.

Service 1957 through 1977 — An additional earnings credit of $300 is granted for each calendar quarter in which any active duty basic pay was received.

Service 1940 through 1956 — Under certain circumstances credits of $160 a month may be received for military service from September 16, 1940 through 1956. These credits can be granted if:

• A veteran was discharged under conditions other than dishonorable with 90 or more days of active service or was released because of a disability or injury received in the line of duty, or
• The veteran is still on active duty, or
• A person is applying for survivors benefits and the veteran died while on active duty.

These pre-1957 credits can't be granted if another Federal benefit is based on the same period of service. However, for active duty after 1956, credits for the period 1951-1956 can be granted even though military retirement based on the same period of service was received.

A veteran can get both Social Security benefits and military retirement. In general, there is no offset against Social Security benefit because of military retirement. And there is no special way to figure Social Security benefit if military retirement is received. A full Social Security benefit is based on covered earnings. However, if in addition to a military benefit a veteran receives a government pension based on a job in which Social Security taxes were not paid (such as a civil service pension), Social Security benefits may be affected.

SOCIAL SECURITY TAXES

Social Security taxes are used to pay for all Social Security benefits. In addition, a portion of such taxes is used to pay for part of the Medicare coverage. General tax revenues, not Social Security taxes, are used to finance the Supplemental Security Income (SSI) program.

Both the employer and the employee pay taxes for Social Security and Medicare. Currently, each party pays 7.65% of the employee's gross salary, up to a limit determined by Congress. For the year 1992, the limit is $55,500. The deduction is usually labeled on a pay slip "FICA," which stands for Federal Insurance Contributions Act, the law that authorized Social Security's payroll tax. A self-employed person pays 15.3% of his/her taxable income into Social Security, up to the same limit of $55,500; however, there are special deductions which may be taken when filing a tax return which are intended to offset this tax rate.

RETIREMENT BENEFIT

The amount of Social Security benefit is based on such factors as date of birth, the type of benefit applied for, and earnings. The benefit is figured as follows:

• SSA determines the number of years of earnings to use as a base.
• These earnings are adjusted for inflation.
• SSA then determines the **average** adjusted earnings based on the number of years figured in step 1.
• The average adjusted earnings are multiplied by percentages in a formula that is specified by law. The formula results in benefits that replace about 42 percent of a person's earnings. This applies to people who had **average** earnings during their working years. The percentage is lower for people in the upper income brackets and higher for those with low incomes because the Social Security benefit formula is weighted in favor of low-income workers who have less opportunity to save and invest during their working years.

A person who has not worked long enough to receive Social Security or receives only a small amount may be eligible for Supplemental Security Income (SSI), which is discussed later.

Benefits may be applied for at any Social Security office. The easiest way to file a claim is to call SSA's toll-free number (1-800-772-1213) ahead of time for an appointment. Applications should be made for disability, survivors, and SSI benefits as soon as one is eligible; it is best to begin processing for retirement benefits about four months before retirement date.

Some of the documents that may be needed when signing up for Social Security include:

- Social Security card (or record of Social Security number)
- Birth certificate
- Children's birth certificates (if they are applying)
- Marriage certificate (if signing up on a spouse's return)
- Applicant's most recent W-2 form, or tax return if self-employed.

Social Security, paid on the third day of the following month, may be deposited directly into a bank account or come to the recipient in the mail. Most people have their benefits deposited in a bank account because it is safer and more convenient than checks. It is also more efficient and saves money for the government. Each January, benefits increase automatically if the cost of living has increased.

Regardless of the recipient's "full" retirement age (which varies with the date of birth), benefits may be received as early as 62. However, if benefits are started early, they are reduced a small percentage for each month before the person's "full" retirement age. For example,if the recipient signs up for Social Security at age 64 and his/her full retirement age is 65, 93.33 percent of the full benefit would be paid. At age 62, the payment would be 80 percent of the full benefit. The percentage reduction will be greater in future years as, beginning in the year 2000, the full retirement age will increase in gradual steps from 65 to 67.

There are disadvantages and advantages to taking benefits before full retirement age. The disadvantage is that the benefit is permanently reduced. The advantage is that benefits are collected for a longer period of time. Each person's situation is different, so payment alternatives should be requested of SSA before the future recipient decides on retirement. (Examples of monthly payments to recipients in various benefit categories are shown in Table 2.)

People who continue to work full time beyond their full retirement age and do not sign up for Social Security until later increase their Social Security benefits in two ways:

- Extra income usually will increase one's "average" earnings, which is the basis for determining the amount of retirement benefit. The higher the average earnings, the higher the Social Security benefit will be.
- A special credit is given to people who delay retirement. This credit, which is a percentage added to the Social Security benefit, varies depending on date of birth. For people turning 65 in 1992, the rate is 4 percent per year. That rate gradually increases in future years, until it reaches 8 percent per year for people turning 65 in 2008 or later. (See Table 3.)

Table 2.
EXAMPLES OF MONTHLY PAYMENTS

Benefit Category	January 1992 Payment
I. *Maximum Social Security benefit*	
Maximum benefit, worker retiring at age 65	$1,088
II. *Average Social Security benefits*	
All retired workers	$ 629
Aged couple, both receiving benefits	$1,067
Widowed mother and two children	$1,251
Aged widow alone	$ 584
Disabled worker, wife, and child	$1,056
All disabled workers	$ 610
III. *Maximum Federal SSI payments**	
Individual	$ 422
Couple	$ 633

Most states provide payments supplementing the federal SSI payment levels for some or all categories of recipients.

Table 3.
INCREASES FOR DELAYED RETIREMENT

Year of Birth	Yearly Percentage Increase*
1916 or earlier	1%
1917-1924	3%
1925-1926	3.5%
1927-1928	4%
1929-1930	4.5%
1931-1932	5%
1933-1934	5.5%
1935-1936	6%
1937-1938	6.5%
1939-1940	7%
1941-1942	7.5%
1943 or later	8%

For example, in the case of a person born in 1943 or later, an extra 8 percent will be added to the benefit for each year's delay in that person's signing up for Social Security beyond his/her full retirement age.

DISABILITY BENEFITS

It is important to note that various kinds of disability benefits are available from Social Security, depending on individual circumstances.

These include:

- People who have earned enough Social Security "credits" to qualify for disability on their own work record;
- Widows and widowers with disabilities who are eligible for benefits on the record of a spouse;
- People with disabilities who have low income and few assets who might be eligible for SSI benefits;
- Disabled children over age 18 who might be eligible for Social Security benefits on the record of a parent, or disabled children at any age who might be eligible for SSI benefits on their own.

Social Security's definition of disability is more specific than the dictionary definition and is generally related to one's ability to work. To qualify for disability from Social Security, one must have a physical or mental impairment that is expected to keep the person from doing any "substantial" work for at least a year. Generally, monthly gross earnings of $500 or more are considered substantial. Or the person must have a condition that is expected to result in death.

This is a fairly strict definition of disability. Unlike many private pension plans or even other government disability programs, Social Security is not intended for a temporary condition. In other words, there is no such thing as a "partial" disability payment from Social Security.

A person who becomes disabled should file for disability benefits as soon as possible by calling or visiting any Social Security office. Processing time will be shortened by having the following medical and vocational information available at the time of application:

- Names, addresses, and phone numbers of doctors and of hospitals, clinics, etc., where treatment has been received
- A summary of where the applicant has worked in the last 15 years and the kind of work performed.

As stated earlier, Social Security's disability rules are different from those of other private plans or government agencies. Therefore, the fact that a person qualifies for disability from another program does not ensure eligibility for Social Security. Further, a doctor's statement indicating disability does not necessarily mean that the person will be automatically eligible for Social Security disability payments.

If SSA decides that an applicant is disabled, in most cases monthly benefits will begin with the sixth full month of disability. (See Table 4 for disability payment estimates.) Disability payments will continue unless the disabling condition improves or a return to "substantial" work becomes possible.

Table 4.
APPROXIMATE MONTHLY BENEFITS IF YOU BECOME
DISABLED IN 1992 AND HAD STEADY EARNINGS

Your Age	Your Family	Your Earnings In 1991				
		$20,000	$30,000	$40,000	$50,000	$55,500 Or More[1]
25	You	$ 745	$ 987	$1,109	$1,231	$1,266
	You, your spouse, and child[2]	1,118	1,480	1,664	1,847	1,899
35	You	740	984	1,105	1,221	1,240
	You, your spouse, and child[2]	1,111	1,476	1,657	1,831	1,860
45	You	739	983	1,086	1,159	1,170
	You, your spouse, and child[2]	1,109	1,475	1,629	1,738	1,755
55	You	739	974	1,044	1,094	1,101
	You, your spouse, and child[2]	1,109	1,462	1,567	1,641	1,652
64	You	746	975	1,034	1,076	1,082
	You, your spouse, and child[2]	1,119	1,463	1,551	1,614	1,623

[1] Use this column if you earn more than the maximum Social Security earnings base.
[2] Equals the maximum family benefit.

Note: The accuracy of these estimates depends on the pattern of your actual past earnings.

Source: "Understanding Social Security", Social Security Admin., Jan. 1992.

FAMILY BENEFITS

When a recipient begins collecting Social Security retirement or disability benefits, family members may also be eligible for payments. For example, benefits can be paid to:

- A husband or wife if he or she is 62 or older (unless he or she collects a higher Social Security benefit on his or her own record)
- A husband or wife at any age if he or she is caring for the recipient's child (the child must be under 16 or disabled)
- Recipient's children, if they are unmarried and: under 18, or under 19 but in elementary or secondary school as a full-time student, or 18 or older and severely disabled (the disability must have started before age 22).

A family member will usually be eligible for a monthly benefit that is up to 50 percent of the recipient's retirement or disability rate, depending upon the number of eligible family members. A spouse is eligible for a share of the 50 percent rate if he or she is 65 or older or caring for a minor or disabled child. If a spouse is under 65 and is not caring for a minor or disabled child, the rate is reduced by a small percentage for each month before age 65. Currently, the lowest reduced benefit is 37.5 percent at 62.

There is a limit to the amount of money that can be paid for family benefits on each Social Security record. The limit varies, but is generally equal to about 150 to 180 percent of the retirement benefit.

If a recipient is divorced (even if remarried), an ex-spouse can be eligible for benefits on the recipient's record. In some situations, he or she could receive benefits even if the primary recipient is not receiving them. In order to qualify, the ex-spouse must:

• Have been married to the primary recipient for at least 10 years
• Be at least 62 years old
• Not be eligible for an equal or higher benefit on his or her own Social Security record, or on someone else's Social Security record
• Be currently unmarried.

If the ex-spouse receives benefits as described above, it does not affect the amount of any benefits payable to the primary recipient or the other family members.

SURVIVORS BENEFITS

When a family breadwinner dies, certain members of the decedent's family may be eligible for benefits on his/her Social Security record if enough credits had been earned. The family members who can collect benefits include:

• A widow or widower who is 60 or older
• Widow or widower who is 50 or older and disabled
• A widow or widower at any age if she or he is caring for a child under 16 or a disabled child
• Children if unmarried and: under 18, or under 19 but in an elementary or secondary school as a full-time student, or 18 or older and severely disabled (the disability must have started before age 22)
• Decedent's parents if they were dependent on the decedent for at least half of thier support.

A special one-time death payment of $255 also will be made if sufficient credits were accumulated. This payment can be made only to certain members of the decendent's family.

If a recipient is divorced (even if remarried), his/her ex-spouse will be eligible for benefits on the recipient's record after death. In order to qualify, the ex-spouse must:

• Be at least 60 years old (or 50 if disabled) and have been married to the primary recipient for at least 10 years
• Be any age if caring for a child who is eligible for benefits on the decedent's record
• Not be eligible for an equal or higher benefit on his or her own record

• Not be currently married, unless the remarriage occurred after 60, or 50 for disabled widows.

The amount payable to survivors is a percentage of the basic Social Security benefit — usually in a range from 75 percent to 100 percent. (See Table 5 for estimates of survivors benefits.)

Table 5.
APPROXIMATE MONTHLY SURVIVORS BENEFITS IF THE WORKER DIES IN 1992 AND HAD STEADY EARNINGS

| Worker's Age | Your Family | Deceased Worker's Earnings In 1991 | | | | |
		$20,000	$30,000	$40,000	$50,000	$55,000 Or More[1]
35	Spouse and 1 child[2]	$1,112	$1,476	$1,658	$1,840	$1,878
	Spouse and 2 children[3]	1,375	1,722	1,934	2,146	2,190
	1 child only	556	738	829	920	939
	Spouse at age 60[4]	530	703	790	877	895
45	Spouse and 1 child[2]	1,110	1,474	1,636	1,752	1,770
	Spouse and 2 children[3]	1,373	1,721	1,910	2,044	2,064
	1 child only	555	737	818	876	885
	Spouse at age 60[4]	529	703	780	835	843
55	Spouse and 1 child[2]	1,108	1,462	1,566	1,640	1,652
	Spouse and 2 children[3]	1,372	1,705	1,828	1,914	1,927
	1 child only	554	731	783	820	826
	Spouse at age 60[4]	528	696	747	782	787

[1] Use this column if the worker earned more than the maximum Social Security earnings base.
[2] Amounts shown also equal the benefits paid to two children, if no parent survives or surviving parent has substantial earnings.
[3] Equals the maximum family benefit.
[4] Amounts payable in 1992. Spouses turning 60 in the future would receive higher benefits.

Note: The accuracy of these estimates depends on the pattern of your actual past earnings.

Source: "Understanding Social Security", Social Security Admin., Jan. 1992.

Similar to payments to family members when the primary recipient is retired or disabled, there is a limit to the amount of money that can be paid each month to survivors. The limit varies, but is generally equal to about 150 to 180 percent of the benefit rate.

Social Security survivors' benefits may affect benefits payable under the optional Department of Defense Survivors Benefit Plan. The Department of Defense or local military retirement advisor should be contacted for more information.

SUPPLEMENTAL SECURITY INCOME (SSI)

Although the SSI program is run by Social Security, the money to pay for SSI benefits does not come from Social Security taxes or Social

Security trust funds. SSI payments are financed by the general revenue funds of the U.S. Treasury.

SSI makes monthly payments to people who have low incomes and few assets. In addition, to obtain SSI the applicant must be: (1) living in the United States; (2) a U.S. citizen or be living in the United States legally; and (3) 65 or older, or blind, or disabled. Children as well as adults can get SSI benefits because of blindness or disability.

Payments for SSI are paid on the first of each month for that month.

To obtain SSI, income and the value of the things owned must be below certain limits. The term "income" means the money income such as earnings, Social Security, or other government checks, pensions, etc. But it also includes "non-cash" items such as the value of free food and shelter.

How much income a recipient can have and still obtain SSI depends on whether or not the recipient works, and in which state he/she resides. Although there is a basic national SSI payment rate, some states add money to the national payment, so they have higher SSI rates and higher income limits than others. The local Social Security office can supply information on the SSI rates and income limits in a particular state.

"Assets" are the things a person owns, but everything owned is not counted in determining SSI eligibility. For example, a person's home and many personal belonging do not count, nor does a car usually count. But assets like cash and bank accounts are included.

An applicant may be able to obtain SSI if the things owned that SSA counts are no more than $2,000 for one person, or $3,000 for a couple. Unlike the income category, these limits do not change from state to state.

People with disabilities, including children, can receive SSI if their income and assets are below the limits discussed above. Most of the rules used to decide if a person has a condition severe enough to qualify for Social Security disability benefits also apply to SSI.

Social Security has recently developed new standards for evaluating disability in children filing for SSI benefits. These new rules are expected to result in more children being qualified for SSI. In cases of a child with a disability or a child who was previously denied for SSI, local Social Security offices should be contacted to apply or re-apply for SSI disability benefits.

MEDICARE/MEDICAID

Medicare is the country's basic health insurance program for people 65 or older and for many disabled people. The Medicare and Medicaid programs should not be confused. Medicaid is a health insurance program for people with low income and limited assets. It is usually run by state welfare or human service agencies. Some people qualify for one or the other; others qualify for both Medicare and Medicaid (neither of which pays for services provided outside the United States).

There are two parts to Medicare:

• Hospital insurance (sometimes called "Part A") — This helps pay for inpatient hospital care and certain follow-up services.

• Medical insurance (sometimes called "Part B") — This helps pay for doctors' services, outpatient hospital care, and other medical services.

Most people get hospital insurance when they turn 65. Qualification is automatic if the applicant is eligible for Social Security or Railroad Retirement benefits. Or someone may qualify on a spouse's (including divorced spouse's) record. Others qualify because they are government employees not covered by Social Security who paid the Medicare portion of the Social Security tax. In addition, a person receiving Social Security disability benefits for 24 months will qualify for hospital insurance. Almost anyone who is eligible for hospital insurance can sign up for medical insurance (Part B). Unlike Part A, which was paid for by a person's tax payments and is free after eligibility has been established, Part B is an optional program that costs $31.80 per month in 1992. Almost everybody signs up for this part of Medicare.

Upon turning 65, a person already receiving Social Security benefits will be automatically enrolled in Medicare (although there is an opportunity to turn down "Part B"). A disabled person will also be automatically enrolled in Medicare after receiving disability benefits for 24 months. ("Part B" may be turned down, if desired.)

A person receiving health care protection under a VA program may find that such health benefits may change or terminate when that person becomes eligible for Medicare. At that time, it would be advisable to contact the VA or a military health benefits adviser for more information. Assistance may be obtained by calling Social Security at 1-800-772-1213 or by visiting any Social Security office.

What does Medicare pay for? Medicare hospital insurance helps pay for: (1) inpatient hospital care; (2) skilled nursing facility care; (3) home health care; and (4) hospice care. Medicare medical insurance helps pay for: (1) doctors' services; (2) outpatient hospital services; (3) home health visits; (4) diagnostic x-ray, laboratory, and other tests; (5) necessary ambulance services; and (6) other medical services and supplies.

What health services does Medicare **not** pay for? Medicare does **not** pay for: (1) custodial care; (2) dentures and routine dental care; (3) eyeglasses, hearing aids, and examinations to prescribe and fit them; (4) nursing home care (except skilled nursing care); (5) prescription drugs; and (6) routine physical checkups and related tests.

BENEFIT LIMITS

There is a provision in the law that limits the amount of money an individual can earn and still collect all Social Security benefits. This provision affects people under the age of 70 who collect Social Security retirement, dependents, or survivors benefits. Earnings in or after the month a person reaches age 70 do not affect Social Security benefits. People who work and collect disability or SSI benefits have different earnings requirements and should report all their income to Social Security.

A recipient under age 65 can earn up to $7,440 in 1992 and still collect all Social Security benefits. However, for every $2 earned over this limit, $1 will be withheld from Social Security benefits.

Recipients aged 65 through 69 can earn up to $10,200 in 1992 and still collect all Social Security benefits. However, for every $3 earned over this limit, $1 will be withheld from Social Security benefits.

Only earnings from a job or net profits if self-employed are counted. This includes compensation such as bonuses, commissions, and vacation pay. It does not include such items as pensions, annuities, investment income, interest, Social Security, veterans, or other government benefits.

QUESTIONS AND ANSWERS

1. **Where is my check?**
    Sometimes mail delivery is late. Allow 3 workdays after the normal delivery date before reporting a lost check to Social Security.

2. **How do I get direct deposit?**
    Call Social Security to arrange direct deposit of your benefit. The teleservice representative will ask you for your Social Security claim number and information about your financial institution, which can be found on a check or bank statement.

3. **How do I change my address?**
    Call Social Security and have available your new address including the ZIP code, your new telephone number, and your Social Security claim number.

4. **How will I know what benefits to report on my income tax return?**
    The Social Security Benefit Statement (Form SSA-1099) shows the amount of benefits you received in the previous year. You only pay income tax on your Social Security benefits if you have other income.

5. **I need proof of what I receive from Social Security. What can I use?**
    Every year you will be sent an SSA-1099 form showing how much

you received from Social Security in the past year. You can use this as proof.

6. **How do I get a new Social Security card or Medicare card?**
    Call Social Security for your new card. Have your Social Security number handy when you call.

7. **Where is my local office?**
    The addresses of Social Security offices are listed in the telephone directory under "U.S. Government" or "Social Security Administration," or you can call the toll-free number to ask for the local office's address.

8. **Why is my neighbor's check more than mine?**
    Benefit computations are based on a person's date of birth and complete work history, so differences are very likely. To protect each person's privacy information about someone else's Social Security record cannot be given out.

9. **Will you please explain this letter I got from you?**
    If a letter leaves you with additional questions, the teleservice representatives can answer them. Some letters will give you a local number to call, or you can call the toll-free number: 1-800-772-1213.

10. **How much can I earn this year?**
    The 1992 earnings limits are $7,440 for people under 65 and $10,200 for people 65-69. Call Social Security if you need to revise your earnings estimate.

11. **Are my benefits figured on my last 5 years of earnings?**
    Retirement benefits are calculated on total earnings during a lifetime of work under the Social Security system. Years of high earnings will increase the amount of the benefit, but no group of years counts more than another group.

12. **Will my retirement pension from my job reduce the amount of my Social Security benefit?**
    If your pension is from work where you also paid Social Security taxes, it will not affect your Social Security benefit. Pensions from work that are not covered by Social Security — for example, the federal civil service or some state or local government systems — may reduce the amount of your Social Security benefit.

13. **What does Medicare cover?**
    The Medicare Handbook provides detailed information about covered services. Your handbook will arrive in the mail close to the time your Medicare entitlement starts.

14. Do I have the doctors' part of Medicare?

Medicare has two parts: hospital insurance and medical insurance. To determine which parts of Medicare you have, look at the entries on your red, white, and blue Medicare card. If you see the words, "Medical Insurance" or "Medical (Part B)," you are covered for the "doctors' part" of Medicare.

15. How do I file a Medicare claim?

You don't need to worry about it. Service providers — doctors, hospitals, medical labs, etc. — take care of submitting Medicare claims.

16. My ex-wife, who has been awarded an alimony payment, has threatened to have my Social Security payment garnished. Can she do this?

Yes, she can. Since 1975 Social Security benefits have been subject to attachment if the recipient fails to make alimony or child-support payments as ordered by the court. The court or other agency having jurisdiction can issue a Garnishment Order that directs the Social Security Administration to: (1) withhold a certain amount of benefits each month and send them to a court or other agency or party to forward to the person entitled to the support payment, or (2) pay the stipulated amount directly to the entitled person. The amount withheld depends on the court order as well as any maximum subject to garnishment under state law.

17. I divorced my husband of 40 years at age 60. Four years later I married a man with minimal Social Security. Meanwhile my ex-husband, who got a large Social Security check, died. Can I draw a benefit based on his account instead of my present husband's?

Yes. Social Security treats widows/widowers and surviving divorced wives/husbands the same with respect to remarriage. Since you were married to your first husband the required ten years, your remarriage took place after you turned 60, and you are now 65, you will receive the larger of: (1) your own full primary benefit from your work record, (2) 100 percent of your deceased former husband's primary benefit, or (3) one-half of your present husband's primary benefit.

VETERANS ORGANIZATIONS

Veterans organizations have existed in the United States almost as long as the U.S. military itself. These organizations have represented the interests of veterans in a number of ways. They have exercised a strong political influence on matters involving veterans. They have strongly supported the U.S. government and its laws. Providing care for veterans, their widows, and other dependents has been another major thrust. The organizations have worked to assure that the memory and the graves of veterans are kept properly. They have provided a focal point for social and local civic activities in which their members have found enjoyment and fulfillment. More recently, veterans organizations have been a source of collective programs (insurance coverage, travel programs, group buying, etc.) which have proven helpful to their members.

The earliest veterans organization of any significance was the Society of the Cincinnati. It was organized in 1783 with none other than George Washington its first president. Subsequently, other organizations were set up to serve veterans of the War of 1812 and the Mexican War. These organizations were devoted almost exclusively to helping indigent or disabled veterans at the local level, while exerting little or no effort to impose political pressure on the veteran's behalf.

The Grand Army of the Republic (GAR) was the first veterans organization of sufficient size to attain the financial strength and political clout to have a truly significant impact upon the nation as a whole. Supported by several hundred thousand Civil War veterans, the GAR served the interests of former Union Army soldiers, sailors, and marines and their widows and other dependents. With membership well in excess of 400,000 at its peak, the GAR was a formidable political force in the Republic Party through the 1890s, credited with introducing and pushing through the first veterans pension legislation of significance. Confederate veterans of the Civil War were provided similar services by the United Confederate Veterans.

Subsequent U.S. military involvements, most notably the Spanish-American War, spawned other veterans organizations in the 1890s. Of these organizations, only the Legion of Valor of the U.S.A. (organized in 1890), the Jewish War Veterans of the U.S.A. (started in 1896), and the Veterans of Foreign Wars (VFW) (whose predecessor organizations were organized in 1899) remain in operation today. The most important of today's veterans organizations, both in terms of influence and membership, are The American Legion, the Veterans of Foreign Wars, and the Disabled American Veterans.

THE AMERICAN LEGION

The American Legion, whose three million members make it the largest of today's veterans organizations, was organized on March 15, 1919, by a group of World War I officers. The Legion's stated goals were to assist veterans and their families in adjusting to a peacetime United States, to promote patriotism, and to foster a common sense of responsibility to the community and the nation.

Following the deep recession after World War I, the Legion in effect became a national employment service, utilizing the facilities of its 11,000 branch offices. It was reported to have obtained more than one million jobs for returning veterans. The Legion also set up rehabilitation programs for disabled veterans and provided representation for many thousands of veterans, their dependents, and their survivors in filing claims for benefits. In the period between World War I and World War II, the Legion is generally acknowledged to have been the predominant spokesman for veterans in dealing with the federal government and legislative efforts. The Legion, in addition to its veterans programs, funds child welfare programs with most of the funds spent for food, clothing, and medical treatment. It also is involved in a variety of other worthwhile local activities. The Legion is credited with playing a leading role in pushing for enactment of the landmark GI Bill of 1944.

DISABLED AMERICAN VETERANS (DAV)

The DAV was formed in 1920 and chartered by Congress in 1932. The stated goal of the 1.05 million member DAV is to represent the official voice of all of America's 2.2 million disabled veterans and their dependents.

The DAV was organized after World War I in response to a serious need for veterans health and benefit programs, especially for disabled veterans. Accordingly, it has focused much of its efforts on promoting reasonable legislation to assist all disabled veterans and their dependents, and to protect legislated rights, a particular concern when public consideration for disabled veterans wanes as war memories recede into the past.

Another key DAV effort is to provide "bread-and-butter" services to disabled veterans. To accomplish this end, the DAV employs some 260 National Service Officers (NSOs) in 67 offices across the U.S. who provide a variety of counseling services to members and nonmembers.

In some cases, the NSOs function as attorneys-in-fact, assisting clients in filing claims for disability compensation, death benefits, pensions, and other benefits. In the year ended June 30, 1991, DAV NSOs interviewed more than 220,000 veterans and their dependents, submitted over 190,000 claims, and secured more than $1.2 billion in new and retroactive benefits for claimants.

The tables which follow list: (1) veterans organizations chartered by Congress and recognized by the VA for representing veterans claims; (2) other veterans organizations recognized by the VA for representing veterans claims; (3) remaining veterans organizations of any size; and (4) the main service features of selected major veterans organizations.

A considerable number of these listed organizations also are noted for their services and assistance to many veterans in many respects; however, we are unable, due to space limitations, to present a more comprehensive picture of each of these organizations at this time.

VETERANS OF FOREIGN WARS (VFW)

The American Veterans of Foreign Service and the National Society of the Army of the Philippines, both organized in 1899, merged in 1914 to form the VFW. The original purpose of the organizations which became the VFW was to secure the rights and benefits for veterans of the Spanish-American War (1898) and the Philippine Insurrection (1899-1902). The current stated objectives of the VFW are: (1) to preserve and strengthen comradeship among VFW members; (2) to assist worthy comrades and their widows and orphans; (3) to perpetuate the memory and military achievements of deceased veterans; (4) to maintain true allegiance and foster patriotism to the U.S.; and (5) to preserve and defend the U.S.

Early VFW achievements included fostering of veterans' compensation benefits and vocational training for disabled veterans and pensions for World War I veterans and their dependents under the War Risk Act of 1917. VFW also was largely instrumental in securing passage of the World War Veteran Act of 1924 (providing for regional Veterans Bureau offices) and creation of the Veterans Administration in 1930. Since World War II, the VFW has either initiated or actively supported every major piece of veterans legislation.

The 2.3 million member VFW provides a national veterans service network to assist veterans and their families in obtaining eligibility to receive federal and state benefits. It also maintains programs for lobbying for improved benefits, for fostering veterans' job preference, and for promoting beneficial service programs in local communities through its 10,500 posts in the U.S., in U.S. territories, and in a dozen foreign countries.

TABLE 1
VETERANS ORGANIZATIONS CHARTERED BY CONGRESS
AND RECOGNIZED BY VA FOR CLAIM REPRESENTATION

American Ex-Prisoners of War
The American Legion
American Red Cross
American Veterans of WWII, Korea
and Vietnam (AMVETS)
Army & Navy Union, USA, Inc.
Blinded Veterans Association
Catholic War Veterans, USA, Inc.
Congressional Medal of Honor
Society of the USA
Disabled American Veterans
Gold Star Wives of America, Inc.
Jewish War Veterans of the USA

Legion of Valor of the USA, Inc.
Marine Corps League
Military Order of the Purple
Heart of the USA, Inc.
Non Commissioned Officers Assoc.
Paralyzed Veterans of America
Polish Legion of American Veterans, Inc.
United Spanish War Veterans
Veterans of Foreign Wars of the
United States
Veterans of World War I of the
USA, Inc.
Vietnam Veterans of America, Inc.

SOURCE: Dept. of Veterans Affairs

TABLE 2
OTHER VETERANS ORGANIZATIONS RECOGNIZED
BY VA FOR CLAIM REPRESENTATION

American Defenders of Bataan
and Corregidor
American G.I. Forum of the US
American Veterans Committee
Army and Air Force Mutual
Aid Association
Fleet Reserve Association
National Amputation Foundation, Inc.
Navy Mutual Aid Association

Regular Veterans Association
Seattle Veterans Action Center
Swords to Plowshares: Veterans
Rights Organization
The Forty & Eight
The Retired Enlisted Association
Vietnam Era Veterans Association
of Rhode Island

SOURCE: Dept. of Veterans Affairs

TABLE 3
OTHER VETERANS ORGANIZATIONS

Air Force Association
Air Force Sergeants Association
Alliance of Women Veterans
American Gold Star Mothers, Inc.
American Military Members Assoc.
American Military Retirees Assoc.
American War Mothers
Association of Ex-POW of the
  Korean War, Inc.
Association of the U.S. Army
Blinded American Veterans Found.
Blue Star Mothers of America, Inc.
Brotherhood Rally of All Veterans
  Organization (BRAVO)
China-Burma-India Veterans
  Association, Inc.
Combined National Veterans
  Association of America
Destroyer-Escort Sailors Assoc.
Italian American War Veterans
  of the USA
Korean War Veterans Assoc., Inc.
Korean War Veterans Memorial
  Advisory Board
Military Chaplains Association
Military Justice Clinic, Inc.
Military Order of the World Wars
NAM-POWS, Inc.
National American Military
  Retirees Association
National Association for Black
  Veterans, Inc.
National Association for
  Uniformed Services
Natonal Association of
  Women Veterans, Inc.
National Assoc. of Atomic Veterans
National Association of Concerned
  Veterans
National Assoc. of Military Widows
National Association of
  Radiation Survivors
National Association of State
  Directors of Veterans Affairs

National Association of State
  Veterans Homes
National Association of Veterans
  Program Administrators
National Congress of Puerto Rican
  Veterans, Inc.
National Incarcerated Veterans Network
National League of Families of American
  Prisoners and Missing in
  Southeast Asia
National Vietnam Veterans Coalition
National World War II Glider
  Pilots Association
Naval Reserve Association
Navy League of the United States
Ninth Infantry Division Association
OSS-101 Association
Past National Commanders
  Organization
Pearl Harbor Survivors Assoc., Inc.
Red River Valley Fighter Pilots
  Association
Reserve Officers Assoc. of the US
Society of Military Widows
The Retired Officers Association
Tuskegee Airmen, Inc.
United States Army Warrant
  Officers Association
U.S. Merchant Marine Veterans of
  World War II
U.S. Submarine Veterans of
  World War II
Veterans of the Vietnam War, Inc.
Veterans United for Strong America
Vietnam Veterans Institute
WAVES National
Wisconsin Vietnam Vets, Inc.
Women Marines Association
Women Air Force Service Pilots,
  WWII
Women's Army Corps Veterans
  Association

SOURCE: Dept. of Veterans Affairs Directory of Veterans Organizations.
NOTE: All source VA listing addresses are available from VA.

ASSOCIATIONS AND ORGANIZATIONS

Organization	Membership Eligibility	Annual Dues	Magazine or Newspaper	Reg. or Local posts	Life Insurance Programs	Health or Hosp. Ins. Programs	Partial listing of other program and/or services
The American Legion 700 N. Pennsylvania Indianapolis, IN 76206 (3 million)	Vets with honor serv. during WWI, II, Korea, Vietnam, Lebanon, Granada, Panama, & S.W. Asia.	$10.00 to $25.00 depending on Posts	"The American Legion" magazine—monthly.	Yes	Yes	Yes	Vets counseling and assist; scholarship guid. and assist; assist to needy children of Vets; Natl. Youth Baseball and Scout programs; National Security, Foreign Relations and Civil Defense programs, Legis progs.
Disabled American Veterans (DAV) 807 Maine Ave. SW Washington, DC 20024 (202) 554-3501 (1,100,000)	All war disabled veterans of the US Armed Forces	$10.00 (average)	"DAV" magazine—monthly.	Yes	No	No	Provides counseling and assistance in obtaining veterans benefits and claims; employment assistance; VA Hospital volunteers; scholarship programs; D saster Relief Fund; Legislative programs.
Veterans of Foreign Wars of the U.S. (VFW) 200 Maryland Ave., NE Washington, DC 20002 (202) 543-2239 (2,000,000)	Any active duty or former member with honorable discharge who has overseas service recognized by campaign medal or ribbon.	$12.00 (average)	"VFW" magazine—monthly	Yes	Yes	Yes	Assistance for any veteran, w/o regard to mbrshp or cost, who has a claim or appeal with VA or DoD; Maintains svc off's in chapters to provide counseling svcs to all vets; Scholarship programs; maintains Home for children of members; legis programs.

ASSOCIATIONS AND ORGANIZATIONS (Continued)

Organization	Membership Eligibility	Annual Dues	Magazine or Newspaper	Reg. or Local posts	Life Insurance Programs	Health or Hosp. Ins. Programs	Partial listing of other program and/or services
Air Force Association. (AFA) 1501 Lee Hwy. Arlington, VA 22209 (703) 247-5800 (200,000)	Membrs/form. membs of Armed Forces. Cur Reserv or Guard spouse, widow or widower of above; others may join as patrons	$21.00	Air Force magazine— monthly.	Yes	Yes	Yes	National and local seminars and symposia on national defense. Air Force activities and aerospace development; local chapters in 350 cities. Visa card, rental car discounts, automobile lease/purchase plan.
Air Force Sergeants Assoc. (AFSA) P.O. Box 50 Temple Hills, MD 20748-0050 (301) 899-3500 (167,000)	Act duty or former enl members of the USAF include Reserve Forces, ANG and Retired AF.	$18.00 eff 1 May 89	"Sergeants" mag—monthly. "Viewpoint" —qtrly.	Yes	Yes	Yes	Discount car rentals; travel service; auto insurance; scholarship grants; Legislative programs; prescription and eyewear programs; Visa card.
American Military Retirees Association (AMRA) Admin. Office—68 Clinton St. Plattsburg, NY 12901 (11,000)	All ret membrs of U.S. Armed Forces include Reserves and active duty with 12 years or more	$18.00	AMRA News Report —quarterly.	Yes	Yes	Yes	Legislative programs, Financial planning service, scholarship awards, Job resume bank, rental car discount, hotel/motel discount.
American Ex-Prisoners of War 3201 East Pioneer Pkwy, #40 Arlington, TX 76010-5396	Ex POW or Family	$15/20	Ex-POW Bulletin Monthly	400	No	No	Medical Research, NSO, VAVS
American Retirees Assoc. 2009 North 14th St., #300 Arlington, VA 22201 (703) 527-3065	Active Duty, Reserve and Retired Members of the Army, Navy, USAF, USMC, Coast Guard & Public Health Service	$25.00	Bi-Monthly Newsletter	Yes	No	No	Sole purpose is reform of the Uniformed Services Former Spouses Protection Act (USFSPA), Public Law 97-252; 10 USC 1408. Also, provides counseling on USFSPA impact to military divorced spouses.

ASSOCIATIONS AND ORGANIZATIONS (Continued)

Organization	Membership Eligibility	Annual Dues	Magazine or Newspaper	Reg. or Local posts	Life Insurance Programs	Health or Hosp. Ins. Programs	Partial listing of other program and/or services
American Veterans of WWII, Korea, & Vietnam (AMVETS) 4647 Forbes Blvd. Lanham, MD 20706 (301) 459-9600 (200,000)	All veterans with active, honorable service any time from 9/16/40	$10.00 $15.00 (varies with post)	The National AMVET magazine quarterly.	Yes	Yes	Yes	Scholarship programs; Veterans Hosp. Volunteer program; blood donor program; counseling program; legislative program.
Coast Guard Chief Petty Officers Association 5520G Hempstead Way Springfield, VA 22151 (703) 941-0395 (9,700)	Any Chief Petty Officer (E-7, 8, 9) of the USCG (active, retired or reserve).	$18.00 check or allot.	"The Chief" magazine— quarterly.	Yes	Yes	Yes	Scholarship awards, legislative program.
Coast Guard Enlisted Association 5520G Hempstead Way, Springfield, VA 22151 C.R. Castor, Chief Admin. (703) 941-0395	Any USCG Enlisted E-6 or below (active, retired, or reserve).	$18.00 check or allot.	"National News" quarterly.	Not yet	Yes	Yes	Scholarship awards, legislative representation
Fleet Reserve Association (FRA) 125 N. West Street Alexandria, VA 22314-2754 (703) 683-1400	All enlisted pers of the Sea Services on AD, in the Fleet Reserve or retired. Off's with at least 1 days AD as enl.	$20.00	"Naval Affairs" magazine— monthly. On Watch ad newspaper bi-monthly	Yes	Yes	Yes	Career counseling and assistance; legislative programs; veterans claims and grievances representation with the VA; assistance with corrections of Naval Records and disability claims. CHAMPUS/Medicare supplemental insurance, term life.
Jewish War Veterans of the U.S. (JWV) 1811 R St., NW Washington, DC 20009 (202) 265-6280 (100,000)	Veterans of wartime service	$25.00	The Jewish Veteran Quarterly	Yes	Yes	Yes	Legislative program; Asst. to veterans; Svc to Homeless; Annual Convention; VA Hosp. Vol. Svc.; Scholarship program for JWV Depens; Blood donor post level programs.

ASSOCIATIONS AND ORGANIZATIONS (Continued)

Organization‡	Membership Eligibility	Annual Dues	Magazine or Newspaper	Reg. or Local posts	Life Insurance Programs	Health or Hosp. Ins. Programs	Partial listing of other program and/or services
Marine Corps Association P.O. Box 1775 MCCDC Quantico, VA 22134 (703) 640-6161	All U.S. Marines	$12 Enl $15 Off	Leatherneck & Gazette	No	Yes	Yes	Book store, MC, Birthday Ball, Supplies.
Marine Corps League P.O. Box 370 Merrifield, VA 22116-3070 (703) 207-9588 (35,000)	All active duty, Reserve or former marines with at least 90 days active duty or with honorable separation or retirement	$10.00 to $20.00 depending on local dets.	Marine Corps League Quarterly.	Yes	Yes	Yes	Auto quote & purch plan, disc lodg prog, auto warranty ext prog. trav asst, disc movg svc, group ins. CHAMPUS & Medicare supple plan. vet svc prog. claims & griev assist. member buying plan, invest progs, no frills auto club, pers legal defender prog.
Marine Corps Reserve Officers' Association (MCROA) 201 N. Washington St., #206 Alexandria, VA 22314 (703) 548-7607 (5,000)	Any Reserve Officer of the USMC on active duty; inactive duty, or retired. Assoc. membership for others with USMC service.	$15.00 to $50.00 dep on grade. Life membership avail.	"The Word" newsletter—bi-monthly.	Yes	Yes	No	Recognition & Awards Program; car leasing and rental; shoppers corner. Accidental Disability and Dismemberment insurance. Group Term Life Insurance, Executive Employment Assistance, Executive & Recruiting Service Assistance Programs.
National Association for Uniformed Services (NAUS) 5535 Hempstead Way Springfield, VA 22151 (703) 750-1342 (50,000)	All members of the uniformed Services: National Guard, active reserve, retired, and veterans and their spouses, widows, widowers and former spouses.	$15.00 ($12.00 widows)	"USJ" bi-monthly.	Yes	Yes	Yes	Legis prog: CHAMPUS/MEDICARE Supple insur, hosp indemnity, accidental death/dismemberment, Term Life, Dental Plan, Legal Svcs Plan, Auto Warranty Plan, Auto and Home Ins, Visa, Pentagon Fed Credit Union, Pharmac. Svcs, Car rentals, Motel Disc., Worldwide Travel Svc. Disabil Ins, Nursing Home Ins. Publications: Uniformed Serv Jour, Legis Guide, and Survivor's Guide.

ASSOCIATIONS AND ORGANIZATIONS (Continued)

Organization	Membership Eligibility	Annual Dues	Magazine or Newspaper	Reg. or Local posts	Life Insurance Programs	Health or Hosp. Ins. Programs	Partial listing of other program and/or services
National Guard Association of the United States (NGAUS) 1 Massachusetts Ave., NW Washington, DC 20001 (202) 789-0031 (51,000)	Any officer or warrant officer who is serving or ever served, honorably in the National Guard.	$14 to $68 depending on grade.	National Guard magazine—monthly.	No	Yes	Yes	Recognition and awards programs; legislative programs; insurance program; CHAMPUS and Medicare supplements; Edward L. Martin Library; Museum of the National Guard
Naval Enlisted Reserve Association (NERA) 6703 Farragut Ave. Falls Church, VA 22042 (703) 534-1329 (16,000)	All enlisted or veterans who have served in the Naval Reserve, Marine Corps Reserve, or Coast Guard Reserve.	$20.00	Bi-Monthly "The Mariner"	Yes	Yes	Yes	Assistance with filing for Naval Reserve retirement; legislative programs; record reviews; group insurance program.
Naval Reserve Association (NRA) 1619 King Street Alexandria, VA 22314-2793 (703) 548-5800 (24,000)	Commis. or warrant officers having served hon. in the Armed Forces & their spouses & widows/widowers.	$25.00 ($60 for 3 yrs.)	"NRA News" Monthly	Yes	Yes	Yes	Professional counseling service; CHAMPUS/Medical Supplement; Record Review service; promotional and service jacket services; legislative program.
Non-Commissioned Officers Association (NCOA) P.O. Box 33610 San Antonio, TX 78265 (512) 653-6161 (175,000)	Reg, ret'd, reserve or Nat'l Guard NCO or petty off's of the Armed Forces & a Vets Div. for honorably sep'd or ret'd vets.	$20.00	NCOA Journal	Yes	Yes	Yes	Legislative Program NCOA Scholarships, Car Rental & New car discount, Counseling Services to members, Job Fair and Resume service, Auto Club and Medical Trust Fund.
Reserve Officers Association (ROA) 1 Constitution Ave. NE Washington, DC 20002 (202) 479-2200 (128,000)	Any officer, active or retired, regular or reserve of the Uniformed Services.	$40.00	"The Officer" magazine—monthly	Yes	Yes	Yes	Congress chartered for Nat'l Secur; supports legis affecting active & Reserve Forces, & retirement; counsels on retirement & career quests or probs; trav services; disc on medals, ribbons, car rent/lease; insur.

ASSOCIATIONS AND ORGANIZATIONS (Continued)

Organization	Membership Eligibility	Annual Dues	Magazine or Newspaper	Reg. or Local posts	Life Insurance Programs	Health or Hosp. Ins. Programs	Partial listing of other program and/or services
The Retired Enlisted Association (TREA) 1111 S. Abilene Court Aurora, CO 80012 (303) 752-0660 (60,000)	Any enlisted, retired from the Armed Forces of the USA for length of svc or perm medically ret'd from the US Armed Forces.	$15.00	"Voice" Monthly Newsletter	Yes	Yes (Term & whole life)	Yes	Var progs: Legis; Vets Counseling and Assist; Scholarship; CHAMPUS & Medicare Supple, Car Rental; Travel Service; Prescription Drug; Counsels member retirement rights, benefits, & privileges; discount eye care program.
The Retired Officers Assoc., (TROA) 201 N. Washington St. Alexandria, VA 22314 (703) 549-2311 (375,000)	Anyone who is or was a commissioned or warrant officer in the active or reserve forces of the Uniformed Services and their widow(er)s.	$20.00	"The Retired Officer Magazine— monthly	Yes	Yes	Yes	Employment assist, including resume writing assist, placement counseling, and computer job ref svc; Legis prog. Insur and supp; Counseling in matters relating to entitlements and benefits; Travel prog; Survivor assist; Disc legal help; Educ assist.
Uniform Services Disabled Retirees (USDB) 5909 Alta Monte NE Albuquerque, NM 87110 (505) 881-4568 (2,000)	All disabled Retirees	$25.00 (new) $15.00 (Renewal)		No	No	No	Correction of unfair law which offsets VA compensation from military retirement pay.
U.S. Army WO Association 462 Herndon Pkwy., #207 Herndon, VA 22070 (703) 742-7727 (4,000)	Army WO retired National Guard, Reserves, and Active Duty.	(Retired) $24.00 Others $36.00	"Newsliner" Newspaper Monthly	Yes	Yes	Yes	Professional membership service to include legislative programs, Professional Development Seminars, awards; legal service, CHAMPUS & car discount programs.
Women's Army Corps Veterans Association P.O. Box 5577 Ft. McLellan, AL 36205 (205) 520-3218 (4,100)	WAC & WAAC; Women in or former members of Army, Army Reserve & National Guard	$8.00	The Channel 10 issues annually	Yes	No	No	Provide svc & spt to vets thru VA Hosp vol prog; annual award to outstanding female ROTC grad in 4 regions ann scholarship award; prom gen welfare of all vets, especially women.

SOURCE: Courtesy of "Retired Military Almanac-1992, 15th Annual Edition"

MILITARY RETIREES

A number of benefits and privileges are available to career military retirees which, with some exceptions, includes all those who have served 20 or more years on active duty and those who have been disabled after 8 years of service. Retirement benefits include retirement pay and health care in military hospitals and facilities, if available, or under the Civilian Health and Medical Program of the Uniformed Services (CHAMPUS). Retirement privileges include the use of military base facilities and commissaries and space available travel. Also, all retirees as veterans also are entitled to VA benefits as well.

RETIREMENT ELIGIBILITY

Regular and reserve commissioned officers, warrant officers, and enlisted members are eligible for retirement with immediate annuity after completing 20 years of **active service**, with mandatory retirement at 30 years. Longer service may be permitted in special circumstances. A member with at least 8 years of service who is unable to perform duties because of a permanent physical or mental disability may be retired if the disability is rated at 30 percent or more. All regular officers, with certain exceptions, are required to retire after reaching 62.

Reserve retirement pay and full retirement benefits are available after age 60 with retirement based on a point system related to years of service and pay grade. It requires point conversion to a minimum of 20 qualifying years for eligibility.

RETIREMENT PAY

Retirement pay is determined by the basic pay rate at the time of retirement multiplied by the years of credited service. The retirement pay for those entering the service before August 1, 1986, is 50 percent of the basic pay for those serving 20 years, plus 2½ percent for each additional year, with the maximum benefit increasing to 75 percent of basic pay.

For those whose service began after August 1, 1986 the retired pay formula is the product of 2.5 times creditable service years, less one percentage point for each year less than 30. Upon reaching 62, the retiree's annuity is recalculated by multiplying the basic pay amount by the 2.5 percent per year times service year formula, and that amount is restored to the member.

Disabled retirement pay generally is based on the degree to which the disabled person is prevented from performing service duties. It is determined by multiplying the basic pay by either the disability percentage or by 2.5 percent per year of active service, whichever is greater. For a permanently disabled person, the minimum benefit is 30 percent of the basic pay, and the maximum benefit is 75 percent of the rate. Disabled retirees who elect to receive veterans' disability from the VA will have their military disability retired pay reduced by the amount received from the VA. (In all cases, retirement pay may be waived, all or in part, to receive VA compensation which is non-taxable.)

Annual pay adjustments are made to accommodate cost-of-living changes as reflected by the Consumer Price Index.

SURVIVOR BENEFIT PLANS

A Survivor Benefit Plan (SBP) was set up under a 1972 law. The SBP is a highly recommended, voluntary program under which a military retiree may elect to receive reduced retirement pay to provide an annuity to an eligible survivor. Although a voluntary program, SBP takes effect automatically on retirement unless the retiree and spouse decline it. Under the plan, a surviving spouse's annuity is calculated at 55 percent of the participant's base annuity until age 62, when it is reduced to 35 percent of the base amount due to spouses' eligibility to receive Social Security survivor benefits. The SBP program includes the following categories of beneficiary coverage:

- Spouse only
- Spouse and children
- Children only
- Former spouse and, where applicable, children
- Person with insurable interest.

There are different rates of premium costs for an SBP plan depending upon the beneficiary. The most common spouse/former spouse premium for those who entered the service before March 1, 1990, is the lower amount of either (a) 6.5 percent of the member's base amount or (b) 2.5 percent of the first $363 of the base amount plus 10 percent of the remaining base amount.

SBP annuities are offset by any non-taxable dependents indemnity compensation (DIC) received from the VA.

A new supplemental SBP plan became effective on April 1, 1992. The new plan permits the purchase of additional amounts of survivor benefit coverage. Information on all aspects of SBP can be obtained from a local Military Finance Center.

HEALTH BENEFITS

Health benefits for military retirees, their spouses, and their dependents, most often can be obtained at Uniformed Services facilities for non-emergency care subject to space and facility availability and medical and dental staff capabilities. (There is a subsistence charge to officers for such inpatient care.) Where such care is not available, retirees and dependents should first rely upon other types of primary coverage health plans to defray costs at civilian hospitals and facilities. If such programs are not available to the retiree, costs for most medical and psychological care will be covered under the Civilian Health and Medical Program of the Uniformed Services (CHAMPUS).

Participation in CHAMPUS is available to all retired members of the Uniformed Services and their spouses and dependents. CHAMPUS covers a wide variety of health care costs but excludes the following:

- Domiciliary or custodial care
- Dental care except that required as a necessary adjunct to CHAMPUS-covered medical or surgical treatment
- Routine physical examination, podiatric, and immunizations
- Eyeglasses and certain prosthetic devices
- Surgery for cosmetic and psychological purposes
- Sex therapy
- Chiropractic, naturopathic, electrolysis, acupuncture, and hair transplants.

It is advisable for retirees to find a health care provider who accepts the CHAMPUS charge as the full fee for the retiree. For those covered under CHAMPUS, there is no deductible charge for inpatient care. For outpatient care, there is an annual deductible cost of $100 per family and a cost of either 25 percnt of the health care provider's billed charge or daily fee, whichever is less. The yearly deductible is based upon a fiscal year extending from October 1 through the following September 30.

Under CHAMPUS, a statement of non-availability of other alternative coverage and a claim form and statement from the health care provider must be filed with CHAMPUS. Most providers have the CHAMPUS claim forms; otherwise, they can be obtained directly from CHAMPUS, Aurora, CO 80045.

For military retirees and dependents, coverage under CHAMPUS terminates at age 65 to be replaced by Medicare.

A retiree's eligibility to receive health care benefits can be readily verified under the Defense Eligibility Reporting System (DEERS). The DEERS program, under which retirees are automatically enrolled, provides a means for minimizing fraudulent use of military health plans. All persons other than retirees must enroll at the nearest uniformed services personnel office.

Satellite primary health care programs (Primary Care for the Uniformed Services, or PRIMUS, and the Navy-established NAVCARE) have been established by the services as walk-in clinics designed to increase access to limited medical care and to reduce medical service backlogs at military facilities. Retirees eligible for CHAMPUS are eligible to use the PRIMUS/NAVCARE centers.

Information on retirees' health care benefits can be obtained from the Health Benefit Advisor at all Uniformed Services hospitals and most clinics.

BASE FACILITY USE

Military retirees and their dependents usually have use of a variety of base facilities. Chief among these are the following:

Officer, NCO, and Enlisted	Libraries
Clubs and Mess Halls	Chapels
Commissaries	Limited Legal Assistance
Theaters	Transient Quarters
Recreation Services	Exchange Stores
Laundry and Dry Cleaning Stores	

These facilities are available to retirees at more than 100 military bases, subject to the availability and adequacy of the facilities.

SPACE AVAILABLE TRAVEL

Retirees, their spouses, and their dependents are eligible to use Military and Airlift Command (MAC) aircraft on flights to and from overseas. This privilege is extended, however, only after all official duty passengers have been accommodated. Retirees are permitted to sign up for up to five destinations. Their names remain on the Space Available register up to 45 days, after which retirees must revalidate their interest if the MAC has not been able to accommodate them. Retirees are charged a $10 fee on one-way trips.

For complete details on military retirement benefits the Retired Military Almanac is an outstanding book at a cost of $5.45. The phone number is (703) 532-1631. Address: P.O. Box 4144, Falls Church, VA 22044.

VA FACILITIES
WHERE TO GO FOR HELP

Information on VA benefits may be obtained from regional offices. Inquiries and requests for service on VA-administered life insurance programs also may be obtained from the regional office and insurance centers in Philadelphia and St. Paul. Special telephone services nationwide include:

Life Insurance 1-800-699-8477

Radiation Helpline 1-800-827-0365

Debt Management Center 1-800-827-0648

Education Loan 1-800-326-8276

Telecommunication Device for the Deaf (TDD) 1-800-829-4833

Many VA medical centers operate outpatient clinics either in the centers or in other locations. Some clinics operate independently of medical centers. All clinics can make referrals for care in VA medical centers.

The following designaitons for medical centers indicate additional programs available: (*) for nursing-home care units; (#) for domiciliaries.

Some national cemeteries can bury only cremated remains or casketed remains of eligible family members of those already buried. Contact the cemetery director for information on the availability of space.

ALABAMA

Medical Centers:
   Birmingham 35233 (700 S. 19th St., 205-933-8101)
   Montgomery 36109 (215 Perry Hill Rd., 205-272-4670)
   *Tuscaloosa 35404 (Loop Rd., East, 205-554-2000)
   *Tuskegee 36083 (205-727-0550)
Clinic:
   Mobile 36604 (1359 Springhill Ave., 205-690-2875)
   Huntsville 35801 (201 Governor's Dr. SW, 205-533-1675)
Regional Office:
   Montgomery 36104 (474 S. Court St., Local 205-262-7781, Statewide 800-827-2046.

Vet Centers:
  Birmingham 35205 (1425 S. 21st St., Suite 108, 205-933-0500)
  Mobile 36604 (951 Government St., Suite 122, 205-694-4194)

ALASKA
  New Anchorage Outpatient Clinic and Regional Office opens in April
    1992 (2925 De Burr Rd., 99508)
Clinics:
  Anchorage 99501 (235 E. 8th Ave., Local 271-2200, Statewide 800-478-
    4400)
  Fort Wainwright 99703 (Bassett Army Hospital, Rm. 262, 907-353-5208)
Regional Office:
  Anchorage 99501 (235 E. 8th Ave., Local 907-279-6116, Statewide 800-
    478-2500); Benefits Office: Juneau 99802 (P.O. Box 20069, Fed. Bldg.,
    Rm. 103, 907-586-7472)
Vet Centers:
  Anchorage 99508 (4201 Tudor Centre Dr., Suite 115, 907-563-6966)
  Fairbanks 99701 (520 5th Ave., Suite 200, 907-456-4238)
  Kenai 99611 (P.O. Box 1883, 907-283-5205)
  Wasilla 99687 (851 E. Westpoint Ave., Suite 109, 907-376-4318)

ARIZONA
Medical Centers:
  *Phoenix 85012 (7th St. & Indian School Rd., 602-277-5551)
  #Prescott 86313 (602-445-4860)
  *Tucson 85723 (3601 S. 6th Ave., 602-792-1450)
Regional Office:
  Phoenix 85012 (3225 N. Central Ave., Local 602-263-5411, Statewide
    800-827-2031)
Vet Centers:
  Phoenix 85004 (141 E. Palm Lane, Suite 100, 602-379-4769)
  Prescott 86301 (637 Hillside Ave., Suite A, 602-778-3469)
  Tucson 85723 (3055 N. 1st Ave., 602-882-0333)

ARKANSAS
Medical Centers:
  Fayetteville 72703 (1100 N. College Ave., 501-443-4301)
  #*Little Rock 72205 (4300 West 7th St., 501-661-1201, 501-661-1202)
Regional Office:
  North Little Rock 72115 (Bldg. 65, Ft. Roots, P.O. Box 1280, Local 501-
    370-3800, Statewide 800-827-2033)
Vet Center:
  North Little Rock 72114 (201 W. Broadway, Suite A, 501-324-6395)

CALIFORNIA

Medical Centers:
   *Fresno 93703 (2615 E. Clinton Ave., 209-225-6100)
   *Livermore 94550 (4951 Arroyo Rd., 415-447-2560)
   *Loma Linda 92357 (11201 Benton St., 714-825-7084)
   *Long Beach 9082 (5901 E. 7th St., 213-494-2611)
#*Palo Alto 94304 (3801 Miranda Ave., 415-493-5000)
   *San Diego 92161 (3350 LaJolla Vilage Dr., 619-552-8585)
   San Francisco 94121 (4150 Clement St., 415-221-4810)
   *Sepulveda 91343 (1611 Plummer St., 818-891-7711)
#*West Los Angeles 90073 (11301 Wilshire Blvd., 213-478-3711)
Clinics:
   Los Angeles 90013 (425 S. Hill St., 213-894-3902)
   Martinez 94553 (150 Muir Rd., 415-372-2000)
   Oakland 94612 (2221 Martin Luther King, Jr. Way, 415-273-7096)
   Redding 96001 (2787 Eureka Way, 916-246-5056)
   Sacramento 95820 (600 Broadway, 916-440-2625)
   San Diego 82108 (Palomar Bldg., 2022 Camino Del Rio North, 619-557-
      6210)
   Santa Barbara 93110 (4440 Calle Real, 805-683-1491)
Regional Offices:
   Los Angeles 90024 (Fed. Bldg., 11000 Wilshire Blvd., counties of Inyo,
      Kern, Los Angeles, Orange, San Bernardino, San Luis Obispo, Santa
      Barbara and Ventura. Direct dial from central Los Angeles 479-4011;
      other areas of these counties 800-827-2013).
   San Diego 92108 (2022 Camino Del Rio North, counties of Imperial,
      Riverside and San Diego, local, 297-8220; other areas of these
      counties, 800-827-2054)
   San Francisco 94105 (211 Main St.; recorded benefits 415-974-0138,
      24-hour availability; Local 415-495-8900, Other Northern California
      areas 800-827-0641)
   Counties of Alpine, Lassen, Modoc and Mono served by Reno, Nev., RO,
      800-827-8014
   Benefits Office: East Los Angeles 90022 (5400 E. Olympic Blvd.,
      Commerce, 310-722-4927)
Vet Centers:
   Anaheim 92805 (859 S. Harbor Blvd., 714-776-0161)
   Burlingame 94010 (1234 Howard—San Mateo, 415-344-3126)
   Commerce 90022 (VA East L.A. Clinic, 5400 E. Olympic Blvd., #120,
      213-728-9966)
   Concord 94520 (1899 Clayton Rd., Suite 140, 415-680-4526)
   Eureka 95501 (305 V St., 707-444-8271)
   Fresno 93721 (1340 Van Ness Ave., 209-487-5660)

Los Angeles 90003 (So. Central L.A., 251 W. 85th Pl., 213-215-2380)
Los Angeles 90025 (West L.A., 2000 Westwood Blvd., 213-475-9509)
Marina 93933 (455 Reservation Rd., Suite E, 408-384-1660)
Oakland 94612 (287 17th St., 415-763-3904)
Riverside 92504 (4954 Arlington Ave., Suite A, 714-359-8967)
Rohnert Park 94928 (6225 State Farm Dr., Suite 101, 707-586-3295)
Sacramento 95825 (1111 Howe Ave., Suite 390, 916-978-5477)
San Diego 92103 (2900 6th Ave., 619-294-2040)
San Francisco 94102 (25 Van Ness Ave., 415-431-6021)
San Jose 95126 (1022 West Hedding, 408-249-1643)
Santa Barbara 93101 (1300 Santa Barbara St., 805-564-2345)
Sepulveda 91343 (16126 Lassen St., 818-892-9227)
Terre Linda 94903 (515 North Gate Blvd., 415-492-8364)
Upland 91786 (313 N. Mountain Ave., 714-982-0416, 800-826-6993)
Vista 92083 (1830 West Dr., Suite 103, 619-945-8941)

COLORADO

Medical Centers:
 *Denver 80220 (1055 Clermont St., 303-399-8020)
 *Fort Lyon 81038 (719-456-1260)
 *Grand Junction 81501 (2121 North Ave., 303-242-0731)
Clinic:
 Colorado Springs 80909 (1785 N. Academy Blvd., 719-380-0004)
Regional Office:
 Denver 80225 (44 Union Blvd., P.O. Box 25126, Local 303-980-1300,
 Statewide 800-827-2043.
Vet Centers:
 Boulder 80302 (2128 Pearl St., 303-440-7306)
 Colorado Springs 80903 (411 S. Tejon, Suite G, 719-471-9992)
 Denver 80204 (1815 Federal Blvd., 303-433-7123)

CONNECTICUT

Medical Centers:
 Newington 06111 (555 Willard Ave., 203-666-6951)
 *West Haven 06516 (W. Spring St., 203-932-5711)
Regional Office:
 Hartford 06103 (450 Main St., Local 203-278-3230; Statewide 800-827-
 0510)
Vet Centers:
 Hartford 06120 (370 Market St., 203-240-3543)
 New Haven 06511 (562 Whalley Ave., 203-773-2232 or 773-2236)
 Norwich 06360 (16 Franklin St., Rm. 109, 203-887-1755)

DELAWARE

Medical Center:
  *Wilmington 19805 (1601 Kirkwood Highway, 302-994-2511)
Regional Office:
  Wilmington 19805 (1601 Kirkwood Highway, Local 302-998-0191, Statewide 800-827-4838)
Vet Center:
  Wilmington 19805 (VAMROC Bldg. 2, 1601 Kirkwood Highway, 302-994-1660)

DISTRICT OF COLUMBIA

Medical Center:
  *Washington, D.C. 20422 (50 Irving St., N.W., 202-745-8000)
Regional Office:
  Washington, D.C. 20421 (941 N. Capitol St., N.E., 202-872-1151)
Vet Center:
  Washington, D.C. 20003 (801 Pennsylvania Ave., S.E., 202-745-8400/8402)

FLORIDA

Medical Centers:
  #*Bay Pines 33504 (1000 Bay Pines Blvd., N., 813-398-6661)
   *Gainesville 32608 (1601 Southwest Archer Rd., 904-376-1611)
   *Lake City 32055 (801 S. Marion St., 904-755-3016)
   *Miami 33125 (1201 N.W. 16th St., 305-324-4455)
   *Tampa 33612 (13000 Bruce B. Downs Blvd., 813-972-2000)
Clinics:
  Daytona Beach 32117 (1900 Mason Ave., 904-274-4600)
  Fort Myers 33901 (2070 Carrell Rd., 813-939-3939)
  Jacksonville 32206 (1833 Boulevard, 904-791-2712)
  Key West 33040 (1111 12th St., Suite 207, 305-538-6696)
  Oakland Park 33334 (5599 N. Dixie Highway, 305-771-2101)
  Orlando 32806 (83 W. Columbia St., 407-425-7521)
  Pensacola 32503 (312 Kenmore Rd., 904-476-1100)
  Port Richey 34668 (8911 Ponderosa, 813-869-3203)
  Riviera Beach 33404 (Executive Plaza, 301 Broadway, 407-827-2204)
Regional Office:
  St. Petersburg 33701 (144 1st Ave. S., Local 612-898-2121, Statewide 800-827-2204).
Benefits Offices:
  Fort Myers 33901 (2070 Carrell Rd., 813-939-3939)
  Jacksonville 32206 (1833 Boulevard, Rm. 3109, 800-827-2204)

Miami 33130 (Federal Bldg., Rm. 120, 51 S.W. 1st Ave., 800-827-2204)
Oakland Park 33334 (5599 N. Dixie Highway, 305-771-2101)
Orlando 32806 (83 W. Columbia St., 407-425-7521)
Pensacola 32503-7492 (312 Kenmore Rd., Rm. 1G250, 800-827-2204)
Riviera Beach 33404 (Executive Plaza, 310 Broadway, 407-845-2800)

Vet Centers:
Ft. Lauderdale 33301 (315 N.E. 3rd Ave., 305-356-7926)
Jacksonville 32202 (255 Liberty St., 904-791-3621)
Lake Worth 33461 (2311 10th Ave., North #13—Palm Beach, 407-585-0441)
Miami 33129 (2700 S.W. 3rd Ave., Suite 1A, 305-859-8387)
Orlando 32809 (5001 S. Orange Ave., Suite A, 407-648-6151)
Pensacola 32501 (15 W. Strong St., Suite 100 C, 904-479-6665)
Sarasota 34239 (1800 Siesta Dr., 813-952-9406)
St. Petersburg 33713 (2837 1st Ave., N., 813-893-3791)
Tallahassee 32303 (249 E. 6th Ave., 904-942-8810)
Tampa 33604 (1507 W. Sligh Ave., 813-228-2621)

GEORGIA

Medical Centers:
*Augusta 30910 (1 Freedom Way, 404-733-0188)
*Decatur 30033 (1670 Clairmont Rd., 404-321-6111)
#*Dublin 31021 (1826 Veterans Blvd., 912-272-1210)
Regional Office:
Atlanta 30365 (730 Peachtree St., N.E., Local 404-881-1776, Statewide 800-827-2939.
Clinic
Savannah 31406 (325 W. Montgomery Crossroads, 912-920-0214)
Vet Centers:
Atlanta 30309 (922 W. Peachtree St., 404-347-7264)
Savannah 31406 (8110 White Bluff Rd., 912-927-7360)

HAWAII

Clinic:
Honolulu 96850 (P.O. Box 50188, 300 Ala Moana Blvd., 808-541-1600)
Regional Office:
Honolulu 96813 (PJKK Federal Bldg., 300 Ala Moana Blvd., Mailing: P.O. Box 50188, Honolulu 96850; Kauai, Lanai, Maui, Molokai 800-827-6549. Direct dial from: Oahu, 541-1000.
Vet Centers:
Hilo 96720 (120 Kelwe St., Suite 201, 808-969-3833)
Honolulu 96814 (1680 Kapiolani Blvd., Suite F, 808-541-1764)

Kailua-Kona 96740 (Pottery Terrace, Fern Blvd., 75-5995 Kuakini Hwy.,
#415, 808-329-0574)
Lihue 96766 (3367 Kuhio Hwy., Suite 101—Kauai, 808-246-1163)
Wailuku 96793 (Ting Bldg., 35 Lunalilo, Suite 101, 808-242-8557)

IDAHO

Medical Center:
  *Boise 83702 (500 West Fort St., 208-336-5100)
Clinic:
  Pocatello 83201 (1651 Alvin Ricken Dr., 208-232-6214)
Regional Office:
  Boise 83724 (Federal Bldg. & U.S. Courthouse, 550 W. Fort St., Box 044,
  Local 208-334-1010, Statewide 800-695-8387)
Vet Centers:
  Boise 83706 (1115 W. Boise Ave., 208-342-3612)
  Pocatello 83201 (1975 S. 5th St., 208-232-0316)

ILLINOIS

Medical Centers:
  Chicago 60611 (Lakeside, 333 E. Huron St., 312-943-6600)
  Chicago 60680 (Westside, 820 S. Damen Ave., P.O. Box 8195, 312-666-
  6500)
  *Danville 61832 (1900 E. Main St., 217-442-8000)
  *Hines 60141 (Roosevelt Rd. & 5th Ave., 708-343-7200)
  Marion 62959 (2401 W. Main St., 618-997-5311)
  #*North Chicago 60064 (3001 Green Bay Rd., 708-688-1900)
Clinic:
  Peoria 61605 (411 Dr. Martin Luther King Dr., 309-671-7359)
Regional Office:
  Chicago 60680 (536 S. Clark St., P.O. Box 8136, Local 312-663-5510,
  Statewide 800-827-0466)
Vet Centers:
  Chicago 60637 (5505 S. Harper, 312-684-5500)
  Chicago Heights 60411 (1600 Halsted St., 708-754-0340)
  East St. Louis 62203 (1269 N. 89th St., 618-397-6602)
  Evanston 60202 (565 Howard St., 708-332-1019)
  Moline 61265 (1529 46th Ave., Rm. #6, 309-762-6954)
  Oak Park 60302 (155 S. Oak Park Ave., 708-383-3225)
  Peoria 61603 (605 N.E. Monroe St., 309-671-7300)
  Springfield 62702 (624 S. 4th St., 217-492-4955)

INDIANA

Medical Centers:
* * Fort Wayne 46805 (2121 Lake Ave., 219-426-5431)
* * Indianapolis 46202 (1481 W. 10th St., 317-635-7401)
* * Marion 46952 (E. 38th St., 317-674-3321)

Clinics:
Crown Point 46307 (9330 Broadway, 219-662-0001)
Evansville 47708 (214 S.E. 6th St., 812-465-6202)

Regional Office:
Indianapolis 46204 (575 N. Pennsylvania St., Local 317-226-5566, Statewide 800-827-0634)

Vet Centers:
Evansville 47711 (311 N. Weinbach Ave., 812-473-5993 or 473-6084)
Fort Wayne 46802 (528 West Berry St., 219-460-1456)
Gary 46408 (2236 West Ridge Rd., 219-887-0048)
Indianapolis 46208 (3833 Meridian, 317-927-6440)

IOWA

Medical Centers:
* \# Des Moines 50310 (30th & Euclid Ave., 515-255-2173)
* Iowa City 52246 (Hwy. 6 West, 319-338-0581)
* \#* Knoxville 50138 (1515 W. Pleasant St., 515-842-3101)

Regional Office:
Des Moines 50309 (210 Walnut St., Local 515-284-0219, Statewide 800-827-7683)

Clinic:
Bettendorf (Quad Cities) 52722 (2979 Victoria Dr., To open May 1992)

Vet Centers:
Des Moines 50310 (2600 Harding Rd., 515-284-4929)
Sioux City 51101 (706 Jackson, 712-255-3808)

KANSAS

Medical Centers:
* \#* Leavenworth 66048 (4201 S. 4th St., Trafficway 913-682-2000)
* * Topeka 66622 (2200 Gage Blvd., 913-272-3111)
* * Wichita 67218 (5500 E. Kellogg, 316-685-2221)

Regional Office:
Wichita 67218 (5500 E. Kellogg, Local 316-264-9123, Statewide 800-827-0445)

Vet Centers:
Wichita 67211 (413 S. Pattie, 316-265-3260)

KENTUCKY

Medical Centers:
* Lexington 40511 (Leestown Rd., 606-233-4511)
  Louisville 40206 (800 Zorn Ave., 502-895-3401)

Regional Office:
  Louisville 40202 (600 Martin Luther King, Jr. Place, Local 502-584-2231, Statewide 800-827-2050)

Vet Centers:
  Lexington 40503 (1117 Limestone Rd., 606-276-5269)
  Louisville 40208 (1355 S. 3rd St., 502-636-4002)

LOUISIANA

Medical Centers:
* Alexandria 71301 (Shreveport Hwy., 318-473-0010)
  New Orleans 70146 (1601 Perdido St., 504-568-0811)
  Shreveport 71101 (510 E. Stoner Ave., 318-221-8411)

Clinic:
  Baton Rouge 70806 (216 S. Foster Drive, 318-389-0628)

Regional Office:
  New Orleans 70113 (701 Loyola Ave., Local 504-589-7191, Statewide 800-827-8022.

Vet Centers:
  Bossier City 71112 (2103 Old Minden Rd., 318-742-2733)
  New Orleans 70116 (1529 N. Claiborne Ave., 504-943-8386)
  Shreveport 71104 (Bldg. 3, Suite 260, 2620 Centenary Blvd., 318-425-8387)

MAINE

Medical Center:
* Togus 04330 (Route 17 East, 207-623-8411)

Regional Office:
  Togus 04330 (Route 17 East, Local 207-623-8000, Statewide 800-827-0794.
  Benefits Office: Portland 04101 (236 Oxford St., 207-775-6391)

Vet Centers:
  Bangor 04401 (352 Harlow St., 207-947-3391)
  Portland 04101 (63 Preble St., 207-780-3584)

MARYLAND

Medical Centers:
  Baltimore 21218 (3900 Loch Raven Blvd., 410-467-9932)

Baltimore 21201 (Prosthetic Assessment Information Center, 103 S. Gay St., 401-962-3934)

* Fort Howard 21052 (N. Point Rd., 410-477-1800)

* Perry Point 21902 (410-642-2411)

Clinic:

Baltimore 21201 (31 Hopkins Plaza, Fed. Bldg., 410-962-4610)

Regional Office:

Baltimore 21201 (31 Hopkins Plaza, Fed. Bldg., Local 410-685-5454, Other areas 800-827-6496); counties of Montgomery & Prince Georges served by Washington, DC, RO 202-872-1151

Vet Centers:

Baltimore 21230 (777 Washington Blvd., 410-539-5511)

Elkton 21921 (7 Elkton Commercial Plaza, South Bridge St., 410-398-0171)

Silver Spring 20910 (1015 Spring St., Suite 101, 301-589-1073 or 589-1236)

MASSACHUSETTS

Medical Centers:

#* Bedford 01730 (200 Spring Rd., 617-275-7500)

Boston 02130 (150 S. Huntington Ave., 617-232-9500)

* Brockton 02401 (940 Belmont St., 508-583-4500)

* Northampton 01060 (421 N. Main St., 413-584-4040)

West Roxbury 02132 (1400 VFW Pkwy., 617-323-7700)

Clinics:

Boston 02114 (251 Causeway St., 617-248-1000)

Lowell 01852 (Old Post Office Bldg., 50 Kearney Sq., 508-453-1746)

Springfield 01103 (1550 Main St., 413-785-0301)

New Bedford 02740 (53 N. Sixth St., 508-999-5504)

Worcester 01608 (595 Main St., 508-793-0200)

Regional Office:

Boston 02203 (JFK Federal Bldg., Government Center, Local 617-227-4600, Other areas 800-827-0520.

Towns of Fall River & New Bedford, counties of Barnstable, Dukes, Nantucket, Bristol, part of Plymouth served by Providence, R.I., RO 800-827-0389

Vet Centers:

Brockton 02401 (1041 Pearl St., 508-580-2730/31)

Boston 02215 (665 Beacon St., 617-424-0065 or 565-6195)

Lowell 01852 (73 East Merrimack St., 617-453-1151)

New Bedford 02740 (468 North St., 508-999-6920)

Springfield 01103 (1985 Main St., 413-737-5167)

Worcester 01605 (108 Grove St., 508-752-3526)

MICHIGAN

Medical Centers:
* Allen Park 48101 (Southfield & Outer Drive, 313-562-6000)
* Ann Arbor 48105 (2215 Fuller Rd., 313-769-7100)
* Battle Creek 49016 (5500 Armstrong Rd., 616-966-5600)
#* Iron Mountain 49801 (H Street, 906-774-3300)
* Saginaw 48602 (1500 Weiss St., 517-793-2340)

Clinics:
Gaylord 49735 (850 N. Otsego, 517-732-7525)
Grand Rapids 49503 (260 Jefferson St., S.E. 616-459-2200)

Regional Office:
Detroit 48226 (Patrick V. McNamara Federal Bldg., 477 Michigan Ave., Local 313-964-5110, Statewide 800-827-1996)

Vet Centers:
Grand Rapids 49507 (1940 Eastern Ave., S.E., 616-243-0385)
Lincoln Park 48146 (1766 Fort St., 313-381-1370)
Oak Park 48237 (20820 Greenfield Rd., 313-967-0040)

MINNESOTA

Medical Centers:
Minneapolis 55417 (One Veterans Dr., 612-725-2000)
#* St. Cloud 56303 (4801 8th St. North, 612-252-1670)

Clinic:
St. Paul 55111 (Fort Snelling, 612-725-6767)

Regional Office:
St. Paul 55111 (Federal Bldg., Fort Snelling, Local 612-726-1454. Other areas, 800-827-0646)
Counties of Becker, Beltrami, Clay, Clearwater, Kittson, Lake of the Woods, Mahnomen, Marshall, Norman, Otter Tail, Pennington, Polk, Red Lake, Roseau, Wilkin served by Fargo, N.D., RO, 800-437-4668)

Vet Centers:
Duluth 55802 (405 E. Superior St., 218-722-8654)
St. Paul 55114 (2480 University Ave., 612-644-4022)

MISSISSIPPI

Medical Centers:
#* Biloxi 39531 (400 Veterans Ave., 601-388-5541)
* Jackson 39216 (1500 E. Woodrow Wilson Dr., 601-362-4471)

Regional Office:
Jackson 39269 (100 W. Capitol St., Local 601-965-4873, Statewide 800-827-2028)

Vet Centers:
> Biloxi 39530 (767 W. Jackson St., 601-435-5414)
> Jackson 39206 (4436 N. State St., Suite A3, 601-965-5727)

MISSOURI

Medical Centers:
> * Columbia 65201 (800 Hospital Dr., 314-443-2511)
> Kansas City 64128 (4801 Linwood Blvd., 816-861-4700)
> * Poplar Bluff 63901 (1500 N. Westwood Blvd., 314-686-4151)
> * St. Louis 63106 (John Cochran Div., 915 N. Grand Blvd., 314-652-4100)
> St. Louis 63125 (Jefferson Barracks Div., 314-487-0400)

Clinic:
> Mt. Vernon 65712 (600 N. Main St., 417-46-4000)

Regional Office:
> St. Louis 63103 (Federal Bldg., 1520 Market St., Local 314-342-1171, Statewide 800-827-0819).
> Benefits Office: Kansas City 64106 (Federal Ofc. Bldg., 601 E. 12th St., 800-827-0819)

Vet Centers:
> Kansas City 64111 (3931 Main St., 816-753-1866 or 753-1974)
> St. Louis 63103 (2345 Pine St., 314-231-1260)

MONTANA

Medical Centers:
> Fort Harrison 59636 (William St. off of Hwy. 12 W., 406-442-6410)
> * Miles City 59301 (210 S. Winchester, 406-232-3060)

Clinic:
> Billings 59101 (1127 Alderson Ave., 406-657-6786)

Regional Office:
> Fort Harrison 59636 (Local: Fort Harrison/Helena 406-447-7975, Statewide 800-827-0508.

Vet Centers:
> Billings 59102 (1948 Grand Ave., 406-657-6071)
> Missoula 59802 (500 N. Higgins Ave., 406-721-4918)

NEBRASKA

Medical Centers:
> * Grand Island 68803 (2201 N. Broad Well, 308-382-3660)
> Lincoln 68510 (600 S. 70th St., 402-489-3802)
> Omaha 68105 (4101 Woolworth Ave., 402-346-8800)

Regional Office:
> Lincoln 68516 (5631 S. 48th St., Local 402-437-5001, Statewide 800-827-6544)

Vet Centers:
> Lincoln 68508 (920 L St., 402-476-9736)
> Omaha 68106 (5123 Leavenworth St., 402-553-2068)

NEVADA

Medical Center:
> * Reno 89520 (1000 Locust St., 702-786-7200)

Clinic:
> Las Vegas 89102 (1703 W. Charleston, 702-385-3700)

Regional Office:
> Reno 89520 (1201 Terminal Way, Local 702-329-9244, Statewide 800-827-8014. Also California counties Alpine, Lassen, Modoc and Mono)

Vet Centers:
> Las Vegas 89101 (704 S. 6th St., 702-388-6368)
> Reno 89503 (1155 W. 4th St., Suite 101, 702-323-1294)

NEW HAMPSHIRE

Medical Center:
> * Manchester 03104 (718 Smyth Rd., 603-624-4366)

Regional Office:
> Manchester 03101 (Norris Cotton Federal Bldg., 275 Chestnut St., Local 603-666-7785, Statewide 800-827-0858)

Vet Center:
> Manchester 03104 (103 Liberty St., 603-668-7060)

NEW JERSEY

Medical Centers:
> * East Orange 07019 (Tremont Ave. & S. Center, 201-676-1000)
> #* Lyons 07939 (Valley & Knollcroft Rd., 201-647-0180)

Clinic:
> Brick 08724 (970 Rt. 70, 908-206-8900)

Regional Office:
> Newark 07102 (20 Washington Pl., Local 201-645-2150, Statewide 800-827-2006.

Vet Centers:
> Jersey City 07306 (115 Christopher Columbus Dr., 201-656-6886 or 656-7484)
> Linwood 08221 (222 New Road, Bldg. 2, Suite 4, 609-927-8387)
> Newark 07102 (75 Halsey St., 201-622-6940)
> Trenton 08608 (318 East State St., 609-989-2260)

NEW MEXICO

Medical Center:
* Albuquerque 87108 (2100 Ridgecrest Dr., S.E., 505-265-1711)

Regional Office:
Albuquerque 87102 (Dennis Chavez Federal Bldg., 500 Gold Ave., S.W., Local 505-766-3361, Statewide 800-827-8019)

Vet Centers:
Albuquerque 87107 (4603 4th St., N.W., 505-345-8366 or 345-8876)
Farmington 87402 (4251 E. Main, Suite B, 505-327-9684)
Santa Fe 87505 (1996 Warner St., Warner Plaza, Suite 5, 505-988-6562)

NEW YORK

Medical Centers:
* Albany 12208 (113 Holland Ave., 518-462-3311)
* Batavia 14020 (Redfield Pkwy., 716-343-7500)
#* Bath 14810 (Argonne Ave., 607-776-2111)
* Bronx 10468 (130 W. Kingsbridge Rd., 212-584-9000)
#* Brooklyn 11209 (800 Poly Place, 718-630-3500)
* Buffalo 14215 (3495 Bailey Ave., 716-834-9200)
#* Canandaigua 14424 (Ft. Hill Ave., 716-394-2000)
* Castle Point 12511 (914-831-2000)
#* Montrose 10548 (Old Albany Post Rd., 914-737-4400)
New York City 10010 (1st Ave. & E. 24th St., 212-686-7500)

Medical Centers:
Northport 11768 (Middleville Rd., Long Island, 516-261-4400)
* Syracuse 13210 (Irving Ave. & University Pl., 315-476-7461)

Clinics:
Brooklyn 11205 (35 Ryerson St., 212-330-7785)
New York City 10001 (252 7th Ave. & 24th St., 212-620-6636)
Rochester 14614 (Federal Ofc. Bldg. & Courthouse, 100 State St., 716-263-5734)

Regional Offices:
Buffalo 14202 (Federal Bldg., 111 W. Huron St., Local 716-846-5191, or 800-827-0619).
New York City 10001 (252 Seventh Ave. at 24th St., Local 212-620-6901; counties of Albany, Bronx, Clinton, Columbia, Delaware, Dutchess, Essex, Franklin, Fulton, Greene, Hamilton, Kings, Montgomery, Nassau, New York, Orange, Otsego, Putnam, Queens, Rensselaer, Richmond, Rockland, Saratoga, Schenectady, Schoharie, Suffolk, Sullivan, Ulster, Warren, Washington, Westchester 800-827-8954).

Benefits Offices:
Albany 12207 (Leo W. O'Brian Federal Bldg., Clinton Ave., Western New York areas, 800-827-0619).

Rochester 14614 (Federal Office Bldg. & Courthouse, 100 State St., 800-827-0619)

Syracuse 13202 (344 W. Genesee St., 800-827-0619) & N. Pearl St., 800-827-8954)

Vet Centers:

Albany 12206 (875 Central Ave., 518-438-2505)

Babylon 11702 (116 West Main St., 516-661-3930

Bronx 10458 (226 East Fordham Rd., Rms. 216-217, 212-367-3500)

Brooklyn 11201 (165 Cadman Plaza, East, 718-330-2825)

Buffalo 14209 (351 Linwood Ave., 716-882-0505 or 882-0508)

New York 10036 (120 West 44th St., 212-944-2931 or 944-2932)

Rochester 14608 (134 S. Fitzhugh St., 716-263-5710)

Staten Island 10301 (150 Richmond Terrace, 718-816-6899 or 816-4499)

Syracuse 13203 (210 North Townsend St., 315-423-5690)

White Plains 10601 (200 Hamilton Ave., 914-682-6850)

Woodhaven 11421 (75-10B 91st. Ave., 718-296-2871)

NORTH CAROLINA

Medical Centers:

*Asheville 28805 (1100 Tunnel Rd., 704-298-7911)

Durham 27705 (508 Fulton St., 919-286-0411)

*Fayetteville 28301 (2300 Ramsey St., 919-488-2120)

*Salisbury 28144 (1601 Brenner Ave., 704-638-9000)

Clinic:

Winston-Salem 27155 (Federal Bldg., 251 N. Main St., 919-631-5562)

Regional Office:

Winston-Salem 27155 (Federal Bldg., 251 N. Main St., Local 919-748-1800, Statewide 800-827-3559.

Vet Centers:

Charlotte 28202 (223 S. Brevard St., Suite 103, 704-333-6107)

Fayetteville 28301 (4 Market Square, 919-323-4908)

Greensboro 27406 (2009 Elm-Eugene St., 919-333-5366)

Greenville 27834 (150 Arlington Blvd., Suite B, 919-355-7920)

NORTH DAKOTA

Medical Center:

Fargo 58102 (2101 Elm St., 701-232-3241)

Regional Office:

Fargo 58102 (655 First Ave. North; 2101 North Elm St.—mail only, Local 701-293-3656, Statewide 800-827-4313)

Vet Centers:

Fargo 58103 (1322 Gateway Dr., 701-237-0942)

Minot 58701 (108 East Burdick Expressway, 701-852-0177)

OHIO

Medical Centers:
#*Brecksville 44141 (10000 Brecksville Rd., 216-526-3030)
  *Chillicothe 45601 (17273 State Route 104, 614-773-1141)
#*Cincinnati 45220 (3200 Vine St., 513-861-3100)
  Cleveland 44106 (10701 East Boulevard, 216-791-3800)
#*Dayton 45428 (4100 W. 3rd St., 513-268-6511)
Clinics:
  Canton 44702 (221 Third St., S.E., 216-489-4660)
  Columbus 43221 (2090 Kenny Rd., 614-469-5146)
  Toledo 43614 (3333 Glendale Ave., 419-259-2000)
  Youngstown 44505 (2031 Belmont, 216-740-9200)
Regional Office:
  Cleveland 44199 (Anthony J. Celebrezze Federal Bldg., 1240 E. 9th St.,
    Local 216-621-5050, Statewide 800-827-8272).
Benefits Offices:
  Cincinnati 45202 (The Society Bank Center, Suite 210, 36 East 7th St.,
    800-827-8272)
  Columbus 43215 (Federal Bldg., Rm. 309, 200 N. High St., 800-827-8272)
Vet Centers:
  Cincinnati 45219 (30 East Hollister St., 513-569-7140)
  Cleveland 44111 (11511 Lorain Ave., 216-671-8530)
  Cleveland Heights 44118 (2134 Lee Rd., 216-932-8471)
  Columbus 43205 (1054 E. Broad St., 614-253-3500)
  Dayton 45402 (6 S. Patterson Blvd., 513-461-9150)

OKLAHOMA

Medical Centers:
  Muskogee 74401 (Honor Heights Dr., 918-683-3261)
  Oklahoma City 73104 (921 N.E. 13th St., 405-270-0501)
Clinic:
  Tulsa 74121 (635 W. 11th St., 918-581-7161)
Regional Office:
  Muskogee 74401 (Federal Bldg., 125 S. Main St., Local 918-687-2500,
    Statewide 800-827-2206).
Benefits Office:
  Oklahoma City 73102 (200 N.W. 5th St., 800-827-2206)
Vet Centers:
  Oklahoma City 73105 (3033 N. Walnut, Suite 101W, 405-270-5184)
  Tulsa 74101 (1855 E. 15th St., 918-581-7105)

OREGON

Medical Centers:
#*Portland 97207 (3710 SW U.S. Veterans Hospital Rd., 503-257-2500)
*Roseburg 97470 (New Garden Valley Blvd., 503-672-4411)
Clinic:
Bandon 97411 (33 Michigan St. SE, 503-347-4736)
Eugene 97403 (138 W. 8th St., 503-425-6481
Portland 97207 (8909 SW Barbur Blvd., 503-244-9222)
Domiciliary:
White City 97501 (Hwy. 62, 503-826-2111)
Regional Office:
Portland 97204 (Federal Bldg., 1220 S.W. 3rd Ave., Local 503-221-2431,
Statewide 800-827-0495)
Vet Centers:
Eugene 97403 (1966 Garden Ave., 503-465-6918)
Grants Pass 95726 (615 N.W. 5th St., 503-479-6912)
Portland 97220 (8383 N.E. Sandy Blvd., Suite 110, 503-273-5370)
Salem 97301 (318 Church St., N.E., 503-362-9911)

PENNSYLVANIA

Medical Centers:
*Altoona 16603 (Pleasant Valley Blvd., 814-943-8164)
#*Butler 16001 (New Castle Rd., 412-287-4781)
#*Coatesville 19320 (Black Horse Rd., 215-384-7711)
*Erie 16501 (135 E. 38th St., 814-868-8661)
*Lebanon 17042 (South Lincoln Ave., 717-272-6621)
*Philadelphia 19104 (University & Woodland Aves., 215-382-2400)
*Pittsburgh 15240 (University Drive C, 412-683-3000)
Pittsburgh 15206 (Highland Dr., 412-363-4900)
*Wilkes-Barre 18711 (1111 E. End Blvd., 717-824-3521)
Clinics:
Allentown 18103 (2937 Hamilton Blvd., 215-776-4304)
Harrisburg 17108 (Federal Bldg., 228 Walnut St., 717-782-4590)
Philadelphia 19102 (1421 Cherry St., 215-597-7244)
Sayre 18840 (Guthrie Square, 717-888-8062)
Regional Offices:
Philadelphia 19101 (RO & Insurance Center, P.O. Box 8079, 5000
Wissahickon Ave., Local 215-438-5225; counties of: Adams, Berks,
Bradford, Bucks, Cameron, Carbon, Centre, Chester, Clinton,
Columbia, Cumberland, Dauphin, Delaware, Franklin, Juniata,
Lackawanna, Lancaster, Lebanon, Lehigh, Luzerne, Lycoming, Mifflin,
Monroe, Montgomery, Montour, Northampton, Northumberland,
Perry Philadelphia, Pike, Potter, Schuylkill, Snyder, Sullivan,

Susquehanna, Tioga, Union, Wayne, Wyoming, York 800-869-8387; recorded benefits information 215-951-5368, 24-hour availability).
Pittsburgh 15222 (1000 Liberty Ave., Local 412-281-4233, Other Western Pennsylvania areas 800-827-0839)

Benefits Office:
Wilkes-Barre 18701 (19-27 N. Main St., 800-869-8387)

Vet Centers:
Erie 16501 (G. Daniel Baldwin Bldg., 1000 State St., Suites 1 & 2, 814-453-7955)
Harrisburg 17110 (1007 North Front St., 717-782-3954)
McKeesport 15132 (500 Walnut St., 412-678-7704)
Philadelphia 19107 (1026 Arch St., 215-627-0238)
Philadelphia 19120 (101 E. Olney Ave., Box C-7, 215-924-4670)
Pittsburgh 15222 (954 Penn Ave., 412-765-1193)
Scranton 18509 (959 Wyoming Ave., 717-344-2676)

PHILIPPINES

Regional Office:
Manila 96440 (1131 Roxas Blvd., APO AP 96440, San Francisco Local 810-521-7521, from U.S. 011632 521-7116, ext. 2577 or 2220)

PUERTO RICO

Medical Center:
*San Juan 00927 (1 Veterans Plaza, Rio Piedras GPO Box 5800, 809-758-7575)

Clinic:
Mayaguez 00708 (Carr. Estatal #2, Frente A Res. Sultana, 809-831-3400)
Ponce 00731 (Reparada Industrial Lot #1, Calle Principal, 809-841-3115)

Regional Office:
San Juan 00936 (U.S. Courthouse & Federal Bldg., Carlos E. Chardon St., Hato Rey, GPO Box 4867, Local 809-766-5141, Island-wide 800-462-4135. Direct dial from U.S. Virgin Islands 800-474-2976)

Vet Centers:
Arecibo 00612 (52 Gonzalo Marin St., 809-879-4510 or 879-4581)
Ponce 00731 (35 Mayor St., 809-841-3260)
Rio Piedras 00921 (Condomino Medical Center Plaza, Suite LC8A & LC9, La Riviera, 809-783-8794)

RHODE ISLAND

Medical Center:
Providence 02908 (Davis Park, 401-273-7100)

Regional Office:
Providence 02903 (380 Westminster Mall, Local 401-273-4910, Statewide 800-827-0389
Vet Center:
Cranston 02920 (789 Park Ave., 401-467-2046 or 467-2056)

SOUTH CAROLINA

Medical Centers:
Charleston 29401 (109 Bee St., 803-577-5011)
*Columbia 29209 (Gamers Ferry Rd., 803-774-4000)
Clinic:
Greenville 29609 (120 Mallard St., 803-232-7303)
Regional Office:
Columbia 29201 (1801 Assembly St., Local 803-765-5861, Statewide 800-827-2035.
Vet Centers:
Columbia 29201 (1313 Elmwood Ave., 803-765-9944)
Greenville 29601 (904 Pendleton St., 803-271-2711)
North Charleston 29418 (5603A Rivers Ave., 803-747-8387)

SOUTH DAKOTA

Medical Centers:
Fort Meade 57741 (I 90/Hwy. 34, 605-347-2511)
#Hot Springs 57747 (Off 5th St., 605-745-4101)
*Sioux Falls 57117 (601 S. Cliff Ave., Suite C, 605-336-3230)
Regional Office:
Sioux Falls 57117 (P.O. Box 5046, 2501 W. 22nd St., Local 605-336-3496, Statewide 800-827-0442)
Vet Centers:
Rapid City 57701 (610 Kansas City St., 605-348-0077 or 348-1752)
Sioux Falls 57104 (601 S. Cliff Ave., Suite A, 605-332-0856)

TENNESSEE

Medical Centers:
*Memphis 38104 (1030 Jefferson Ave., 901-523-8990)
#*Mountain Home 37684 (Sidney & Lamont St., 615-926-1171)
*Murfreesboro 37129 (3400 Lebanon Rd., 615-893-1360)
Nashville 37203 (1310 24th Ave., South, 615-327-4751)
Clinics:
Chattanooga 37411 (Bldg. 6300 East Gate Center, 615-855-6550)
Knoxville 37923 (9047 Executive Park Dr., Suite 100, 615-549-9319)

Regional Office:
 Nashville 37203 (110 9th Ave. South, Local 615-736-5251, Statewide 800-827-2026.

Vet Centers:
 Chattanooga 37404 (425 Cumberland St., Suite 140, 615-752-5234)
 Johnson City 37601 (703 South Roan St., 615-928-8387)
 Knoxville 37914 (2817 East Magnolia Ave., 615-971-5866)
 Memphis 38104 (1835 Union, Suite 100, 901-722-2510)

TEXAS

Medical Centers:
 *Amarillo 79106 (6010 Amarillo Blvd., West, 806-355-9703)
 *Big Spring 79720 (2400 S. Gregg St., 915-263-7361)
 #*Bonham 75418 (1201 E. Ninth, 903-583-2111)
 #*Dallas 75216 (4500 S. Lancaster Rd., 214-376-5451)
 *Houston 77030 (2002 Holcombe Blvd., 713-791-1414)
 *Kerrville 78028 (3600 Memorial Blvd., 512-896-2020)
 Marlin 76661 (1016 Ward St., 817-883-3511)
 San Antonio 78284 (7400 Merton Minter Blvd., 512-617-5300)
 #*Temple 76504 (1901 S. First, 817-778-4811)
 #*Waco 76711 (4800 Memorial Dr., 817-752-6581)

Clinics:
 Beaumont 77701 (3385 Fannin St., 409-839-2480)
 Corpus Christi 78405 (5283 Old Brownsville Rd., 512-888-3251)
 El Paso 79925 (5919 Brook Hollow Dr., 915-540-7892)
 Laredo 78043 (2359 E. Saunders Ave., 512-725-7060)
 Lubbock 79410 (4902 34th St., #10, 806-796-7900)
 Lufkin 75901 (1301 Frank Ave., 409-637-1342)
 McAllen 78501 (2101 S. Rowe Blvd., 512-618-7100)
 San Antonio 78229 (9502 Computer Dr., 512-641-2672)
 Victoria 77901 (2710 E. Airline Dr., 512-572-0006)

Regional Offices:
 Houston 77054 (2515 Murworth Dr., Local 713-664-4664, counties of Angelina, Aransas, Atacosa, Austin, Bandera, Bee, Bexar, Blanco, Brazoria, Brewster, Brooks, Caldwell, Calhoun, Cameron, Chambers, Colorado, Comal, Crockett, DeWitt, Dimitt, Duval Edwards, Fort Bend, Frio, Galveston, Gillespie, Goliad, Gonzales, Grimes, Guadalupe, Hardin, Harris, Hays, Hidalgo, Houston, Jackson, Jasper, Jefferson, Jim Hogg, Jim Wells, Karnes, Kendall, Kenedy, Kerr, Kimble, Kinney, Kleberg, LaSalle, Lavaca, Liberty, Live Oak, McCulloch, McMullen, Mason, Matagorda, Maverick, Medina, Menard, Montgomery, Nacog-doches, Newton, Nueces, Orange, Pecos, Polk, Real, Refugio, Sabine, San Augustine, San Jacinto, San Patrico, Schleicher, Shelby, Starr,

Sutton, Terrell, Trinity, Tyler, Uvalde, Val Verde, Victoria, Walker, Waller, Washington, Webb, Wharton, Willacy, Wilson, Zapata, Zavala, 800-827-2021)

Waco 76799 (1400 N. Valley Mills Dr., local, 817-772-3060, all other counties not listed under Houston, 800-827-2102)

Bowie County (served by Little Rock, AR, RO, 800-827-2033, other counties, 800-792-3271)

Benefits Offices:

Dallas 75242 (U.S. Courthouse & Federal Ofc. Bldg., 1100 Commerce St., 800-827-2012)

Fort Worth 76102 (819 Taylor St., 800-827-2012)

Lubbock 79401 (Federal Bldg., 1205 Texas Ave., 800-827-2012)

San Antonio 78229-2041 (3601 Bluemel Rd., 512-225-5511, 800-827-2021)

Vet Centers:

Amarillo 79109 (3414-E Olsen Blvd., 806-376-2127)

Austin 78723 (3401 Manor Rd., Suite 102, 512-476-0607)

Corpus Christi 78404 (3166 Reid Dr., Suite 1, 512-888-3101)

Dallas 75244 (5232 Forest Lane, Suite 111, 214-361-5896)

El Paso 79903 (2121 Wyoming St., 915-542-2851)

Fort Worth 76104 (1305 W. Magnolia, Suite B, 817-921-3733)

Houston 77004 (4905A San Jacinto, 713-522-5354 or 522-5376)

Houston 77007 (8100 Washington Ave., Suite 120, 713-880-8387)

Laredo 78041 (6020 McPherson Rd. #1, 512-723-4680)

Lubbock 79410 (3208 34th St., 806-743-7551)

McAllen 78501 (1317 E. Hackberry St., 512-631-2147)

Midland 79703 (3404 West Illinois, Suite 1, 915-697-8222)

San Antonio 78212 (231 W. Cypress St., 512-229-4025)

UTAH

Medical Center:

*Salt Lake City 84148 (500 Foothill Blvd., 801-582-1565)

Regional Office:

Salt Lake City 84147 (P.O. Box 11500, Federal Bldg., 125 S. State St., Local 801-524-5960, Statewide 800-827-8016.

Vet Center:

Provo 84601 (750 North 200 West, Suite 105, 801-377-1117)

Salt Lake City 84106 (1354 East 3300, South, 801-584-1294)

VERMONT

Medical Center:

*White River Junction 05001 (N. Hartland Rd., 802-295-9363)

Regional Office:
    White River Junction 05001 (N. Hartland Rd., Local 802-296-5177, State-
    wide 800-827-6558)
Vet Centers:
    South Burlington 05401 (359 Dorset St., 802-862-1806)
    White River Junction 05001 (Gilman Office Center, Bldg. #2, Holiday Inn
    Dr., 802-295-2908)

VIRGINIA

Medical Centers:
    #*Hampton 23667 (Emancipation Dr., 804-722-9961)
    *Richmond 23249 (1201 Broad Rock Rd., 804-230-0001)
    *Salem 24153 (1970 Roanoke Blvd., 703-982-2463)
Regional Office:
    Roanoke 24011 (210 Franklin Rd., S.W., Local 703-982-6440; Northern
    Virginia counties of Arlington & Fairfax, cities of Alexandria, Fairfax,
    Falls Church served by Washington, D.C., RO 202-872-1151. Other
    areas 800-827-2018)
Vet Centers:
    Norfolk 23505 (7450-1/2 Tidewater Dr., 804-587-1338)
    Richmond 23220 (3022 W. Clay St., 804-353-8958)
    Roanoke 24016 (320 Mountain Ave., S.W. 703-342-9726)
    Springfield 22150 (7024 Spring Garden Dr., Brookfield Plaza, 703-866-
    0924)

VIRGIN ISLANDS

Vet Centers:
    St. Croix 00820 (United Shopping Plaza, Suite 4—Christiansted, 809-
    778-5553 or 778-5755)
    St. Thomas 00801 (Havensight Mall, 809-774-6674)

WASHINGTON

Medical Centers:
    *Seattle 98108 (1660 S. Columbian Way, 206-762-1010)
    Spokane 99208 (N. 4815 Assembly St., 509-328-4521)
    #*Tacoma 98493 (American Lake, 206-582-8440)
    *Walla Walla 99362 (77 Wainwright Dr., 509-525-5200)
Regional Office:
    Seattle 98174 (Federal Bldg., 915 2nd Ave., Local 206-624-7200, State-
    wide 800-827-0638)
Vet Centers:
    Seattle 98122 (1322 East Pike St., 206-442-2706)

Spokane 99201 (West 1708 Mission St., 509-327-0274)
Tacoma 98408 (4801 Pacific Ave., 206-473-0731)

WEST VIRGINIA

Medical Centers:
*Beckley 25801 (200 Veterans Ave., 304-255-2121)
Clarksburg 26301 (Milford/Chestnut Sts., 304-623-3461)
Huntington 25704 (1540 Spring Valley Dr., 304-429-6741)
#*Martinsburg 25410 (Route 9, 304-263-0811)

Regional Office:
Huntington 25701 (640 Fourth Ave., Local 304-529-5720, Statewide 800-827-2052; counties of Brooke, Hancock, Marshall, Ohio served by Pittsburgh, Pa., RO)

Vet Centers:
Beckley 25801 (101 Ellison Ave., 304-252-8220 or 252-8229)
Charleston 25311 (1591 Washington St. East, 304-343-3825)
Huntington 25701 (1014 6th Ave., 304-523-8387)
Martinsburg 25401 (138 West King St., 304-263-6776/7)
Morgantown 26505 (1191 Pineview Dr., 304-291-4001)
Princeton 24740 (905 Mercer St., 304-425-5653 or 425-5661)
Wheeling 26003 (1070 Market St., 304-232-0587, ext. 271)

WISCONSIN

Medical Centers:
Madison 53705 (2500 Overlook Terrace, 608-256-1901)
#*Milwaukee 53295 (5000 W. National Ave., 414-384-2000)
*Tomah 54660 (County Trunk E, 608-372-3971)

Clinic:
Superior 54880 (Tower Ave., 715-392-9711)

Regional Office:
Milwaukee 53295 (5000 W. National Ave., Bldg. 6, Local 414-383-8680, Statewide 800-827-0464)

Vet Centers:
Madison 53703 (147 South Butler St., 608-264-5343)
Milwaukee 53208 (3400 Wisconsin, 414-344-5504)

WYOMING

Medical Centers:
*Cheyenne 82001 (2360 E. Pershing Blvd., 307-778-7550)
Sheridan 82801 (Fort Rd., 307-672-3473)

Regional Office:
    Cheyenne 82001 (2360 E. Pershing Blvd., Local 307-778-7396, Statewide
    800-827-3188)
Vet Centers:
    Casper 82601 (111 S. Jefferson, 307-235-8010)
    Cheyenne 82001 (3130 Henderson Dr., 307-778-7370)

DOMICILIARY CARE

Federal and state governments maintain homes to provide care for veterans disabled by age or disease who are not in need of acute hospitalization or skilled nursing services provided by nursing homes. Usually, such veterans are ambulatory and physically capable of tending to their personal needs, but without adequate means of financial support.

FEDERAL DOMICILIARY CARE

The first federally supported domiciliary began operation after the Civil War following congressional authorization for the construction of soldiers homes. The first soldiers home, the National Home for Disabled Volunteer Soldiers, began operation in Togus, Maine, in 1867. Other veterans homes for disabled veterans were constructed in the 1800's at Pikesville, Maryland, and Little Rock, Arkansas. Over the ensuing 90 years, federal domiciliaries have been established in a number of locations. (See VA facilities listing beginning on page 145).

The VA has set forth physical and mental criteria required for veterans to be cared for in its domiciliary homes. The veteran must be able to carry out the following functions:

- Perform all bathroom-related activities and/or control body elimination by using prosthesis
- Dress with minimum assistance
- Self-feed
- Be ambulatory or able to use a wheelchair effectively
- Assist in maintaining and operating living quarters
- Make rational and competent decisions regarding remaining at or leaving the facility.

With regard to eligibility for domiciliary care, the VA has stated that "domiciliary care, as the term implies, is the provision of a home, with such ambulant medical care as is needed. To be entitled to domiciliary care, the applicant must consistently have a disability, disease or injury which is essentially chronic in type and is producing disablement of such a degree and probably persistency as will incapacitate from earning a living for a prospective period."

Eligible veterans must have served in the active military forces, must not have received a dishonorable discharge, must be sufficiently incapacitated to prevent earning a living, and must have no adequate means of support. Priorities for acceptance into a VA domiciliary depend on whether the veteran has a service-incurred or aggravated disability, if the veteran served in wartime, income, and whether compensation is being paid.

The United States Naval Home and the United States Soldiers' and Airmen's Home have many of the features of VA-operated domiciliaries although neither are under VA jurisdiction. Legislation passed in 1990 incorporated both homes into an independent federal entity, the Armed Forces Retirement Home. They are managed locally by advisory boards.

A 25% "user fee" is assessed on applicants receiving federal annuities, including military retirement pay, VA compensation, civil service retirement or Social Security benefits.

Legislation which became effective in November 1991 amended admissions criteria for both homes as follows:

- *Retirees* must be 60 years of age (previously there was no age requirement).
- Up to one-half of service can be commissioned (previously commissioned time did not count).
- No requirement for Regular service (previously there was a requirement for Regular Army or Regular Air Force service).
- Veterans unable to earn a livelihood due to a non-service-connected disability must have served in a war theater or received hostile fire special pay (previously there was no requirement for being in the war theater, only for service during wartime).
- Female veterans who were volunteers prior to 1948 (WAAC and WAC) are now eligible (previously they were not eligible because they were not Regular).
- Other veterans with compelling reasons are eligible under criteria established by the Home Board.

For admissions information, write or call: **U.S. Soldiers' and Airmen's Home**, Admission Office, Washington, D.C. 20317 (1-800-422-9988) or the **U.S. Naval Home**, 01800 E. Beach Blvd., Gulfport, Miss. 37507 (601-896-3110).

UNITED STATES NAVAL HOME

The United States Naval Home is a modern, eleven-story building containing 580 rooms. First established in 1833, the Naval Home was relocated to Gulfport, Mississippi, in 1976. It is essentially a large "family home," operated to serve the living needs of Navy and Coast Guard veterans. Residents must be able to manage their personal finances, care for their rooms, and conduct normal living activities without assistance. Although residents are required to be self-sufficient when admitted, they are provided all possible assistance within the Naval Home's capabilities. The Home has a limited medical care facility, but all residents are solely responsible for any additional medical care which may be needed.

UNITED STATES SOLDIERS' AND AIRMEN'S HOME

The United States Soldiers' and Airmen's Home is a home for distinguished enlisted men and warrant officer veterans who served in the Army and Air Force. The Home, located in Washington, D.C., was created as a federal entity. The 300-acre Home includes 640 modern single rooms with complete living, dining, medical, and recreational facilities and activities.

The Home is not supported by taxpayers' funds, being completely supported by monthly deductions from those eligible for membership and from interest earned on trust funds and other sources.

OTHER HOUSING ALTERNATIVES

Each of the services has established facilities to provide military widows, retirees, and others who qualify, with housing and other accommodations designed primarily for the aged and those in need of comfort, security, and companionship. The Air Force Enlisted Men's Widows and Dependents Home Foundations, Inc., receives the main portion of its funding from the annual Air Force Assistance Fund Campaign.

Knollwood, formerly the Army Distaff Hall, containing 245 units and located in Washington, D.C., was opened in 1962 and is operated by the Army Distaff Foundation, Inc. Eligibility for residence is limited to retired military officers and their widows, mothers, daughters, sisters or mothers-in-law.

Vinson Hall, opened in 1969 in McLean, Virginia, is operated by the Navy Marine Coast Guard Residence Foundation. It is a residence community for retired sea service officers, their dependents, and surviving spouses. There are 255 apartment living units, an infirmary, a dining room and many other amenities.

Air Force Village, located in San Antonio, Texas, has been open since 1970 to widows of Air Force officers, retired Air Force officers (single or with spouse) and young widows of Air Force officers with or without children during an adjustment period of up to one year. There are 374 apartment living units and a health care facility including a licensed skilled care 68-bed nursing home. Village II has 316 residential apartments and construction of a 92-unit garden home addition is under way. Retired officers of all uniformed services are eligible for residency at both villages.

The Air Force Enlisted Men's Widows and Dependents Home Foundation, Inc., in Fort Walton Beach, Florida, is the parent organization of Teresa Village, a 123-unit complex, and Bob Hope Village, which consists of 256 apartments. Any widow or widower, age 55 or older, whose spouse was a retired enlisted person from the Regular Air Force, Air National Guard, or Air Force Reserve, is eligible to reside in the facilities. Younger widows may be admitted under special circumstances, and a limited number of retired couples, age 62 or older, may be admitted.

STATE DOMICILIARY CARE

Congress established the State Veterans Home Program in 1888. That program still provides federal financing to states to construct and operate veterans homes. Prior to that legislation, some states built homes to meet the needs of Civil War veterans. The VA supports state veterans homes to meet the needs of a growing population of aging veterans. VA support of the program amounts to as much as 65 percent of construction costs as well as providing regular payments to defray the cost of caring for veterans in state homes. In 1987 the VA provided state homes $40.3 million in construction grants and $66.9 million in veteran-support payments.

Thirty-six states maintain homes for veterans. Requirements for accepting applicants vary among the states, especially as they relate to income, length of state residency, and admittance of family members. Following is a list of state veterans homes; those which accept female veterans and/or dependents are indicated.

ARKANSAS
  Arkansas Veterans Home, Little Rock 72204 (501-370-3820)
CALIFORNIA
  Veterans' Home of California, Yountville 94599*
COLORADO
  The Monte Vista Golden Age Center, Homelake 81135 (303-625-0842)**
CONNECTICUT
  Veterans' Home and Hospital, Rocky Hill 06067 (203-721-5892)
FLORIDA
  Veterans' Home of Florida, Lake City 32055 (904-758-0600)
GEORGIA
  Georgia War Veterans' Home, Milledgeville 31061 (912-453-4751)

IDAHO
Idaho State Veterans Home, P.O. Box 7765, Boise 83707 (208-334-5000)
ILLINOIS
Illinois Soldiers' and Sailors' Home, Quincy 62301 (217-228-9625)**
INDIANA
Indiana State Soldiers Home, Lafayette 57901 (317-463-1502)**
IOWA
Iowa Soldiers' Home, Marshalltown 50158 (515-242-5331)**
KANSAS
Kansas Soldiers' Home, Fort Dodge 67843 (913-296-3976)**
LOUISIANA
Louisiana War Veterans Home, P.O. Box 748, Jackson 70748 (504-634-5265)*
MAINE
Maine Veterans' Home, State House Station 105, Augusta 04333 (207-289-4060)
MARYLAND
Maryland Veterans Home, Charlotte Hall 20622 (410-884-8171)
MASSACHUSETTS
Soldiers' Home, Chelsea 01824 (617-727-3578)
Soldiers' Home, Holyoke 01040 (617-727-3578)**
MICHIGAN
Michigan Veterans Facility, Grand Rapids 49505 (517-373-3130)**
Michigan Veterans Facility, Marquette 49855 (517-373-3130)**
MINNESOTA
Minnesota Veterans Home, Minneapolis 55417 (612-721-0600)**
Hastings Veterans Home, Hastings 55033 (612-458-8500)
MISSOURI
State Federal Soldiers' Home of Missouri, St. James 65559 (314-751-3779)**
MONTANA
Montana Soldiers' Home, Columbia Falls 59912 (406-892-3256)**
NEBRASKA
Nebraska Veterans Home, Grand Island 68803 (308-382-9420)**
Nebraska Veterans Home, Norfolk 68702 (402-644-3177)**
Nebraska Veterans Home, Scottsbluff 69361 (308-632-3381)**
Nebraska Veterans Home, Omaha 68164 (402-595-2180)**
NEW HAMPSHIRE
New Hampshire Soldiers' Home, Tilton 03276 (603-624-9230)
NEW JERSEY
New Jersey Veterans Memorial Home, Menlo Park 08837 (908-603-3000)
New Jersey Veterans Memorial Home, Paramus 07652 (201-967-7676)
New Jersey Veterans Memorial Home, Vineland 08360 (609-696-6400)
NEW MEXICO
Truth or Consequences Veterans Center, Truth or Consequences 87901 (505-827-6300)

NEW YORK
New York State Women's Relief Corps Home, Oxford 13830 (518-474-3752)**

NORTH DAKOTA
North Dakota Veterans Home, Lisbon 58054 (701-683-4125)*

OHIO
Ohio Soldiers' and Sailors' State Soldiers' Home, Sandusky 44870 (419-625-2454, ext. 231)*

OKLAHOMA
Oklahoma Veterans Center, Ardmore 73402 (405-223-2266)
Oklahoma Veterans Center, Sulphur 73086 (405-622-2144)
Clinton Veterans Center, Clinton 73601 (405-323-5540)

PENNSYLVANIA
Pennsylvania Soldiers' and Sailors' Home, Erie 16512 (814-871-4531)**
Holidaysburg Veterans Home, Holidaysburg 16648 (814-696-5357)**
Southeastern Pennsylvania Veterans Home, Spring City 19475 (215-948-2401)**

RHODE ISLAND
Rhode Island Veterans Home, Providence 02900 (401-277-2488)*

SOUTH CAROLINA
War Veterans Home, Columbia 29201 (803-734-0200)

SOUTH DAKOTA
South Dakota State Soldiers' Home, Hot Springs 57747 (605-745-5127)**

VERMONT
Vermont Home in Vermont, Bennington 05201 (802-442-6353)**

WASHINGTON
State Soldiers Home and Colony, Orting 98360 (206-893-2156)

WEST VIRGINIA
Barboursville Veterans Home, Barboursville 25504 (304-736-1027)*

WISCONSIN
Wisconsin Veterans' Home, King 54946 (608-266-1311)*

WYOMING
Wyoming Soldiers' and Sailors' Home, Buffalo 82834 (347-684-5519)**

Admits female veterans
**Admits female veterans and certain dependents*

VETERAN POPULATION AGE DATA

As of March 31, 1990 the median age of the 27 million veterans was 55.1 years. The number of veterans under 45 years old was 8.4 million (31 percent of the total), 11.5 million veterans (43 percent) were 45-64 years old, and 7.1 million (26 percent) were 65 years old and over.

Veterans who served during WWI represented the oldest segment of the veteran population with a median age of 93.0 years. The next oldest group was WWII veterans with a median age of 68.3 years. Post-Vietnam era veterans were the youngest subgroup of the veteran population with a median age of 30.9 years.

The veteran demographic studies projected that by the turn of the century the present number of veterans of 27 million will fall to 24 million and by 2040 will be down to 13 million. And although the total number of veterans will be downward, the number of veterans 65 and older will increase from the current 6.7 million to over 9 million by 1999.

The World War II veterans number of 9.3 million are currently the largest group of living veterans, and Vietnam era veterans are second, with 8.3 million. By 1993 Vietnam era veterans will be the largest group.

Estimated Number of Veterans Living in U.S.
And Puerto Rico By Age — March 31, 1990

Age	ALL VETERANS MEN AND WOMEN (In thousands)			WOMEN VETERANS ONLY (In Thousands)		
	Total All Veterans	Wartime Veterans Total	Peacetime Veterans Total	Total Women Veterans	Wartime Veterans Total	Peacetime Veterans Total
All Ages	*27,001*	*20,754*	*6,247*	*1,217.8*	*681.1*	*536.7*
Under 20 yrs.	1	—	1	0.1	—	0.1
20-24 years	281	—	281	25.1	—	25.1
25-29 years	977	—	977	107.4	—	107.4
30-34 years	1,570	363	1,208	165.8	32.5	133.3
35-39 years	1,946	1,575	371	140.1	85.7	54.4
40-44 years	3,586	3,458	128	100.3	82.4	17.8
45-49 years	2,634	1,777	857	72.1	35.5	36.7
50-54 years	2,442	869	1,573	60.7	22.2	38.6
55-59 years	3,086	2,541	544	78.1	52.8	25.3
60-64 years	3,387	3,270	116	73.2	53.4	13.9
65-69 years	3,453	3,413	41	178.3	160.1	18.1
70-74 years	2,158	2,120	38	98.5	82.0	16.5
75-79 years	895	852	43	56.2	39.7	16.5
80-84 years	375	339	36	34.3	20.5	13.8
85 yrs. & over	209	177	33	27.7	14.4	13.3
Median age	55.1	59.7	46.9	49.9	63.0	35.2

LEGISLATION

Selected Legislation of Interest to Veterans
(102nd Congress - 1st Session 1991)

The following is a listing of selected legislation enacted by the first session of the 102nd Congress in 1991. The listing is not all-inclusive but rather is representative of legislative efforts that deal with a number of issues of special interest to veterans.

Legislation Enacted into Law

P.L. 102-3 (H.R. 3) 02/06/91 Veterans Compensation Amendments of 1991.

Provides a 5.4% cost of living adjustment in the rates of disability compensation and dependency and indemnity compensation (DIC) effective January 1, 1991.

P.L. 102-4 (H.R. 556) 03/18/91 Agent Orange Act of 1991.
Codifies the actions of the Secretary of Veterans Affairs in compensation for chlorcane, non-Hodgkins' lymphoma and soft-tissue sarcomas suffered by veterans during the Vietnam conflict.

Authorizes the National Academy of Sciences to conduct a comprehensive review of available and future data on the long term health effects of herbicide exposure and report its finding to the Secretary. The Secretary is required to take action on NAS's recommendations.

P.L. 102-12 (H.R. 555) 03/18/91 Soldiers and Sailors Civil Relief Act Amendments of 1991.

Amends the Soldier's and Sailors' Civil Relief Act of 1940 regarding increased rental allowance maximum, and provides suspension of liability and health insurance reinstatement for persons called to active duty.

P.L. 102-25 (S 725) 04/06/91 Persian Gulf Conflict Supplemental Authorization and Personnel Benefits Act of 1991; Persian Gulf War Veterans' Benefit Act; Persian Gulf Conflict Higher Education Assistance Act.

Defines Gulf War period as beginning August 2, 1990 and will end by presidential proclamation. Also increases GI Bill benefits on the 3 to 6 year active duty and 2 year active duty enlistments. National Guard and

Reserve Montgomery GI Bill Benefits are increased. Provides VA guaranteed home loan eligibility after 90 days for active force members. Increases the maximum SGLI and VGLI life insurance programs from $50,000 to $100,000. The bill also includes other matters.

P.L. 102-27 (H.R. 1281) 04/10/91 Dire Emergency Supplemental Appropriation for Consequences of Operation Desert Shield/Desert Storm, Food Stamps, Unemployment Compensation Administration, Veterans Compensation and Pensions, and Other Urgent Needs Act of 1991.

Provides additional funds for service personnel compensation, veterans compensation and all of the above as indicated in the bill title.

P.L. 102-54 (H.R. 232) 06/13/91 Veterans Benefits Amendment.

Authorizes, through a four-year demonstration project, transitional housing for homeless veterans in the VA compensated work therapy program. Provides VA notification, information, and counseling to veterans who default on VA-guaranteed home loans about the effect of, and alternatives to foreclosure.

P.L. 102-72 (H.R. 2521) 11/26/91 Defense Appropriations Act.

Includes $20 million for cooperative VA/DoD research programs to be made available as a transfer to VA's medical and Prosthetic Research appropriation. Bill also includes $600,000 for post traumatic stress disorder treatment centers in Hawaii and Greensburg, PA to study the effects of war on service persons.

P.L. 102-82 (H.R. 153) 08/06/91 Veterans Judicial Review Amendments of 1991.

Provides that laws requiring (1) a judge to refrain from taking part in any case in which his impartiality may be questioned, and (2) that courts adopt procedures for the conduct of any judge of the court. Both should apply to the Court of Veterans Appeals.

P.L. 102-86 (H.R. 1047) 08/14/91 Veterans Benefits Improvement Act.

Liberalizes eligibility for coverage in cases of ionizing radiation exposure to atomic weapons testing to include Reserve and National Guard Members. Restores eligibility for burial and DIC compensation for veterans who die as a result of service-connected disabilities. Protects veterans current disability ratings from reduction solely due to changes in the schedule for rating disabilities.

P.L. 102-127 (S 868) Veterans Educational Assistance Amendments of 1991.

Improves education assistance benefits for members of the reserve components who served on active duty during the Persian Gulf War, and to improve and clarify the eligibility of certain veterans for employment and training assistance.

P.L. 102-152 (H.R. 1046) 11/12/91 Veterans Benefits Improvement Act.

Provides a 3.7% increase in the rates of compensation for service-connected disabilities and of dependency and indemnity compensation (DIC) for survivors of veterans who die as a result of service-connected disabilities. Increases are effective as of December 1, 1991 to be received in the January checks.

THE PRESIDENT'S CABINET
MEMBERS WITH VETERAN STATUS

George Bush, President — Navy
Dan Quayle, Vice President — National Guard
James A. Baker, Department of State — Marine Corps
Jack Kemp, Housing & Urban Development — Army
James D. Watkins, Energy — Navy
Edward Derwinski, Veterans Affairs — Army
Samuel K. Skinner, Chief of Staff — Army
(plus 12 members — non-veteran status)

VETERANS COMMITTEES, 102ND CONGRESS

Senate Veterans' Committee — Room SR-414, Washington, D.C. 20510, Telephone (202) 224-9126

Democrats:
A — Alan Cranston, CA Chairman
A — Dennis De Concini, AZ
A — George Mitchell, ME
— Jay Rockefeller, WV
— Bob Graham, FL
A — Daniel Akaka, HI
AF — Thomas Daschle, SD

Republicans:
AF — Arlen Specter, PA Ranking Mbr.
A — Alan Simpson, WY
A — Strom Thurmond, SC
CG — Frank Murkowski, AK
N — James Jeffords, VT

There are no Subcommittees

House Committee On Veterans' Affairs — Room 335, Cannon HOB, Washington, D.C. 20515, Telephone (202) 225-3527

Democrats:
A — G.S. Montgomery, MS Chairman
N — Don Edwards, CA, Vice Chairman
— Douglas Applegate, OH
MC — Lane Evans, IL
— Timothy J. Penny, MN
— Harley O. Staggers, WV
A — J. Roy Bowland, CA
ANG — Jim Slattery, KS
ANG — Claude Harris, AL
— Joseph P. Kennedy, MA
— Elizabeth J. Patterson, SC
A — George E. Sangmeister, IL
— Ben Jones, CA
— Jill Long, IN
AF — Pete Peterson, FL
— Chet Edwards, TX
— Maxine Waters, CA
AR — Bill Brewster, O
— Owen B. Pickett, VA
— Pete Geren, TX

Republicans:
N — Bob Stump, AZ Ranking Member
A — John Paul Hammerschmidt, AK
A — Chalmers P. Wylie, OH
— Chris Smith, NJ
A — Dan Burton, IN
AF — Michael Bilirakis, FL
A — Thomas J. Ridge, PA
ANG — Craig James, FL
AF — Cliff Stearns, FL
— Bill Paxon, NY
N — Floyd Spence, SC
N — Richard Nichols, KS
— Richard John Santorum, PA

House Subcommittees:
1. Hospital and Health Care
2. Compensation, Pension and Insurance
3. Oversight and Investigations
4. Education, Training and Employment
5. Housing and Memorial Affairs

Veteran Status
A — Army
N — Navy
AF — Air Force
MC — Marine Corps
AR — Army Reserves
ANG — Air National Guard
CG — Coast Guard

DISABILITY CASES BY WAR
September 1990

	Service Connected	Non-service Connected
World War I	3,449	14,666
World War II	876,359	417,970
Korean Conflict	208,517	96,647
Vietnam Era	651,756	32,748
Peacetime	444,191	—
TOTAL	**2,184,262**	**562,040**

WHICH OF THESE PAY LEVELS WAS YOUR PAY WHEN IN SERVICE?
MONTHLY BASIC PAY SCALE (Rounded Dollars)
(-2 = under 2 years)

		1942 Years Service		1949 Years Service		1959 Years Service		1969 Years Service		1979 Years Service		1989 Years Service		1992 Years Service	
		-3	3	-2	4	-2	4	-2	4	-2	4	-2	4	-2	4
Officer															
LtCol/CDR	O-5	$292	$306	$456	$456	$474	$540	$635	$798	$1,304	$1,637	$2,258	$2,835	$2,537	$3,185
Maj/LCDR	O-4	250	263	385	385	400	455	536	696	1,100	1,428	1,904	2,472	2,139	2,778
Capt/LT	O-3	200	210	314	328	326	415	498	659	1,022	1,361	1,769	2,339	1,988	2,629
1LT/LTJG	O-2	167	175	249	278	259	370	399	588	891	1,208	1,542	2,092	1,733	2,351
2LT/LT	O-1	150	158	214	242	222	314	343	474	773	973	1,339	1,685	1,505	1,893
Officers over 4 years enlisted duty															
	O-3E	—	—	328	328	—	415	—	659	—	1,351	—	2,339	—	2,629
	O-2E	—	—	278	278	—	370	—	589	—	1,208	—	2,092	—	2,351
	O-1E	—	—	242	242	—	314	—	474	—	973	—	1,685	—	1,893
Warrant Officer															
Chief Warrant	W-3			291	291	303	348	461	506	946	1,039	1,638	1,799	1,841	2,022
Chief Warrant	W-2	175	184	255	255	265	307	404	450	829	922	1,434	1,597	1,612	1,794
Warrant	W-1	150	158	211	211	219	285	337	418	690	857	1,195	1,485	1,343	1,668
Enlisted															
Sgt/CPO	E-7	166	173	198	206	206	250	304	391	693	802	1,227	1,422	1,378	1,598
Sgt/PO1	E-6	137	143	169	176	176	225	262	345	598	708	1,056	1,250	1,187	1,405
Sgt/PO2	E-5	115	120	139	154	146	205	226	305	525	630	927	1,104	1,041	1,240
CPL/PO3	E-4	94	98	117	132	122	170	190	272	505	608	864	1,041	971	1,170
PFC/SEA	E-3	79	83	96	110	99	141	138	219	485	554	814	928	915	1,043
PV2/SA	E-2	65	68	83	98	86	108	113	159	467	467	784	784	881	881
PVT/SR	E-1	60	63	80	95	83	105	110	146	419	419	699	699	786	786

Basic pay only, however, there are any number of additional amounts for flight, sea, submarine, hazard, hostile fire, etc.

AMERICA'S WARS

(All figures as of October 1, 1991)

American Revolution (1775-1784)
Participants 290,000
Deaths in Service 4,000
Last Veteran, Daniel F. Bakeman, died 4/5/1869, age 109
Last Widow, Catherine S. Damon, died 11/11/06, age 92
Last Dependent, Phoebe M. Palmeter, died 4/25/11, age 90

War of 1812 (1812-1815)
Participants 287,000
Deaths in Service 2,000
Last Veteran, Hiram Cronk, died 5/13/05, age 105
Last Widow, Carolina King, died 6/28/36, age not available
Last Dependent, Esther A.H. Morgan, died 3/12/46, age 89

Mexican War (1846-1848)
Participants 79,000
Deaths in Service 13,000
Last Veteran, Owen Thomas Edgar, died 9/3/29, age 98
Last Widow, Lena James Theobald, died 6/20/63, age 89
Last Dependent, Jesse G. Bivens, died 11/1/62, age 94

Indian Wars (Approx. 1817-1898)
Participants 106,000
Deaths in Service 1,000
Last Veteran, Fredrak Fraske, died 6/18/73, age 101

Civil War (1861-1865)
Participants (Union) 2,213,000
Deaths in Service (Union) 364,000
Participants (Conf.) 1,000,000*
Deaths in Service (Conf.) . . . 133,821*
Last Union Veteran, Albert Woolson, died 8/2/56, age 109
Last Confederate Veteran, John Salling, died 3/16/58, age 112

(*Authoritative statistics for Confederate Forces not available. Estimated 28,000 Confederate personnel died in Union prisons.)

Spanish-American War (1898-1902)
Participants 392,000
Deaths in Service 11,000
Living Veterans 1

World War I (1917-1918)
Participants 4,744,000
Deaths in Service 116,000
Living Veterans 65,000

World War II (9/16/40 thru 7/25/47)
Participants . . . . 16,535,000[a]
Deaths in Service 406,000
Living Veterans . . . . 8,469,000[b c]

Korean Conflict (6/27/50 thru 1/31/55)
Participants . . . . 6,807,000[a d]
Deaths in Service 55,000
Living Veterans . . . . 4,726,000[b c e]

Vietnam Era (8/5/64 thru 5/7/75)
Participants . . . . 9,200,000[d]
Deaths in Service 109,000
Living Veterans . . . . 8,303,000[b e h]
(Current living veterans figures reflect a revision of data.)

Persian Gulf War (Start date 8/2/90)*
Participants** . . . . 569,000[f]
Deaths in Service . . . . 1,783[g]
Living Veterans . . . . 264,000[h]
*The official start of the war is 8/2/90; the ending date has not yet been established. Data provided are as of 10/1/91.

America's Wars Total (thru 10/1/91)
War Participants [#] 40,328,341
Deaths in Service 1,082,783
Living War Veterans 20,370,000
Living Ex-
  Servicemembers 26,629,000
6 million limited VA benefits

**DoD committed troops in the Gulf.

(Continued on next page)

NOTE: Figures on the number of living veterans reflect final 1980 Census data and include only veterans living in the U.S. and Puerto Rico. Detail may not add to total shown due to rounding.

VETERANS AND DEPENDENTS ON THE COMPENSATION AND PENSION ROLLS AS OF OCTOBER 1, 1991

	Veterans	Children	Parents	Surviving Spouses
Civil War (80% Union)..........	—	37	—	3
Indian Wars....................	—	2	—	8
Spanish-American War[i]	1	566	—	2,278
Mexican Border	58	26	—	622
World War I....................	13,231	10,335	10	150,959
World War II	1,226,336	27,469	14,038	384,657
Korean Conflict	303,958	8,333	6,460	74,513
Vietnam Era...................	697,811	25,176	12,507	75,757
TOTAL......................	**2,709,500[j]**	**86,407[k]**	**38,642[l]**	**731,469[m]**

FOOTNOTES:
\#   Persons who served in more than one war period are counted only once.
a   1,476,000 served in World War II and the Korean Conflict.
b   Includes 255,000 who served in World War II, the Korean Conflict, and the Vietnam Era.
c   Includes 611,000 who served in both World War II and the Korean Conflict.
d   887,000 served in the Korean Conflict and the Vietnam Era.
e   Includes 327,000 who served in both the Korean Conflict and the Vietnam Era.
f   At Mid-February, 1991.
g   During Fiscal Year 1991.
h   Includes 47,000 who served in both the Persian Gulf War and the Vietnam Era.
i   The only living Spanish-American War veteran receives benefits under World War II.
j   Includes 468,084 peacetime veterans with service between January 31, 1955, and August 5, 1964; peacetime veterans with service beginning after May 7, 1975 and all other peacetime periods; 20 World War I Retired Emergency Officers and 2 Peacetime Special Acts.
k   Includes 14,463 children of deceased peacetime veterans.
l   Includes 5,627 parents of deceased peacetime veterans.
m   Includes 42,852 surviving spouses of deceased peacetime veterans.

Source: Dept. of Veterans Affairs.

102ND CONGRESS — VETERAN STATUS — WARTIME & PEACETIME SERVICE

The following is a list of members of Congress who have veteran status deriving from either, or both, wartime and peacetime service. The listing identifies the members by name, party affiliations, state, branch and years of military service.

HOUSE:

Alexander, Bill	D-AR - Army - 51-53
Anderson, Glenn M.	D-CA - Army - 43-45
Archer, Bill	R-TX - AF - 51-53
Aspin, Les	D-WI - Army - 66-68
Aucoin, Les	D-OR - Army - 61-64
Bacchus, James	D-FL - Army - 71-72*
Ballenger, Cass	R-NC - NAC - 44-45
Barnard, Doug, Jr.	D-GA - Army - 43-45
Bateman, Herbert H.	R-VA - AF - 51-53
Bennett, Charles E.	D-FL - Army - 42-47
Bereuter, Douglas K.	R-NE - Army - 63-65
Bevill, Tom	D-AL - Army - 43-46
Bilbray, James	D-NV - ANG - 55-63
Bilirakis, Michael	R-FL - AF - 51-55
Blaz, Ben	R-Guam - USMC - 51-80
Bliley, Thomas J., Jr.	R-VA - Navy - 52-55
Boehlert, Sherwood L.	R-NY - Army - 56-58
Bonior, David E.	D-MI - AF - 68-72
Brewster, Bill	D-OK - AR - 68-71
Brooks, Jack	D-TX - USMC - 42-46
Broomfield, W. S.	R-MI - AAC - 42
Brown, George E., Jr.	D-CA - Army - 42-46
Burton, Dan	R-IN - Army - 56-57
Bustamante, A. G.	D-TX - Army - 54-56
Callahan, H.L.	R-AL - Navy - 52-54
Campbell, Ben N.	D-CO - AF - 52-54
Carper, Thomas R.	D-DE - Navy - 68-73*
Chandler, Rod	R-WA - ANG - 59-64
Clay, William	D-MO - Army - 53-55
Clement, Bob	D-TN - Army - 64-71*
Clinger, Bill, Jr.	R-PA - Navy - 51-55
Coble, Howard	R-NC - CG - 52-56*
Coleman, Ronald D.	D-TX - Army - 67-69
Conyers, John, Jr.	D-MI - Army - 52-53*
Coughlin, Lawrence	R-PA - USMC - 51-52*
Cox, John	D-IL - Army - 69-70
Coyne, William J.	D-PA - Army - 55-57
Cramer, Bud	D-AL - AR
Crane, Philip	R-IL - Army - 54-56
Cunningham, Randy	R-CA - Navy - 67-87
Dannemeyer, W. E.	R-CA - Army - 52-54
DeFazio, Peter A.	D-OR - AF - 67-71
De La Garza, E.	D-TX - Navy - 45-52**
Dellums, Ronald V.	D-CA - USMC - 54-56
De Lugo, Ron	D-VI - Army - 48-50
Dickinson, W. L.	R-AL - Navy - 43-46
Dingell, John D.	D-MI - Army - 44-46*
Dixon, Julian C.	D-CA - Army - 57-60
Dornan, Robert K.	R-CA - AF - 53-58
Duncan, John J., Jr.	R-TN - ARNG - 70-86

Dwyer, Bernard J.	D-NJ - Navy - 40-45
Early, Joseph D.	D-MA - Navy - 55-57
Edwards, Don	D-CA - Navy - 42-45
Emerson, Bill	R-MO - AFR - 64-
English, Glenn	D-OK - AR - 65-71
Erdreich, Ben	D-AL - Army - 63-65
Evans, Lane	D-IL - USMC - 69-71
Faleomavaega, E.	FH Am.Sam-Army-66-69*
Fascell, Dante B.	D-FL - Army - 41-46*
Fish, Hamilton, Jr.	R-NY - NR - 44-46
Ford, William D.	D-MI - Navy - 44-46*
Frost, Martin	D-TX - AR - 66-72
Gaydos, Joseph M.	D-PA - NR - 44-46
Gekas, George	R-PA - Army - 53-55
Gephardt, Richard	D-MO - AFNG - 65-71
Gibbons, Sam	D-FL - Army - 41-45
Gilchrest, Wayne	R-MD - USMC - 64-68
Gillmor, Paul	R-OH - AF - 65-66
Gilman, Benjamin A.	R-NY - AAC - 42-45
Gonzalez, Henry	D-TX - Army - WW II
Goodling, William	R-PA - Army - 46-48
Goss, Porter J.	R-FL - Army - 60-62
Green, Bill	R-NY - Army - 53-55
Guarini, Frank J.	D-NJ - NR - 44-47
Hall, Ralph M.	D-TX - Navy - 42-45
Hammerschmidt, J.P.	R-AR - Army - 42-45*
Hancock, Melton D.	R-MO - AF - 51-53*
Hansen, James V.	R-UT - Navy - 51-53
Harris, Claude J.	D-AL - ANG - 67-
Hatcher, Charles F.	D-GA - AF - 58-62
Hayes, James A.	D-LA - AFNG - 68-74
Hoagland, Peter	D-NE - Army - 64-66
Hobson, David	R-OH - AF - 62-63*
Hochbrueckner, G.	D-NY - Navy - 56-59
Hopkins, Larry J.	R-KY - USMC - 54-56
Horton, Frank J.	R-NY - Army - 41-46
Houghton, A., Jr.	R-NY - USMC - 45-46
Hubbard, Carroll, Jr.	D-KY - ANG - 62-70
Hunter, Duncan L.	R-CA - Army - 69-71
Hutto, Earl Dewitt	D-FL - Navy - 44-46
Hyde, Henry J.	R-IL - Navy - 44-46
Inhofe, James	R-OK - Army - 54-56
Jacobs, Andrew, Jr.	D-IN - USMC - 50-52
James, Craig T.	R-FL - ANG - 63-69
Jefferson, W.	D-LA - Army - 72
Jenkins, Ed	D-GA - CG - 52-55
Johnston, H. A., III	D-FL - Army - 53-55
Kleczka, Gerald D.	D-WI - ANG - 63-69
Kolbe, Jim	R-AZ - Navy - 67-69*
Kolter, Joseph P.	D-PA - AF - 44-45
LaFalce, John J.	D-NY - Army - 65-67

Lagomarsino, R.	R-CA - Navy - 44-46		Regula, Ralph S.	R-OH - Navy - 44-46
Lancaster, H. M.	D-NC - Navy - 67-70*		Rhodes, John J. III	R-AZ - Army - 68-70
LaRocco, Larry	D-ID - Army - 69-72		Ridge, Thomas J.	R-PA - Army - 68-70
Laughlin, Greg H.	D-TX Army - 64-69*		Riggs, Frank	R-CA - Army - 72-75
Leath, J. Marvin	D-TX - Army - 54-56		Roberts, Pat	R-KS - USMC - 58-62
Lehman, Richard H.	D-CA - ANG - 70-76		Roe, Robert A.	D-NJ - Army - 43-46
Lehman, William	D-FL - AAC - 42-46		Rogers, Harold	R-KY - ANG - 56-64
Lent, Norman F.	R-NY - NR - 52-54		Rostenkowski, Dan	D-IL - Army - Korea
Lewis, Tom	R-FL - AF - 43-54		Roth, Toby	R-WI - AR - 63-69
Lightfoot, Jim Ross	R-IA - Army - 55-56*		Rowland, J. Roy	D-GA - Army - 44-46
Lipinski, William O.	D-IL - AR - 61-67		Roybal, Edward R.	D-CA - Army - 44-45
Livingston, R.	R-LA - Navy - 61-63		Sangmeister, G.	D-IL - Army - 51-53
McCandless, Alfred	R-CA - USMC - 45-52**		Savage, Gus	D-IL - Army - 43-46
McCloskey, Francis	D-IN - AF - 57-61		Schaefer, Dan	R-CO - USMC - 55-57
McCollum, Bill	R-FL - Navy - 69-72*		Scheuer, James H.	D-NY - Army - 43-45
McCurdy, David	D-OK - AFR - 69-72		Schiff, Steven	R-NM - ANG - 69-
McDermott, James A.	D-WA - Navy - 68-70		Schulze, Richard T.	R-PA - Army - 51-53
McMillan, J. Alex III	R-NC - Army - 54-56		Serrano, Jose E.	D-NY - Army - 64-66
Machtley, Ronald K.	R-RI - Navy - 70-75*		Shuster, E. G.	R-PA - Army - 54-56
Manton, Thomas J.	D-NY - USMC - 51-53		Sisisky, Norman	D-VA - Navy - 45-46
Markey, Edward	D-MA - AR - 68-73		Skaggs, David E.	D-CO - USMC - 68-71*
Martin, David O'B.	R-NY - USMC - 66-70		Skeen, Joseph R.	R-NM - Navy - 45-46*
Martinez, M. G.	D-CA - USMC - 47-50		Slattery, Jim	D-KS - ANG - 70-75
Mazzoli, Romano	D-KY - Army - 54-56		Slaughter, D.F., Jr.	R-VA - Army - 43-47
Michel, Robert	R-IL - Army - 42-46		Smith, Neal	D-IA - AAC - 42-45
Miller, John R.	R-WA - Army - 60-61		Solomon, G. B. H.	R-NY - USMC - 50-51
Mineta, Norman Y.	D-CA - Army - 53-56		Spence, Floyd D.	R-SC - Navy - 52-54
Moakley, John	D-MA - Navy - 43-46		Spratt, John M., Jr.	D-SC - Army - 69-71
Mollohan, Alan B.	D-WV - Army - 70-80		Stark, Fortney H.	D-CA - AF - 55-57
Montgomery, G.V.	D-MS - Army - 43-52**		Stearns, Cliff	R-FL - AF - 63-67
Moorhead, Carlos J.	R-CA - Army - 42-45		Stokes, Louis	D-OH - Army - 43-46
Morrison, Sid	R-WA - Army - 54-56		Stump, Bob	R-AZ - Navy - 43-46
Mrazek, Robert J.	D-NY - Navy - 67-68		Sundquist, Don	R-TN - Navy - 57-59
Murphy, Austin J.	D-PA - USMC - 44-46*		Tanner, John S.	D-TN - Navy - 68-72*
Murtha, John P.	D-PA - USMC - 52-67**		Taylor, Gene	D-MS - CGR - 70-83
Myers, John T.	R-IN - Army - 45-46		Thomas, Craig	R-WY - USMC - 55-59
Natcher, William H.	D-KY - Navy - 42-45		Thomas, Robert L.	D-GA - AFNG - 68-72
Nowak, Henry J.	D-NY - Army - 57-62		Thorton, Ray	D-AR - Navy - 50-53
Olin, James R.	D-VA - Army - 43-46		Torres, Esteban E.	D-CA - Army - 49-53
Ortiz, Solomon P.	D-TX - Army - 60-62		Towns, Edolphus	D-NY - Army - 56-58
Packard, Ronald C.	R-CA - Navy - 57-59		Traxler, Bob	D-MI - Army - 53-55
Panetta, Leon E.	D-CA - Army - 64-66		Udall, Morris	D-AZ - AAC - 42-46
Pease, Donald J.	D-OH - Army - 55-57		Valentine, Tim	D-NC - AAC - 44-46
Peterson, Pete	D-FL - AF - 54-80		Volkmer, Harold L.	D-MO - Army - 55-57
Pickle, J. J.	D-TX - Navy - 42-45		Walker, Robert S.	R-PA - ANG - 67-73
Porter, John E.	R-IL - AR - 58-64		Weiss, Ted	D-NY - Army - 46-47
Poshard, Glenn	D-IL - Army - 62-65		Williams, Pat	D-MT - Army - 60-61*
Pursell, Carl D.	R-MI - Army - 57-59		Wilson, Charles	D-TX - Navy - 56-60
Quillen, James H.	R-TN - Navy - 42-46		Wolf, Frank	R-VA - Army - 61-62*
Ramstad, Jim	R-MN - AR - 68-74		Wylie, Chalmers	R-OH - Army - 43-45*
Rangel, Charles B.	D-NY - Army - 48-52		Yates, Sidney R.	D-IL - Navy - 44-46
Ravenel, Arthur	R-SC - USMC - 45-46		Young, C. W.	R-FL - ANG - 48-57
Ray, Richard B.	D-GA - Navy - 44-45		Young, Don	R-AK - Army - 55-56
Reed, Jack	D-RI - Army - 71-79		Zeliff, Bill	R-NH - Army - 58-64

SENATE:

Akaka, Daniel K.	D-HI - Army - 45-47
Adams, Brock	D-WA - Navy - 44-46
Bentsen, Lloyd	D-TX - AAC - 42-59**
Bingaman, Jeff	D-NM - AR - 68-74
Boren, David L.	D-OK - ANG - 68-75
Bradley, Bill	D-NJ - AFR - 67-78
Brown, Hank	R-CO - Navy - 65-66
Bryan, Richard H.	D-NV - Army - 59-60*
Bumpers, Dale	D-AR - USMC - 43-46
Burns, Conrad	R-MT - USMC - 54-56
Chafee, John H.	R-RI - USMC - 42-52**
Coats, Dan	R-IN - Army - 66-68
Cochran, Thad	R-MS - Navy - 59-61
Craig, Larry	R-ID - Army - 70-72
Cranston, Alan	D-CA - Army - 44-46
Daschle, Thomas A.	D-SD - AF - 69-72
DeConcini, Dennis	D-AZ - Army - 59-60*
Dixon, Alan J.	D-IL - Navy - 45-46
Dodd, C. J.	D-CT - Army - 69-75
Dole, Robert	R-KS - Army - 43-48
Durenberger, D.	R-MN - Army - 55-57
Exon, J. James	D-NE - Army - 41-45*
Ford, Wendell H.	D-KY - Army - 44-46*
Fowler, Wyche	D-GA - Army - 63-65
Garn, Edwin J.	R-UT - Navy - 56-60*
Glenn, John H., Jr.	D-OH - USMC - 42-65
Gore, Albert, Jr.	D-TN - Army - 69-71
Gorton, Slade	R-WA - AF - 53-56*
Harkin, Tom	D-IA - Navy - 62-67*
Hatfield, Mark O.	R-OR - Navy - 43-46
Heflin, Howell	D-AL - USMC - 42-46
Heinz, H. John III	R-PA - AF - 63-69
Helms, Jesse A.	R-NC - Navy - 42-45
Hollings, Ernest	D-SC - Army - 42-45
Inouye, Daniel K.	DF-HI - Army - 43-47
Jeffords, James	R-VT - Navy - 56-59*
Johnston, J., Jr.	D-LA - Army - 56-59
Kasten, Robert W., Jr.	R-WI - AF - 67*
Kennedy, Edward M.	D-MA - Army - 51-53
Kerrey, Bob	D-NE - Navy - 66-69
Kerry, John	D-MA - Navy - 67-70
Kohl, Herbert	D-WI - ANG - 58-64
Lautenberg, Frank R.	D-NJ - Army - 42-46
Lugar, Richard G.	R-IN - Navy - 57-60
McCain, John	R-AZ - Navy - 58-81
Mitchell, George J.	D-ME - Army - 54-56
Moynihan, Daniel P.	D-NY - Navy - 44-47
Murkowski, Frank H.	R-AK - CG - 55-56
Nickles, Don	R-OK - ANG - 70-76
Nunn, Sam	D-GA - CG - 59-60*
Pell, Claiborne	D-RI - CG - 41-45
Pressler, Larry	R-SD - Army - 66-68
Robb, Charles	D-VA - USMC - 61-70

Roth, W. V., Jr.	R-DE - Army - 43-46
Rudman, Warren	R-NH - Army - 52-54
Sanford, Terry	D-NC - Army - 42-46*
Sasser, James R.	D-TN - ANG - 48-60
Seymour, John	R-CA - USMC - 55-59
Simon, Paul	D-IL - Army - 51-53
Simpson, Alan	R-WY - Army - 54-56
Smith, Robert	R-NH - Navy - 65-69
Specter, Arlen	R-PA - AF - 51-53
Stevens, Ted	R-AK - NAC - 43-46
Symms, Steven D.	R-ID - USMC - 60-63
Thurmond, Strom	R-SC - Army - 42-46
Wallop, Malcolm	R-WY - Army - 55-57
Warner, John W.	R-VA - Navy - 44-52**
Wirth, Timothy E.	D-CO - AR - 61-67

*Additional Reserve Service
**Split in years of Service

AAC — Army Air Corps
AF — Air Force
AFNG — Air Force National Guard
AFR — Air Force Reserve
ANG — Army National Guard
AR — Army Reserve
CG — Coast Guard
CGR — Coast Guard Reserve
MCR — Marine Corps Reserve
NAC — Naval Air Corps
NR — Naval Reserve
USMC — Marine Corps

World War II — 1940-47
Korea — 1950-55
Vietnam Era — 1964-75

To call any of the Senators or Congressmen phone 202-224-3121.

To call the White House phone 202-456-1414.